Struggling in the Land of Plenty

Struggling in the Land of Plenty

Race, Class, and Gender in the Lives of Homeless Families

Anne R. Roschelle

LEXINGTON BOOKS
Lanham • Boulder • New York • London

Published by Lexington Books
An imprint of The Rowman & Littlefield Publishing Group, Inc.
4501 Forbes Boulevard, Suite 200, Lanham, Maryland 20706
www.rowman.com

6 Tinworth Street, London SE11 5AL

British Library Cataloguing in Publication Information Available

Library of Congress Cataloging-in-Publication Data

ISBN 978-1-7936-0076-9 (cloth : alk. paper)
ISBN 978-1-7936-0077-6 (electronic)

♾️™ The paper used in this publication meets the minimum requirements of American National Standard for Information Sciences Permanence of Paper for Printed Library Materials, ANSI/NISO Z39.48-1992.

To my brother Steve—thanks for Existentialism, Beat Poetry, the Allman Brothers Band, and for always having my back.

Table of Contents

Acknowledgments

I am forever indebted to all the homeless families who generously shared their stories with me, and changed my life forever. Thanks, Jeanie, for trusting me. I am infinitely grateful to Glenna Spitze, Karyn Loscocco, and Chris Bose, all of whom have contributed to my professional development in innumerable ways. As graduate advisors, they taught me the rigors of sociological research and how to demand excellence from myself and my students. Most importantly, their actions taught me what it means to be a feminist mentor—a tradition I continue in their honor. Over the last twenty years, Glenna, Karyn, and Chris have continued to provide intellectual support and friendship. I can never repay Jennifer Turpin, who welcomed me to the University of San Francisco as I embarked on my new career. Jenny was a wonderfully supportive colleague and friend who's had the greatest impact on the trajectory of my career. It was Jenny who encouraged me to publish my dissertation as a book, something I never would have done without her encouragement. The publication of *No More Kin* gave me visibility within our discipline and provided me with research opportunities I would never have had otherwise. As Chair of the Sociology Department, Jenny allowed me the freedom to conduct my fieldwork and engage in anti-poverty activism. She truly promoted the Jesuit mission of social justice. As a result, I have spent my entire career as a scholar-activist.

Thank you to Courtney Lachapelle Morales, the Associate Acquisitions Editor at Lexington Books. Courtney believed in this book immediately and was incredibly responsive and supportive throughout the process. She has been a delight to work with, and I couldn't ask for a more wonderful editor. I appreciate all the work my inspiring undergraduate research assistants Sara Walenta, Amanda Tolive Wall, Sami Grober, and Tim Allan did over the years on this and other projects with me.

Survival in academia would not be possible without my extended kinship network. I would like to thank my parents Stan and Irma, my brothers Steve and Riche, and Steve's partner Deby for their endless encouragement and for not incessantly asking—so when is your book coming out? I miss you mom. My dad's partner Linda Willner and her daughter Nancy have been a fun addition to the family. My cousins Samuel and Gale Poulten, their kids Benari and Geordarna, Gee's husband Chris Constant, and their delightful daughter Rhodes keep the spirit of Aunt Bernice alive and envelop me in love and family locally. I cannot believe my great fortune that Gee ended up in the Hudson Valley and that Chris and his family are so welcoming. Writing with my good friends Maura Toro-Morn, Elisa Facio, and Sharina Maillo-Pozo have been highlights of my academic career. I cannot express the depth of my gratitude to my San Francisco friendship network. Karen Bouwer spent hours on the phone listening me to process the painful experiences I recount in the book, offering support and keeping me sane. Karen, Loie Lorentzen, Tracy Seeley, Esther Madriz, Mike Webber, Pedro-Lange Churion, Kathryn Nasstrom, Berndette Barker-Plummer, Rob Elias, and of course Jenny. You made life in the Bay Area a blast.

Aside from the cost of living, the major reason for moving back to upstate New York was to return to my beloved Catskill Mountains, magnificent swimming holes, and my wonderful friends. Marcia Tolive, my sister from another mother, allowed me to be Fairy Earth Mother (the white middle-class hippie chick equivalent of a *comadre* or *other mother*) to her wonderful daughters Sarah and Amanda. Spending the last twenty years with Sarah and Amanda as they grew into amazing, bad-ass women and getting to know their partners, Duncan and Rick, has been magical. Having Amanda attend SUNY New Paltz, working as my research assistant on this book, and driving up to see Sarah in Plattsburgh, solidified our adult relationship and created an unbreakable bond. I can't wait to be a Fairy Earth Grandmother in the next few years, when she and Rick have kids. Marcia, our college buddy Brenda Grober, and I have had many adventures over the last forty years and never pass up an opportunity to see *Dead and Company* (formerly the *Grateful Dead*). To my extraordinary Priestess friend Pamela Cubbage with whom I shared backpacking and travel adventures beyond comparison; so glad you found your spiritual path. Thanks Chris Nemeth and Adrienne Bonilla for all the holiday fun over the years. To my extraordinary flamenco guitar playing friend Maria Zementauski and her kick-ass partner Gina Chapman, let's keep the New Year's Eve cocktails flowing and the kayaks meandering. To my New Paltz inner circle—İlgü Özler, Brian Obach, Sunita Bose, Karl Bryant, Suse Volk, Laura Dull (editor extraordinaire), Vanessa Plumly, Omar Nagi, Heather Morrison, Sharina Maillo-Pozo, Luz Porras, Leigh Weaver, and Peter Kaufman (I'll miss you P.K.), I can never adequately express the depth of my gratitude for your friendship. To my bandmates in *Questionable Author-*

ities, I appreciate your willingness to allow me to play mediocre flute, dance with abandon, and scream punk songs at our shows. To all my friends— thank you for coming over to move the furniture before every dance party, for showing up on Halloween with the greatest costumes imaginable (except for Sunita—you get a pass—especially since you made me your third sister), for going to music festivals and theater productions, for hiking, biking, and swimming together and for Brian and İlgü who never fail to leave me incomprehensible, but much loved, voice messages from music venues around the globe. Thanks for the trips to Turkey, India, Cuba, Guatemala, France, Germany, and Hungary that some of us took together. To my newest friend Vanessa, who is always up for a last-minute adventure and is a total smartass (like me), you will be deeply missed as you embark on your new career in Wisconsin. It is infinitely comforting to be part of this incredible community of friends who have my back, fight for social justice, and continue to find joy in an increasingly dismal world. You are my family.

Lastly I would like to thank *The Underground Girls*. To Nico, whose unconditional love kept me warm on raw San Francisco summer nights and then on frigid winter nights in the Hudson Valley. To Velvet, (Joey) Ramona, and Stormy Monday—I couldn't have asked for better companions and especially to Ramona and Stormy—the two best lap cats that ever existed. To Chester and Axle, sorry the girls wouldn't let you into the band—maybe that's why your lives were so short-lived. Thanks for keeping me cozy.

Introduction

THE CITY BY THE BAY

I arrived in San Francisco in August 1994 ready to embark upon my new career as a sociology professor. I couldn't believe my great fortune at getting a job in such an amazing city. I was thrilled to be in a beautiful and culturally vibrant environment. Views of Golden Gate Park, the Pacific Ocean, and the Marin Headlands surrounded me. The city itself was well-manicured, clean, and easily navigable. My new colleagues at the University of San Francisco were supportive and welcoming. For a moment I thought I had landed in paradise. However, I very quickly began to notice cracks in the flawless façade. I moved to the legendary Haight Ashbury, which was brimming with history, music, nostalgia, and a seemingly infinite number of homeless individuals. Every time I stepped out of my apartment I was endlessly panhandled by friendly and often very clever individuals. I was frequently regaled with imaginative tales of misadventure and misfortune by the more recognizable cast of characters. There were a variety of homeless street people in my community, including homeless youths and runaways, young adults, and older, more hard-core homeless men and women. I became increasingly disturbed by the ubiquitous sight of homeless street people throughout San Francisco and the heartless policy of ticketing and arresting them for quality-of-life violations. Rather than see the homeless as a public nuisance, I saw them as a reflection of social structural inequality and of increasing poverty. However, I soon learned that there was also a significant population of homeless families who were less obviously identifiable and typically went unnoticed. The majority of homeless families in San Francisco consisted of young women and their children. Homeless families frequently remain hidden because they have access to shelters, residential motels, and transitional housing. In addition, many homeless women and children double up with family members, sleeping on couches and on floors rather than in public spaces. When homeless mothers and their children do appear in public, they are less noticeable because they typically have access to showers and donated clothing, transgressing the stereotype of rancid-smelling, disheveled street people. Despite outward appearances, the lives of homeless women and children, particularly those who are chronically homeless, are also intensely bleak and chaotic. As I got to know scores of homeless families in San Francisco, it became clear that there were two types of homeless families in San Francisco; families that experienced brief spells of homelessness and families that were chronically homeless. Families that had short-lived stints of homelessness often experienced a precipitating crisis that led directly to their homelessness. For some families the loss of a job or housing caused their homelessness. For other families the onset of a serious illness, whether of a parent or child was another. In general, these families were highly functional, were able to find housing and employment, and rarely returned to the family shelters. Alternatively, there was a hard-core group of persistently homeless families in San Francisco that cycled in and out of homelessness over the course of several years. These chronically homeless single mothers had prolonged histories of exposure to and experience with physical and sexual violence and were overwhelmed by drug and alcohol abuse, physical and mental health problems, and long-term unemployment. This book focuses on habitually homeless mothers who represent the most destitute of the homeless familial population. Although the life stories of these women are bleak and do not represent all homeless mothers, they are reflective of the experiences of chronically homeless families, and they need to be told. The women I spoke to were desperate to come out of the shadows and be made visible.

With that in mind, this book is about the rise in homeless families in the 1990s, using San Francisco as a case study. Specifically, the book focuses on the causes of familial homelessness in the Bay Area and its devastating impact on women and children. My intention is to make the experiences of chronically homeless women and children visible and to give voice to a marginalized and frequently silenced population. Although San Francisco is a unique city, and I cannot generalize my qualitative findings to other locales, the rise in familial homelessness in the Bay Area in the 1990s is analogous to what was happening throughout the country at the end of the twentieth century. As the gap between rich and poor widened, low-income women and children fell through the cracks and became homeless in unprecedented numbers (Collins and Bilge 2016). Examining the proliferation of family homelessness at the dawn of the new millennium provides a historical link to the current crisis that has worsened over the last three decades and continues to persist.

THE RESEARCH SITE: A HOME AWAY FROM HOMELESSNESS

The research site where I collected my data on homeless families[1] is an organization in San Francisco called A Home Away From Homelessness. Home Away is a non-profit organization that provides services to homeless families in San Francisco living in low-income housing, residential motels, transitional housing, family shelters, and foster care. The program was founded in 1994 in partnership with the National Park Service and their tandem organization the Golden Gate National Parks Conservancy. Home Away programs include a Beach House in Marin County, shelter support services, a Crisis Hotline, a Family Drop-in center, a Mentorship Program, and, in conjunction with the San Francisco Unified School District, an After-school Educational Program. I began my fieldwork in the fall of 1995 and continued until the summer of 1999 when I moved back to upstate New York. Over the course of my fieldwork approximately 100 five- to eighteen-year-old kids went to the Beach House each year. Of these kids, 50 percent were female and 50 percent were male. The racial ethnic composition of families participating in Home Away programs was 40 percent African American, 30 percent white, 20 percent Latinx[2] and 10 percent multi-racial. During my four-year ethnography nearly 1,000 children and their parents participated in Home Away programs. Although these data were collected in the late 1990s they are still highly relevant and provide a snapshot into an important historical moment. These data provide much needed insight into the social dynamics that produced the significant rise in homeless families that began at the turn of the new millennium and continues unabated.

None of the kids participating in Home Away programs were runaways or homeless youth living independently. Although all of the kids lived with at least one parent, many of them were victims of parental neglect and ultimately had to fend for themselves. In addition, many kids had various physical, emotional, and developmental problems. Given the chaos that characterizes the lives of homeless children, it is not surprising that they suffered from extensive physical and social deficits (Bassuk and Gallagher 1990; Rafferty 1991; Rafferty and Shinn 1991). Like their children, many of the homeless mothers in my study also had physical and emotional problems. In addition, a large majority of them came from severely impoverished communities, had histories of drug and alcohol abuse, and suffered from physical and sexual violence. Given the wretched conditions under which these women lived, it is not surprising that they had substance abuse and emotional problems (Bassuk and Gallagher 1990; Taylor and Barusch 2004). However, it is important to note that many of the women in my research did not become homeless as a result of drug or alcohol abuse. Rather, for many women in my study, their substance abuse problems began or escalated as a result of becoming homeless. Finally, a large majority of parents utilizing Home Away services were single mothers, although there were some two-parent families that periodically participated in Home Away programs.

My fieldwork consisted of participant observation at the Beach House, the Afterschool Education Program, and the Family Drop-in Center. In addition, I attended meetings at numerous social service agencies and conducted observational research at transitional housing facilities, residential motels, and homeless shelters throughout the Bay Area. After the passage of the Personal Responsibility and Work Opportunity Reconciliation Act (PRWO-RA) in 1996, I attended welfare reform workshops and CalWORKs[3] seminars with homeless mothers. In addition, I conducted thousands of hours of informal interviews with parents and kids, sometimes asking leading questions (Gubrium and Holstein 1997), other times just listening. Although I rarely took notes during these conversations, it was sometimes necessary to immediately record significant comments or noteworthy events. On those occasions I slipped out of the room unnoticed and quickly jotted down field notes. I did not regularly employ this strategy because scrutinizing disenfranchised individuals in such an intrusive way might make them feel inhibited and would certainly inspire mistrust between us. I spoke my field notes and my interpretations of the day's events into a tape recorder immediately after working with the families. I usually spent about two hours recreating the particularities of the day, recounting interactions I observed, articulating conversations I overheard, and reciting direct quotes into the tape recorder. Throughout this process I would critically analyze and synthesize the material as it unfolded. Overall, I conducted formal interviews with ninety-seven homeless and formerly homeless parents and their children. All taped formal and informal interviews were transcribed word-for-word.

Contrary to the pervasive discourse of the homeless as transients in search of undeserved social services, most of the families in my research were from northern California. Although there were a few families from southern California and the Pacific Northwest, they relocated to the Bay Area to be near relatives. Most of the families came from poor backgrounds and became homeless as a result of intimate partner violence, chronic illness, underemployment, and a lack of stable housing. Many Home Away families were in contact with their extended kinship networks and received emotional support. However, because network members were also typically impoverished, they were rarely able to provide economic support. Some homeless families periodically crashed with relatives but those relatives ran the risk of being evicted from their own low-income housing if caught. As the housing market got increasingly tighter, landlords and representatives of the Housing Authority were more likely to kick out tenants who violated occupancy restrictions. When families could not double up with relatives, they moved to residential motels, stayed in family shelters, and often ended up in substandard apartments in violent neighborhoods.

GROUNDED THEORY

Throughout my fieldwork I engaged in grounded theory. Grounded theory is a methodological strategy for collecting and analyzing qualitative data that allows researchers to construct theories as they emerge from the data. Essentially grounded theory enables researchers to collect data, construct levels of theoretical abstraction directly from that data, and create analytic categories to understand that data in a cyclical process (Charmaz 2006). In their seminal work on grounded theory, Glaser and Strauss (1967) recommend that researchers refrain from doing an extensive literature review and free themselves from the shackles of social theory before entering the field. They promoted this idea as a way of preventing researchers from imposing their preconceived ideas onto the research site. However, given my background in feminist and critical race epistemology and methodology, I did not enter the field as a blank slate. I did in fact conduct an extensive literature review and entered the field with an eye toward examining the intersections of race, class, and gender. Nonetheless, throughout my fieldwork I did employ the guiding principles of grounded theory. For example, during the first year of my fieldwork it became clear that the initial questions I was asking about movement out of homelessness were inappropriate. Throughout my research, I continuously analyzed and synthesized events in the field as they occurred. This strategy allowed me to see unexpected themes and trends emerge and make connections between them. The data generated new theoretical insights which in turn led to new analyses. As this process unfolded, I constructed codes that helped define and categorize the data which in turn led to new questions and interpretations of that data. I utilized theoretical sampling, which makes possible the emergence of more detailed theoretical categories through persistent examination of unanswered questions and conceptual gaps (Charmaz 2000, 2002). I then used selective coding to organize the data, which allowed me to "use the most frequently appearing initial codes to sort, synthesize, and conceptualize large amounts of data" (Charmaz 2002, 684). This technique helped me to evaluate the fit between the emerging theoretical framework and the empirical reality of my respondents. Throughout this process I also engaged in free-writing to more deeply analyze the data and make it more conceptually sophisticated and theoretically driven (see Charmaz 2006; Roschelle and Kaufman 2004). After a year of data collection, I completely changed the focus of my research based on what I learned from the women in the field. I realized that it was inappropriate to focus on whether or not Home Away programs provided an escape from homelessness and was a conduit for upward mobility. Given the enormous social structural inequality that impinged on these families, it would be unfair to expect Home Away programs to mitigate poverty and homelessness. Instead, based on conversations with respondents, I began to focus on how families became homeless, the chronic nature of their homelessness, and the strategies they used to survive.

METHODOLOGICAL CHALLENGES: FEMINIST AND CRITICAL RACE EPISTEMOLOGY

Gaining entrée into disenfranchised communities can sometimes be difficult, particularly for white middle-class researchers like me. Obtaining access into the familial homeless community was easier than expected. I developed a strong rapport with both parents and kids by spending considerable time with them at a variety of locations. Entrée was further facilitated by Sally, a formerly homeless woman, who was the designated House Mother. Sally was married and had one son. Her family lived in a residential motel in the Tenderloin district. Both Sally and her husband Rick had long-term problems with drug addiction. When I met Sally she was clean and was volunteering at the Club House. She was always very kind to me and introduced me to many parents. Because Sally was previously homeless, the parents trusted her implicitly. One day I gave Sally an old microwave oven that I no longer needed. Since she lived in a residential motel she had no cooking facilities. About three weeks after I gave her the microwave, Jeanie told me that Rick had stolen their rent money to buy heroin and that Sally sold the microwave to supplement the rent. Jeanie said that Sally was embarrassed but would talk to me about it. When Sally told me the story I responded by saying "I wish I had more stuff to give you to sell." After years of dealing with judgmental service providers and criminal justice personnel, Sally was astounded by my response. She expected me to chastise her for selling the microwave and for not using it to cook for her son. I told her that once I give someone a gift it is not my place to tell them what to do with—it was her microwave. It had simply not occurred to me to infantilize her and contribute to her shame. Instead, I treated her like an adult who was confronted with a difficult choice. My response to Sally solidified our relationship, and from that moment on she provided unlimited entrée into the community of homeless families in San Francisco. Sally regularly conveyed to the families her support for and fondness of me. Whenever anyone new came to the club house Sally would say "this is Dr. Annee, she is writing a book about us. You should talk to her, she is really cool." When some homeless parents responded with skepticism, Sally assured them I was not judgmental and that I would listen to their life stories with respect and empathy. This legitimacy was crucial because it allowed homeless women to be interviewed and observed in the context of their social group interactions. Spending time with homeless mothers in their everyday settings minimizes the artificiality that often exists between researchers and their respondents. Further, such an approach provides a forum for parents and their children to express their world view in an uninhibited manner (Charmaz 2000). Over the years, many parents discussed the painful details of their lives because of Sally's encouragement and because of my relationship with their kids.

Participating in impromptu conversations was another strategy that captured the ways women managed their devalued social status. These gatherings, which I taped and later transcribed verbatim, were not focus groups because they had neither an identifiable agenda nor a formal mediator (Morgan 2002; Stewart and Shamdasani 1990). Rather, these were freewheeling conversations that allowed me to "remain as close as possible to accounts of everyday life while trying to minimize the distance between [herself] and [the] research participants" (Madriz 2000, 838). These conversations were particularly appropriate because they allowed for the expression of ideas in which individuals felt comfortable speaking up (Denzin 1986; Frey and Fontana 1993). Furthermore, talking with homeless women in relaxed group settings, in which the respondents feel safe, minimizes the inherent power differential between the researcher and the respondents (Eder and Fingerson 2002) and gives voice to those who have been systematically oppressed (Madriz 2000).

As a feminist ethnographer, I paid careful attention to the devalued social position of my respondents, so as not to exploit them further. In addition, because I came from an activist background, I saw my role as an advocate for these families, not simply as an objective observer. Homeless women and children are among the most disenfranchised people in American society. Chronically homeless mothers typically come from impoverished backgrounds, are undereducated, have often been victims of physical and sexual abuse, and are predominately women of color. As a result, homeless women are often demonized as drug-addicted, undeserving, welfare cheats. Therefore, it is crucial to identify and chronicle the ways in which homeless families construct meaning in their lives and not assume that they experience social reality uniformly (Charmaz 2000, 522). I used several methodological strategies to discover the multiplicity of experiences among homeless families. Interviewing by comment was one strategy I found particularly useful. Interviewing by comment is essentially eavesdropping on conversations as they naturally unfold. These conversations are not answers to researchers' questions, so they provide insight into personal information often obscured from researchers (Snow and Anderson 1993; Snow, Zurcher, and Sjoberg 1982). This technique allowed me to understand the meanings homeless families ascribed to particular elements of their lives and to develop interpretations of those constructed meanings (Holstein and Gubrium 1995; Warren 2002).

Another way to minimize power differentials inherent in the research process is to be self-reflexive (Atkinson 1990; Clifford and Marcus 1986).

Reflexivity was particularly important to me due to the precarious social structural location of the families in my study. Throughout the project, I remained aware of how I interacted with and treated homeless family members (Heyl 2001). I paid particular attention to the political, material, and cultural context of my research (Bourdieu 1996), and was cognizant of how my race, class, and gender location impacted the research itself (Wasserfall 1997). I consciously resisted reproducing hegemonic colonial relationships that often characterize interactions between privileged researchers and disenfranchised respondents of color. To facilitate dismantling this hierarchy, I treated respondents with respect, I never used pedantic language; I developed questions based on the discursive expressions of parents and their children (Charmaz 2002; Stanfield 1993) and acknowledged respondents' interpretations of their social reality.

Along with reflexivity, I was also attentive to the complexities of representation, articulated by feminist ethnographers (Alcoff 1994; Heyl 2001; Mohanty 1991). Although feminists aspire to give respondents a voice by conveying their experiences, it is ultimately the researcher who determines which narratives get selected for consumption. In order to avoid reproducing hegemonic images of homeless families, I present a wide variety of experiences among diverse families from different racial ethnic and cultural backgrounds. By presenting the narratives of chronically homeless women with differing perspectives, I minimized the risk of imposing my own viewpoint onto their life stories and thereby reproducing unequal discursive power relations (Stacey 1988; Roschelle, Toro-Morn, and Facio 2010). There are different strategies of representation in ethnographic writing. Some ethnographers present a small but select sample of respondents who represent the larger sample. Although this strategy provides an in-depth look at several individuals, I am often left wondering about the other people in the research are. Others provide narratives from a large array of respondents who appear once or twice, never to be heard from again. This style provides readers with more voices from the field but prevents readers from getting to know respondents intimately. In order to present a diverse array of stories in which readers have the chance to form a deep relationship with particular respondents, I have combined these approaches. Some respondents appear once or twice to highlight a particular point, while others appear throughout the book. Because homeless families share a similarly devalued social position they do not experience that social position uniformly.[4] It is the unique storytelling of each individual that conveys the nuances of their experiences.[5]

RACE, CLASS, AND GENDER:
THEORIZING THE INTERSECTIONS

Over the last three decades feminist scholars have been theorizing about the centrality of race, class, and gender in daily life (Anderson and Collins 1992; Collins 1986 1990; Collins and Bilge 2016; Blea 1992; Chow, Wilkinson, and Zinn 1996; Dill 1983; Glenn 1985 1999; hooks 1981; Roschelle 1997 2008; Sacks 1989; Smith 1983; Zinn 1990). Black feminists were the first to examine the interlocking nature of race, class, and gender class oppression which shifts the investigative focus from merely explicating elements of race, gender, or class oppression to determining what the links are among these systems. This integrative approach treats the interaction among multiple systems as the object of study. Instead of simply adding to existing theoretical paradigms by inserting previously excluded variables, black feminists developed new theoretical interpretations of the interaction itself (Collins 1990; Davis 1981; Dill 1983). Because other women of color have been historically disenfranchised (Smith and Tienda 1988), this theoretical perspective, with its focus on the linked nature of oppression is also applicable to their experiences. (Collins 1990; Glen 1985; Zinn 1990).

Transnational feminists extended the analysis of gender inequality proffered by U.S. feminists of color by articulating the importance of examining the daily lives of women in developing nations in the context of the colonial relations that shape their oppression. In addition, they insisted that hegemonic feminists refrain from standardizing the experiences of non-western and racial ethnic women. Ultimately, using "women" as a universal category of analysis de-historicizes them and obscures their race, class, religion, nation, culture, and ideological differences (Mohanty 1991). Although my research focuses on impoverished U.S. women of color, transnational intersectionality is a useful analytic tool because it underscores the importance of contextualizing the experiences of women and avoiding the tendency to homogenize their experiences (Alcoff 1994; Anzaldúa 1990; Bannerji 1995; DeVault 1999 Mohanty 1991; Vrushali 2011).

In addition to theorizing about race, class, and gender, proponents of the intersectionality perspective assert that when building and testing empirical models, race, class, and gender must become the center of the analysis, not simply another set of variables to be examined. However, intersectionality theory has remained elusive and can be somewhat difficult to apply to one's research findings. Therefore, feminist scholars have recently advocated for a more coherent and systematic theoretical paradigm to guide research (Choo and Ferree 2010; Collins and Bilge 2016; Davis 2008; Ken 2007 2010; McCall 2001; Roschelle, Toro-Morn, Facio 2010). According to Ken (2010), race, class, and gender must be interrogated as fundamental organizing principles of society. Because of the ways in which race, class, and gender structure our lives, they become the source of both oppression and of privilege. Race, class, and gender are not merely demographic categories, nor are they simply categories of identity. Rather, race, class, and gender organize social practices, institutions, and social structural arrangements. These practices, institutions, and arrangements socially construct race, class, and gender in mutually constitutive and interdependent ways. Race, class, and gender shape social structures but are also themselves social structures. Ultimately, Ken (2010) argues that race, class, and gender influence social reality which in turn shapes subsequent events in a particular social context. San Francisco provides an excellent context for understanding the rise of homelessness among women and children in the 1990s. Collins and Bilge (2016) extend this analysis by focusing on particular domains of power to articulate how social institutions have structured race, class, and gender inequality over the last thirty years. Using the structural domain of power as one analytic tool, they illustrate that income inequality increased exponentially in the 1990s, resulting in an unparalleled racialized and gendered wealth gap. My research is particularly relevant now because it illustrates how social structural inequality and gendered violence in impoverished communities of color in San Francisco in the 1990s led to an unprecedented rise in familial homelessness. Empirically examining the particular social dynamics that forced women and their children onto the streets during the 1990s provides a historical link to the causes and consequences of the crisis in familial homelessness that continues to persist.

An important component of intersectionality theory is the recognition that race, class, and gender are shifting categories of oppression and that individuals do not react uniformly to social structural constraints. In addition, individuals are not simply passive receptacles of social structure. Rather, they have the ability to intervene in their world and make choices about their actions; what Anthony Giddens (1984) calls *agency*. According to Giddens, it is therefore essential to examine the dialectical relationship between individual responsibility and social structural constraints. However, people's agency is constrained by their social structural position. Clearly, people do make choices and resist oppression; however, where they are situated in the social hierarchy shapes their perspectives on life. These perspectives, what Pierre Bourdieu called *habitus*, reinforce the social structural locations of individuals in an interactive way. These often unconscious perspectives seem normative and typically go unquestioned. Habitus are internalized social structures that appear simply as common sense, but actually reflect race, class, and gender divisions in the social hierarchy. As a result, these perspectives continue to shape the social structure which in turn continues to shape individuals' lives. Because individual behavior reflects these normative perspectives, it often has the unintended consequence of reproducing social structural inequality. Ultimately, individuals' perspectives shape the structural locations of race, class, and gender and impact the institutional forces that contribute to their continued formation (Ken 2010; Bourdieu 2003; Bourgeois 1995; Ritzer and Goodman 2004).

As a sociologist faced with the brutal realities of poverty, I found myself vacillating between a purely individual approach to the violence I witnessed and a purely structural one. The first time I observed cigarette burn scars on the back of a young child I was overwhelmed with rage at her mother. When I witnessed the appalling conditions under which homeless families were forced to live, I regarded them as victims of an unjust economic system. Throughout my field experience I sought to untangle the complicated relationship between social structure and individual agency. I also thought a lot about hegemony and the way it functions to maintain race, class, and gender inequality. Unfortunately, I have no definitive answers. I believe that poverty is a violent and powerful force in people's lives. I also believe that people do make choices, but that those choices, and their consequences, are constrained by their social structural location. Over the course of my fieldwork I saw first-hand how social conditions impinged on individual actions. While I absolutely do not condone child abuse, I now understand how the overwhelming inhumanity and devastation of poverty can lead a mother to hurt her child. Based on these considerations, the theoretical analysis of my research is on the intersection of gender, race, and class inequality as fundamental organizing principles of society. Ultimately, my goal is to illustrate how socially structured race, class, and gender inequality influences the daily lives of homeless families in San Francisco and how their subsequent experiences are then shaped by race, class, and gender inequality in an interactive process.

CULTURE VERSUS SOCIAL STRUCTURE

There is a long-standing debate in sociology regarding the primacy of social structure versus culture in the creation and perpetuation of poverty. Structural theorists point to economic inequality and historical racism as the causes of poverty. Proponents of the structural perspective argue that slavery, migration, and the development of an inequitable class structure should be the focus of analysis. Cultural theorists examine cultural norms and behaviors as the causes of poverty, not economic inequality. The cultural perspective dates back to the 1920s when E. Franklin Frazier began to characterize poor African Americans as inherently pathological. He blamed high rates of poverty, unemployment, and low educational attainment on out-of-wedlock births and the rejection of marriage, rather than on structural inequality (Frazier 1939). Ironically, his work was quite progressive at the time. Frazier was attempting to disprove the widely held belief in African American biological inferiority. In addition, he questioned the idea that all black families were uniformly disorganized by examining the role of class differences in behavior. In his attempt to demonstrate that black families were not monolithic, Frazier presented low-income black families as inherently pathological. The ideology of impoverished African Americans as deviant became fixed in the public imagination.

During the 1960s the cultural approach to understanding poverty re-emerged. In 1965 Daniel Patrick Moynihan published his report *The Negro Family—The Case for National Action*. Moynihan portrayed the black community as being characterized by female-headedness, high rates of illegitimacy, divorce, matriarchy, economic dependence, unemployment, delinquency, and crime. Moynihan argued that the "tangle of pathology" confronting the black community was caused by unstable black families (Mathis 1978; Martin and Martin 1978; Dodson 1988). His focus on African American women as responsible for black poverty resulted in the creation and perpetuation of the myth of the black matriarch. This pernicious myth continues to plague black women in discussions of poverty, welfare reform, and black family life. Moynihan argued that the precarious nature of low-income black families was a direct result of female-dominated, and thus dysfunctional, households that commonly existed within the black community (Moynihan 1965; Allen 1978; Martin and Martin 1978; Staples 1981). Matriarchal families were blamed for unemployment, low educational attainment, poverty and were considered detrimental to the personality development of black children (Rainwater 1966; Martin and Martin 1978). Although Moynihan was genuinely concerned with urban poverty, he rejected racism as a pivotal force in the perpetuation of poverty by asserting that the tangle of pathology was "capable of perpetuating itself without assistance from the white world" (Zinn 1989, 858).

During the 1960s the work of anthropologist Oscar Lewis (1959, 1966), who studied poverty in Mexico and Puerto Rico, also became popularized. In fact, he coined the term "the culture of poverty" when referring to the cultural norms of his Mexican respondents. His theoretical framework was subsequently applied to Latinixs in the United States. As in studies of the black family, the culture of poverty approach to Latinix families was also predicated on an assumption of the superiority of white middle-class culture and the devaluation of all other family forms (Staples and Mirandé 1980; Roschelle 1997). However, unlike studies of the black family, this approach to understanding Latinix families focused on male dominance and female passivity as the key to explaining Latinix family disorganization. The primary focus of this perspective was on the debilitating effects of *machismo* (the spiritual, physical, and sexual, domination of men over women). Social and economic inequality experienced by Latinixs was blamed solely on the patriarchal structure of the Latinix family (Mirandé 1985). In addition, these sociologists argued that low-income Latinixs have distinctive values, aspirations, and psychological characteristics that inhibit their achievement and produce behavioral deficiencies that keep them impoverished. These deficiencies result in a perpetual cycle of poverty (Zinn 1989) and a fundamental rejection of marriage. (Andrade 1982; Mirandé 1985; Ybarra 1983). Paradoxically, culture of poverty theorists asserted that African Americans must achieve a patriarchal family structure as a means of transcending their pathological conditions, while simultaneously arguing that this same patriarchal structure is responsible for the impoverished conditions of Latinix families.

During the 1970s a new cultural perspective that focused on the strength of black and Latinix communities emerged. This framework, known as the strength resiliency perspective, was an attempt by scholars of color to refute the negative stereotypes of the previous decade. A discussion of this perspective is beyond the scope of this book (for an in-depth analysis of the strength resiliency perspective, see Roschelle 1997). What is important is that these scholars provided an analysis of historically based cultural norms that were positive and that contributed to the survival of black and Latinix communities confronting poverty. In addition, these scholars provided a scathing critique of Moynihan's work. *The Moynihan Report*, which focused almost exclusively on negative cultural norms, was derided as racist. His lack of a structural analysis of poverty angered many progressive scholars. As the economy continued to worsen and the gap between rich and poor widened during the 1980s, liberal sociologists seemed reluctant to interrogate urban poverty for fear of being labeled racist.

When William Julius Wilson's book *The Truly Disadvantaged: The Inner City, the Underclass, and Public Policy* was published in 1987 he was attacked for focusing too heavily on cultural norms. I remember being mystified by this critique since the central argument of the book is that the loss of the production economy (i.e., manufacturing jobs in highly racialized northeastern central cities), is directly responsible for the rise in poverty-related social problems. While it is true that he briefly discussed some negative elements of culture, the book systematically analyzed how job loss and concentrated poverty affect African Americans. It is true, however, that despite Wilson's recognition of the unique experience of men of color in the labor market, his policy recommendations were devoid of a racial (and gender) component. Ultimately, Wilson was unfairly aligned with culture of poverty theorists. The message was clear; any discussion of the relationship between urban poverty and cultural norms was dangerous.

To make matters worse, a vicious debate about the term "underclass" emerged. Journal articles and editorials were written. I have no doubt that if the book were published now the tweets would be flying and people would spend endless hours blogging about it. As a feminist graduate student I recognized the profundity of language, (my older brother Steve still winces and then auto-corrects himself when he uses the term "girl" to refer to anyone over 18 in front of me) but as a young activist I was angered by the amount of time people spent debating this term. While I agree the term "underclass" is infinitely problematic, what was more problematic were the conditions under which people of color in inner city America were forced to live. I kept waiting for people to organize and fight against poverty and the welfare state. Not only was there an absence of political activism from within academe, there was a dearth of research on urban poverty conducted by progressive scholars. In fact, the overwhelming majority of research on black and Latinix poverty during the 1980s was conducted by conservative scholars who were unapologetic in their racialized discourse. Much of their research focused on teenage and nonmarital pregnancy, criminality, violence, welfare dependency, and a lack of normative family values. Poor families of color were vilified as pathological; it seemed that once again "culture" was the cause of poverty and was code for "deviant" (Mead 1992; Murray 1984).

Many progressive sociologists began examining poverty and racism in the 1990s as a way to take back the research on urban poverty and to reject the reemerging culture of poverty approach proffered by these conservative analysts. The bulk of this research focused on social structure and institutional racism to the exclusion of culture. Some scholars have recently suggested that sociologists refrained from analyzing culture to avoid being labeled racist. Others argue that, particularly in quantitative research, culture is difficult to measure (Small Harding and Lamont 2010). For those of us doing on-the-ground research on poverty, it is difficult to ignore the overwhelming power of social structural inequality. Cultural norms do matter, but they are often overshadowed by the exigencies of poverty. Throughout my own career I have used intersectionality theory as a way to include both culture and social structure in my analyses. In fact, I examined the role of cultural norms and social structural inequality on the loss of extended kinship networks among black and Latinix families in my book *No More Kin: Exploring Race, Class, and Gender in Family Networks*. Therefore, the renewed focus on culture (see, for example: Fosse 2010; Lamont, Beljean and Clair 2014; Small Harding and Lamont 2010; Vaisey 2010) is of interest to me.[6] However, we must be careful not to revert back to the ideological position that culture is the cause of poverty. While it is clear to me that different racial ethnic groups do indeed have unique cultural norms, these norms are not responsible for poverty. Rather, cultural norms provide the context for how people navigate their social structural position. Throughout the book intersectionality provides a framework from which to interrogate the interconnection between culture and social structure in the lives of homeless families.

REPRESENTATIONS OF HOMELESS FAMILIES

One of the most daunting challenges to writing a book on homeless families is presenting the realities of their lives without reinforcing stereotypic images of poverty. For the last several years I have been agonizing over what stories to tell and how to tell them. I do not want my book to perpetuate already pervasive stereotypes of low-income women and their children. However, I believe it is my responsibility to portray an accurate account of the experiences of chronically homeless families in San Francisco. In the past, social scientists have sometimes refrained from presenting negative behavior for fear of reproducing stereotypic assumptions about the poor. In addition, the use of qualitative methods that are not ethnographic limits the amount of time investigators spend in the field. As a result, these researchers do not get to know respondents viscerally and merely scratch the surface of their experiences. The unwillingness of some sociologists to fully interrogate destructive behavior among the poor has recently come under scrutiny (Wacquant 2002). Rather than ignoring the sometimes brutalizing behavior that exists among the poor, I will contextualize it within an analysis of poverty. If social scientists want to effect meaningful social change, we must anchor problematic behavior like child abuse, domestic violence, and drug use within the context of poverty and social structural oppression Subsequently, this book examines deleterious behaviors found among homeless families and analyzes them within the context of gender, race, and class inequality. However, I also do not want to contribute to what Philippe Bourgois calls the "pornography of violence" (1995, 18). While I believe it is essential to depict the ravages of poverty accurately, this book is not meant to be titillating, nor is it meant to be a touristic journey through the urban ghetto. Rather, this book is intended to present the myriad experiences of persistently homeless families, in order to contribute to thoughtful social policy that will lead to positive social change.

STRUCTURE OF THE BOOK

This book chronicles the rise of familial homelessness in San Francisco at the end of the twentieth century. San Francisco is undeniably a unique city with a distinct character. Nevertheless, San Francisco has undergone similar wide-ranging macroeconomic shifts and concomitant changes in family structure, found in other U.S. cities Therefore, using San Francisco as a case study will provide insight into why familial homelessness increased throughout the United States during the 1990s and the consequences of that increase. Only by chronicling the oftentimes unbearable stories of homeless women and children can we empathize with their anguish and begin to construct appropriate social policy. With that in mind the next three chapters examine a variety of causes for increased familial homelessness. Chapter 1, "San Francisco: The Best City on Earth" examines macrostructural changes in the economy, including urban development, declining wages, increased housing costs, and the loss of low-income housing. Chapter 2, "Home is Where the [Broken Heart] Is" focuses on the violence of poverty. This chapter examines the gendered and racialized violence of poverty experienced by homeless mothers in San Francisco. Women in this research have endured physical and sexual violence as children and are typically victims of adult intimate partner violence. This chapter presents the excruciating narratives of violence and degradation suffered by homeless women. Their lived experiences illustrate that, for many women of color, becoming homeless is a direct result of racialized poverty and chronic family violence. Chapter 3, "The Unraveling Social Safety Net," discusses welfare reform and the impact of this radical legislation on homeless families. Chapter 4, "The Tattered Web of Kinship," investigates how the erosion of traditional social support and extended kinship networks has pushed low-income families further over the edge into homelessness. Chapter 5, "Life's A Bitch: The Everyday Struggle for Survival," examines the various strategies homeless families use to navigate the city, create kinship networks with other homeless families, and access institutional forms of social support as a means of survival. Chapter 7, "Paradise Lost: The Lived Experiences of Homeless Kids," presents the life stories of San Francisco's homeless kids and the meanings they ascribe to their poverty and homelessness. The conclusion is a discussion of "A Home Away From Homelessness" and the delicate balancing act required to provide non-regimented programs that allow for autonomy among families, while maintaining safety and calmness. This final chapter ends with an economic update of San Francisco as it relates to topics presented throughout the book.

NOTES

1. There are different definitions of homelessness currently used by particular government agencies. The most restrictive definition is utilized by the Department of Housing and Urban Development (HUD). HUD focuses primarily on homeless people living on the streets, in shelters, in vehicles, or other places not meant for human habitation. This definition does not include people doubling up with family or friends, nor does it include families who are precariously housed in residential motels, campgrounds, or trailer parks. In addition, HUD counts of the homeless, which are conducted in January on a single night across the country, provide only a snapshot of homelessness on a given night at one point in the year. In 2009 the HUD definition was expanded with the passage of the Homeless Emergency Assistance and Rapid Transition to Housing (HEARTH) Act to include people escaping domestic violence, children, and runaway and homeless youth. However, this population is even more difficult to count using the Point-in-Time method. A more inclusive definition of homelessness is used by The Departments of Education, Health and Human Services, Labor, Justice, and Agriculture and provides a more accurate portrayal of the extent of homelessness, particularly among children and families. Throughout the book when I refer to homeless families or homeless children, I

use the McKinney-Vento Homeless Assistance Act definition first signed into law in 1987 and reauthorized in 2009. This definition of homelessness includes children, families, and individuals who lack a fixed regular and adequate nighttime residence and who live in public or private places that are not designed for human beings (e.g., car, park, abandoned building), temporary shelters or transitional housing (including motels and hotels), are doubled up with family or friends, are in imminent danger of losing their housing, are facing eviction action, or lack the resources or support networks necessary to obtain housing. In addition, families with children are defined as homeless if they have experienced a long-term period of living without permanent housing, have experienced persistent instability and frequent moves, and can be expected to remain precariously housed as a result of chronic health or mental health conditions, disabilities, substance abuse, histories of domestic violence or childhood abuse, the presence of children or youth with a disability, or multiple barriers to employment. Families who are fleeing domestic violence, dating violence, sexual assault, or stalking are also considered homeless (Bassuk, et al. 2014).

2. When referring to both Latinas and Latinos, I will use the term Latinix, which is gender neutral and inclusive of trans, queer, nonbinary, gender nonconforming, or genderfluid individuals. However, since the respondents in my sample all identified as cisgender, when referring specifically to women or men I will use the terms Latina and Latino respectively, to indicate respondents' cisgender identity. For the same reasons, I also use she/he/they when referring to men and women in general.

3. The California Work Opportunity and Responsibility to Kids (CalWORKs) was created by the California State Legislature in 1997 as a response to the 1996 Personal Responsibility and Work Opportunity Reconciliation Act (PRWORA) and is essentially the state's version of Temporary Aid to Needy Families.

4. For a more detailed discussion of the research design and methodology, see Roschelle and Kaufman (2004).

5. Having said that, I did edit many of the quotes for readability and to preserve the subtlety of what was said. It is very difficult to convey the meaning behind an utterance by simply reproducing verbatim tape transcriptions. Without seeing the body language or hearing the intonation of an individual's voice, the meanings of their words can get lost when converted to the written page. Therefore, I omitted repetitive phrases, incomplete thoughts, and fragmented sentences, to maintain the meaning of the original utterance. In addition, I deleted unnecessary verbiage (like, uh, um, ya know etc.) because it resulted in incoherent sentences and is distracting to readers. Nonetheless, I tried to maintain the grammatical form and expressive language used by respondents so as not to change the meaning of their words.

6. For a scathing critique of this resurgent focus on culture, see Stephen Steinberg's 2011 article "Poor Reason" in the *Boston Review*.

Chapter One

San Francisco: The Best City on Earth

I was born and raised in San Francisco, have lived here all my life. I've seen a lot of changes in these neighborhoods. Even back in the day when things were really bad at least you knew you could always find a place to live. Now only rich folk can afford this city and the rest of us are being squeezed out like toothpaste at the end of a crusty old tube.—Jeremiah

POVERTY AND HOMELESSNESS

At the conclusion of the twentieth century the U.S. economy was booming. Interest rates were down, the stock market was up, unemployment was low, and inflation was under control. Policy makers, political pundits, and media moguls reminded us daily of our nation's prosperity.[1] However, not everyone in the United States was enjoying this newfound affluence. Beginning in the 1980s the gap between the rich and poor began to widen significantly and poverty rates among women and children skyrocketed. In 1995, the first year of my fieldwork, 36.4 million people lived in poverty, representing 13.8 percent of the overall population. This statistic exposes the breadth of poverty; however, it does not provide specific details of exactly who is poor. To understand how poverty is distributed in America, we need to look at more comprehensive data. In 1995, the poverty rate was 8.5 percent for non-Hispanic whites, 29.3 percent for African Americans, and 30.3 percent for Hispanics.[2] These data indicate that poverty is racialized with people of color among the most disadvantaged. When we examine the data for non-married women who live with their children, the statistics become even more disturbing. Poverty rates among mother-only families are much higher than they are for two-parent families. For example, only 5.6 percent of married couples lived in poverty, while 32.4 percent of female-headed families did. In addi-

19

tion to being racialized, poverty is also clearly gendered. The 1995 census did not include poverty rates for father-only families, which is alarming, since research has consistently shown that father-only families are much less likely to be impoverished than mother-only families (Cherlin 2013). When we look more closely at racial ethnic differences, we once again see that families of color are significantly more disadvantaged than white families. For mother-only families with no spouse present the poverty rates were 26.6 percent for white families, 45.1 percent for African American families, and 49.4 percent for Hispanic origin families. Perhaps the most disturbing aspect of poverty in American is the number of children who are destitute. Forty percent of individuals under eighteen were living in poverty in 1995. Considering that people in this age group only made up about one-fourth of the total population, this figure is staggering. Even more troubling is the fact that 23.7 percent of children under the age of six lived in poverty. For children under six living in mother-only families, 61.8 percent of them were poor, compared to 11.1 percent of kids in married-couple families (U.S. Census Bureau 1996). It might be tempting to look at these data and assume that the solution to poverty is for women to simply get married. However, research has shown that even if low-income single mothers married the fathers of their children, they would still have higher poverty rates than women who are currently married (Sigle-Rushton and McLanahan 2002; Thomas and Sawhill 2002).

One manifestation of increased poverty is the rise in homelessness among women and children that occurred during the 1990s. In 1987, women with children comprised 9 percent of the urban homeless population (Burt 1992). By 1997, that figure increased to 34 percent (Burt et al. 1999). By the end of the twentieth century, the percentage of the homeless that were women and children had reached 40 percent (Burt, et al. 1999; U.S. Conference of Mayors 2001). In less than a decade, while some Americans were enjoying unprecedented affluence, homelessness among women and children increased dramatically. This chapter examines macroeconomic shifts in the occupational structure and in the housing market in San Francisco, illustrating how these social structural forces combined to cause homelessness among families.

HISTORICAL MACROSTRUCTURAL CHANGES

Transformations in the economy and in the labor market have had a significant impact on inner-city urban neighborhoods throughout the United States. Massive economic changes since the end of World War II have resulted in a major shift from a manufacturing economy to an information processing and service economy. While these economic shifts, which have redistributed work in national and regional economies, affect all workers, they have more serious consequences for workers of color who are concentrated in the hardest-hit industries (Wilson 1987). In San Francisco, these economic shifts were exacerbated by the development of the downtown beginning in the 1960s. This massive urban development, combined with the loss of manufacturing jobs, had a profound impact on employment. Throughout the 1960s and 1970s blue-collar and low-skilled jobs declined substantially. Although overall employment rates rose in San Francisco during this period, manufacturing jobs were replaced by jobs requiring more education in real estate, insurance, retail, and finance (Cohen 1981; Hartman 2002). By the mid-1970s San Francisco became a center of international commerce and banking. As white-collar jobs proliferated, so did office construction. Between 1960 and 1981, 30 million square feet of new office buildings were added to the downtown. As San Francisco was becoming a major participant in the nation's corporate economy, low-income residents were being ousted from their downtown neighborhoods (Hartman 2002).

Another significant factor in the transformation of San Francisco was the expansion of the tourism and convention industries. In the mid-1960s the San Francisco Redevelopment Agency and the San Francisco Convention & Visitors Bureau began development of the Yerba Buena Center in the South of Market neighborhood. This neighborhood had historically been home to unskilled and semi-skilled workers. In addition, residents included transients, hoboes, seasonal workers, and casual laborers who lived in lodging houses and hotels. South of Market was a thriving (albeit poor) neighborhood that provided goods and services to approximately 4,000 low-income residents who lived there until they were displaced by this massive construction project (Hartman 2002).

Urban renewal also profoundly affected the landscape of San Francisco. Redevelopment projects occurred throughout the 1960s in which residents were essentially evicted from their homes. For example, in the Western Addition neighborhood more than four thousand, mostly African American and Asian families were dispersed throughout the Bay Area as their homes were "redeveloped." The Golden Gateway Project, located in the downtown area, demolished the homes of 200 single men and 25 families living near the waterfront. In the Fillmore district, a primarily African American neighborhood, 13,500 people were forced out of their homes, some of whom had only recently moved there after being expelled from the Western Addition. Residents in the primarily African American neighborhood of Bayview-Hunter's Point were also being systematically dislocated. Overall, approximately 6,000 housing units were destroyed in redevelopment areas and were replaced by only 662 units of low- or moderate-income housing. The displacement of the poor and the increasingly tight housing market for low-income families in the 1960s and 1970s was the forerunner of the massive housing crisis that reemerged during my fieldwork (Hartman 2002) and unrelentingly continues.

CONTEMPORARY MACROSTRUCTURAL CHANGES

As macroeconomic shifts in the job market continued unabated, employment opportunities in San Francisco changed considerably. Throughout the 1990s, the dot-com boom created high-paying jobs for well-educated white people. The majority of employees working at start-ups and at established internet companies were recent transplants to the city, often making obscene amounts of money. These jobs provided sick pay, health insurance, and hefty retirement plans (Borsook 1999). In direct contrast were newly created jobs in the service economy, which grew more than any other segment of the labor market. By the middle of the 1990s only 15 percent of the city's total workforce was employed in blue-collar jobs (Hartman 2002). By 1999, 49 percent of new jobs created were *very low-income* occupations including: janitors, retail sales, guards, cashiers, waiters and waitresses, home health care workers, hand packers and packagers, cooks, domestics, and hotel maids. These jobs were highly racialized and a majority of the workers were men and women of color. *Low-income* jobs such as secretaries and salespeople made up 9 percent of new jobs (Frank 1999). Many of these jobs paid only minimum wage and rarely included health insurance or other benefits. Individuals employed as waiters or waitresses were often not paid minimum wage because their salaries were presumably offset by tips. As jobs in the lowest-paying sector of the labor market increased, it became increasingly difficult for people to survive economically. In addition, salary differences between employees in the dot-com industry and the service economy contributed to unbridled inequality. In fact, between 1994 and 1996 the gap between rich and poor in San Francisco increased by 40 percent (Borsook 1999).

In addition to declining wages, housing costs in San Francisco simultaneously skyrocketed. By the mid-1990s San Francisco had among the highest housing costs in the country (Frank 1999). During the first year of my fieldwork the median rent for a two-bedroom apartment was $1,100. Over the course of the next four years, rents increased drastically. In 1996 the median rent for a two-bedroom apartment was $1,350 and in 1997 it increased to $1,600. According to the San Francisco Planning Department, by 1999 the median monthly rent for a two-bedroom apartment was $2,500. Based on the federal guidelines of 30 percent income going to rent, an individual would have to make roughly $100,000 per year to afford a $2,500-a-month apartment. More appalling is the fact that a person earning minimum wage would have to work 174 hours per week to afford $2,500 a month (Hartman 2002). Given that there are only 168 hours in a week, this is utterly absurd.

In addition to exorbitant rents, the lack of available housing was catastrophic in the mid-to-late 1990s. When I moved to San Francisco in 1994, the vacancy rate was about 2 to 3 percent, meaning that 97 to 98 percent of the units were unavailable. Within a year, the vacancy rate was estimated to be lower than 1 percent. Most experts agree that a vacancy rate of 4 to 6 percent is necessary for a healthy housing market and that consistently low vacancy rates reflect serious housing shortages (Frank 1999). As a result, renting an apartment was a nightmare, particularly for low-income women with children. Potential renters had to provide detailed credit reports, job histories, and references. In addition, landlords required first and last month's rent as well as a security deposit. Numerous people showed up for each vacant apartment, often with homemade cookies, gift certificates, and other bribes. As a result, landlords would only rent to the most desirable tenants, preferably individuals with white-collar jobs and no kids. Scores of newly transplanted dot-comers moved into previously working-class neighborhoods, displacing long-tern residents. Subsequently, it became increasingly difficult for low-income women to find stable housing, leading many to become homeless.

In addition to outrageous rents, another problem leading to increased family homelessness was the loss of Single Room Occupancy (SRO) hotels, also called residential motels. The demolition of residential motels started during the Yerba Buena Development Project and continued well into the 1990s. During the construction of the Yerba Buena Center approximately forty-eight SROs containing about 3,200 residents were demolished. Many of these hotels extended past South of Market into the Tenderloin, parts of the Mission District, and into Chinatown, home to many low-income residents. Between 1975 and 1979 the city lost another 6,098 residential hotel rooms. From 1997 to 1999 an additional 1,200 residential hotel rooms were destroyed by fires and conversion to apartments (Hartman 2002; Nieves 1999).

In addition to the loss of residential motels, there was a significant decline in public housing during the course of my fieldwork. When I moved to San Francisco, there were 36 public housing projects, with approximately 6,000 apartments. In addition, there were about 6,000 units of privately owned low-rent Section 8 housing with waiting lists of 7–10 years.[3] Between 1996 and 1998 thousands of public housing residents were evicted when several of these dilapidated units were destroyed. This massive loss of low-income housing was happening throughout urban America. During the 1980s, President Reagan decreased the Housing and Urban Development (HUD) budget by 80 percent. As a result, by 1985, there was only enough low-income housing for half the overall low-income population (Wasserman, and Clair 2010). In San Francisco people were initially excited that barely habitable units were being rebuilt. However, the total number of new units built did not equal the number destroyed. For example, in Hayes Valley, the original housing project had 463 units prior to demolition but only had 195 units when rebuilt. Another housing project in the Western Addition had 500 original units replaced with only 353. The Housing Authority had a waiting list of 14,000 families in 1999, subsequently, the loss of this many units of low-income housing was disastrous. A disturbing outcome of this process was that many residents were forced to leave the city in search of housing. Displaced tenants were given Section 8 vouchers. However, given the insanely low vacancy rates, a large majority of them could not find Section 8 housing. Over one-third of the families expelled from Hayes Valley and 30 percent of the families evicted from Bernal Heights left the city. Since almost half of all families in public housing in San Francisco were African American, there was a concomitant reduction in the city's black population (Hartman 2002).

In addition to public housing projects, San Francisco also had approximately 10,000 privately owned, government-subsidized low- and moderate-income rental units throughout the city. These units were called "expiring use projects" because they were built under a low-interest federal loan program that allowed developers to prepay the mortgage after twenty years and thus evade government rent controls. Throughout California about 11,000 of these apartments had their rents increased to market rates. In San Francisco, a disproportionate number of these apartments were in the poorest neighborhoods in the city, including the Tenderloin, Western Addition, and Bayview-Hunters Point. The loss of these low-income apartments has been catastrophic for poor women and children throughout San Francisco and has contributed to their homelessness.

THE CRUSHING IMPACT OF HISTORICAL MACROSTRUCTURAL CHANGES ON FAMILIES

These conditions come together in the unique stories of homeless women and children who were directly impacted by these profound macrostructural changes. Their poignant stories reveal the interconnection between individuals and the broader social structure. Through their narratives, the racialized and gendered nature of poverty will become evident. The analytic framework of intersectionality theory will illuminate how race, class, and gender inequality, which is deeply embedded in American society, has a profound impact on families' ability to thrive.

During my fieldwork a common theme of frustration with the changing landscape of San Francisco emerged. Respondents consistently expressed their disgust with how elite San Francisco was becoming and with their ability to make a living wage and to afford housing. Because most of the respondents in my research were from San Francisco, they experienced these changes first-hand. Older respondents were more cognizant of the historical transformations of the city, but even women in their twenties remembered a time when their families, although poor, were securely housed. Many of the individuals I interviewed blamed gentrification, urban development, and low wages on their homelessness. Jeremiah and Effie, a married African American couple in their mid-forties who had recently become homeless, had vivid memories of San Francisco prior to the massive structural upheaval of the last thirty years. They discussed their experiences with me at great length.

Jeremiah: I grew up in a poor family but we always had a safe place to live and my parents always had work. We lived in the Western Addition where lots of black families lived. My whole family lived there—cousins, aunts, and uncles—everyone was poor but everyone had a home.

Effie: I grew up with just my mom and two sisters. My dad died when I was a little girl. My mother worked as a waitress and as a maid. She didn't make a lot of money but it was enough for us to survive. We could pay the rent. And as J said, even though all our friends and neighbors were poor, we lived in apartments in the projects—we had homes.

Jeremiah: In the 1960s, when I was about ten or eleven the city started these big urban renewal projects. I remember there were huge signs hanging on the fences in front of all the construction sites. Urban Renewal in big bold letters—like it was some great thing they were doing to help us *poor Negroes! You* know that is what they used to call us black folks back then. Anyway—we knew better—we called it urban removal cuz we knew we would be getting kicked out of our neighborhoods. We didn't believe the hype and we were right.

Effie: Ain't that the truth! After they finished knocking down all those buildings and putting up new ones it seemed like half the neighborhood was gone. You have to remember Annee that in the 1960s black people were organizing and standing up for our rights. It made white people nervous so they tried to get rid of us. After they finished rebuilding the Western Addition most of my neighbors got scattered all over the city and a lot of them moved to Oakland.

Jeremiah: Yeah, Effie and I were lucky because both our families found apartments in other neighborhoods. Even though a lot of people left the city we were able to stay. In those days you would never become homeless. You would either move to Oakland or find another housing project in San Francisco. Even the poorest families had a roof over their heads.

There was always some kind of shelter—even if it was in one of those hotels in the Tenderloin.

Effie: After we got married we found a place together in Hayes Valley. We both worked and had our two kids. Over the years we watched the neighborhood change from mostly black and kind of poor to mostly white and kind of rich. This happened all over the city. So many neighborhoods that had black and Latin families got more and more white and more and more expensive. When they started to rebuild our housing project two years ago we got kicked out. They told us we could move back once it was finished but in the meantime we had no place to live. They gave us a Section 8 voucher but there is like a ten-year waiting list or something for Section 8 housing. We couldn't afford to pay rent anywhere; even a dump costs a fortune. That is how we ended up at the Hamilton [family shelter].[4] If we didn't have kids we would be living in Golden Gate Park. I hate those yuppies—they moved here and we ended up homeless.

Jeremiah: Effie is right. The rents have gone crazy in the last ten years. You know they ruined this city. All the so-called urban renewal did was make it impossible for working people like us to survive. The jobs don't pay enough—not like when I was a kid. My dad worked in a factory and belonged to the union. Those jobs paid decent wages and had benefits. Families could survive. Now, all the jobs are low-paying service jobs. Plus, there are not enough housing projects anymore, rents are crazy high, and there are all these homeless families. I never imagined I would ever be homeless. I work hard and have always supported my family. It's not right. All these rich white yuppies have taken over the city.

I spoke to Jeremiah and Effie after the completion of the Hayes Valley housing project that had been converted to stratified[5] housing to find out if they got an apartment. Jeremiah told me "oh yeah, they finished the project in Hayes Valley, it looks great—we didn't get an apartment, we're still homeless!" Jeremiah and Effie were the oldest respondents in my study. As such, they provide a unique perspective on the impact of the macrostructural shifts that occurred over the last thirty years. Jeremiah's comment that even "back in the day when things were really bad at least you knew you could always find a place to live" is a common theme among homeless families in the Bay Area.[6] His statement exemplifies that, despite the presence of grinding poverty, families would not have become homeless twenty or thirty years ago.

Historical redevelopment and gentrification in San Francisco exacerbated already existent racial and economic inequality. In particular, the demolition of low-income housing units in San Francisco resulted in the loss of over 50 percent of the African American population over a thirty year period. This monumental shift in the racial composition of the city had profound implications for its remaining black residents who are residentially segregated and make up a large percentage of the city's poor. In addition, the urban renewal that began in the 1960s and was reinvigorated in the 1990s, paved the way for the influx of wealthy white elites who seem to have taken over the city. Redevelopment policy in San Francisco is one example of how race and class structure people's lives and is the source of both oppression and of privilege. For African Americans, urban development and low-wages converged at the intersection of race and class, and further disempowered an already vulnerable population, while simultaneously privileging white middle-class residents who benefited from redevelopment.

THE CRUSHING IMPACT OF CONTEMPORARY
MACROSTRUCTURAL CHANGES ON FAMILIES

Throughout the course of my research, there was widespread agreement among respondents that even the most impoverished families would never have become homeless "back in the day." This viewpoint was expressed by women in their twenties and early thirties, who grew up poor, but whose families were securely housed during the massive urban development of the 1960s and 1970s. Their perspective is not a naïve romanticization of the past, but in fact, reflects empirical reality. During the mid-1990s evictions were at an all-time high and over 70 percent of those ousted from their homes left the city. These young mothers had no resources available to relocate, so they turned to family shelters. This first generation of homeless mothers attributed their homelessness to current macrostructural shifts occurring throughout the Bay Area. Gentrification and urban development, low-wage service-economy jobs, skyrocketing rents, and a lack of low-income housing were frequently mentioned as causes of their homelessness. When asked how she became homeless, Adela, a Latina mother of two in her early twenties said:

> I just can't afford to live here no more. The city keeps changing so much. They keep fixing things up so the tourists wanna come but it's hella expensive and I don't make much money. I worked in a dry cleaning store for three years but I only made minimum wage. I hated that job so much—I worked on my feet all day long with no breaks, but I stayed there so I could support my kids. After a while I couldn't afford to pay my rent and buy food and pay my other bills. Stuff is so expensive now. I kept paying the rent late so my landlord kicked me out. Now I'm homeless. I can't find a cheap apartment anywhere—even in the worst neighborhoods—they cost a fortune. There are no more apartments in housing projects anymore. They keep knocking 'em down and building 'em back with less apartments in them. I mean, they look really nice—pretty gardens, little backyards, no more graffiti—now the tourists aren't afraid to go

into those neighborhoods—but how does that help me? This city is for rich
people now. How are we supposed to survive?

Similarly, Marlene, an African American woman, expressed her frustration
with the shifting landscape of San Francisco and the inability of wages to
keep pace with increasing rents.

> I worked in a school cafeteria for about a year and then I worked as a teacher's
> aide for a while. The pay was so shitty I could barely pay my bills. I tried to
> pay my rent on time but after a while I just couldn't do it anymore. I had to buy
> food for Tamika and Jerold and pay for the bus to get to work. We got put out.
> I am so tired of struggling—it is so hard to live. All these rich white people
> have come here and made it impossible for us to survive. I grew up here and
> was always poor but there were plenty of places to live. We had the projects,
> we had houses in poor neighborhoods—no one with kids was put out on the
> street. But Da Mayor—all he cares about is looking smooth and making mon-
> ey for the city.[7] Just cuz he's black doesn't mean he cares about us. He just
> wants those rich white people to come here and bring their money with them.
> He doesn't care how that changes our neighborhoods or that poor people can't
> afford their rent. He'd probably be happy if we all just moved out of the city—
> then he can say look at me I took out the trash!

Donna expressed a similar sentiment when she explained:

> This city is out of control. All these fancy new buildings going up all over
> downtown—oh excuse me in *SOMA*! What the fuck is SOMA—just because
> you give a place a nickname doesn't make it right to kick people out. I get it—
> South of Market—my neighborhood was always south of Market Street but it
> is where I lived. There were crappy apartments, and junkies, and prostitutes,
> and yeah, it was kind of dangerous. But I could afford to live there on my
> waitress salary. All of a sudden they start building lofts and condos for those
> asshole computer nerds and film people and suddenly they call my neighbor-
> hood SOMA. That doesn't give them to right to kick me out. But that is what
> they did. I got evicted and they tore down my building and now I live in the
> Franciscan.[8] FUCK SOMA!

Adela, Marlene, and Donna do not espouse the formal discourse endemic
to gentrification and urban development. Nonetheless, it is clear from their
stories that they do have a critique of how they have been impacted by these
large-scale changes in San Francisco. All three women expressed disgust
with the influx of white elites who have driven up the cost of living, changed
the character of their neighborhoods, and have caused rents to skyrocket. As
homeless mothers, they have a visceral understanding of the impact of urban
development and low-wages on individual families.

The critique offered by these three women is shared by many homeless
mothers throughout San Francisco. The gentrification of the Mission District

is particularly relevant for homeless Latinas in San Francisco, and highlights the dramatically changing terrain of the city. In the Mission District urban development was heightened by the explosion of the dot-com industry and a rapid influx of affluent, white interlopers. Irish families predominated in the Mission until the 1960s when Mexican immigrants began to arrive. Mexican immigrants and their children made up the bulk of the neighborhood until the 1980s. In the 1980s refugees from civil wars in El Salvador and Nicaragua arrived, further solidifying the Mission as a thriving Latinix and Latin American immigrant community. At the conclusion of the 1980s, the Mission was one of the few remaining working class neighborhoods in the city (Keating 2003). However, with the arrival of dot-com companies in the 1990s, the Mission District became one of the most brutally gentrified enclaves in San Francisco. For example, during the mid-1990s approximately 48 percent of Mission residents were Latinix and 70 percent of inhabitants were renters. As internet companies moved in Latinixs were systematically displaced. Commercial property was not subject to rent control. As a result, between 1997 and 1999 commercial real estate prices increased 47 percent. Despite non-commercial rent control laws, landlords found ways around tenants' rights (Borsook 1999). By the end of the decade over 1,000 Latinix families had been dislocated. Between 1993 and 2000 the number of rental evictions tripled from 965 to 2,730. In the span of two years (1996-1998), owner move-in evictions increased from 433 to 1,253.[9] By 1998 over two hundred dot-com companies had moved into the Mission and as a result over 50 percent of the local businesses failed. These businesses were owned by Mission residents and catered to the low-income Latinix population (Mirabel 2009). The dot-com boom resulted in what local activist Kevin Keating (2003) called an "internet-spawned housing crisis." Along with the influx of internet start-up companies came an increase in upscale restaurants catering to the new hipster class. As the neighborhood became trendier and more highly educated, affluent white people from outside of the dot-com industry also began moving in. As a result of this rapid and unrelenting gentrification, rents increased considerably. Residents of the Mission became enraged and began to fight back. Keating and a small group of neighborhood activists created the Mission Yuppie Eradication Project. This grassroots organization plastered anti-yuppie posters all over the neighborhood, encouraging residents to vandalize yuppie vehicles and upscale restaurants. Although there were other forms of housing activism in the neighborhood, the Mission Yuppie Eradication Project reflects the intensity of anger over the unabashed destruction of what was a thriving working-class and low-income Latinix community. This fury was shared by impoverished mothers who lived in the Mission prior to becoming homeless. The following impromptu focus group conversation reflects the bitterness and resentment homeless Latina mothers felt at being displaced by callous yuppies in the computer industry who radically altered their community.

Annee: All three of you lived in the Mission District before becoming homeless. Can you tell me what happened in your neighborhood and if that had any connection to your becoming homeless?

Rita: Hell yeah, what happened in our neighborhood is exactly why we became homeless. My family came here from Mexico before I was born. My family lived on Guerrero Street when I was growing up. It was all Mexicans and then people from Central America. Everyone spoke Spanish and we had a real sense of community. After high school, I got my own apartment and lived above a store on Valencia. It was real cheap and I could afford the rent. Before I had my kids I worked and then when I had Nestor I went on welfare for two years. I went back to work when Nestor was two and worked for another year. When I had Ceci, I went back on welfare for another two years and then went back to work. I worked pretty steady at a bunch of different jobs but the longest one was as a nursing assistant in a nursing home. The pay sucked but I could pay the rent and feed my kids. A lot of people in the neighborhood were like me—poor but surviving. Then those computer dudes started moving into the neighborhood. It was so fast—we could see the neighborhood changing before our eyes. The guy who owned the store I lived above went out of business which was really sad because he had that business for thirteen years. Then someone bought the building and we got evicted. A computer business moved in and we just got kicked out. And we weren't the only ones who got evicted. A lot people from my neighborhood got kicked out of their apartments over the last few years. The rents are so high everywhere in the city so most of them moved to the East Bay. Now even Oakland is getting too expensive so many of them had to move to Stockton and live two hours away. I couldn't move that far away, my family is here, my job is here, and I can't afford a car.

Claudia: The same thing happened to me and Luis. We both grew up in the Mission and all of our family lived in the neighborhood. We had our kids and I stayed home to take care of them. Luis worked at Kaiser[10] as an orderly. He worked his ass off but was so underpaid. They treated him like shit too. Sometimes he would work a second job just to make a little extra money. We sort of lived week to week but we could always pay the rent and always had enough food for the family. Even though we were struggling, we had a good family—our life was good. Then the neighborhood started to change—it got you know—gentrified they call it. All of a sudden there were young white people moving into our neighborhood.

They didn't speak Spanish and they were really rude to us—like we weren't as good as them. They started buying buildings and all these new internet business started to move in. As Rita said it happened really fast—it seemed like it was overnight. All of a sudden there were all these expensive restaurants and fancy stores that none of us could afford. The rents kept going up and families that lived here their whole lives had to move out. Families we knew from school and church started to disappear—they had to move out of the city. It was awful; people were forced out of their homes. It was really horrible for the immigrants from Central America. A lot of them came to the city about ten to fifteen years ago and now they have to move again. It was like they were leaving home and immigrating all over again. Can you imagine how painful that is?

Carmen: I hate those fucking yuppies. I wish they would die. We always had white people living in our neighborhood. Some of them spoke Spanish but not all of them. But they were cool—they tried to be part of the community. They didn't look down their noses at us. They appreciated what we created here—and of course they loved the weather![11] A lot of them were poor artists and writers and community organizers—you know the type—they ride their bikes everywhere and recycle. But they cared about the neighborhood and were good people. Those computer assholes only care about themselves and how much money they can make. They moved in here like they owned the place—which is pretty sad because now they do. They bought up everything they could get their greedy little hands on and they kicked out whoever was in their way. The artists, the activists, us locals—what the fuck do they care? Not about me and my family. Our rent kept going up after they started moving in and we couldn't afford it. I never understood what happened because there is supposed to be rent control. But the rent went up anyway and we got evicted, and now we are homeless. They couldn't care less. That is why people started to fuck with their cars and try to scare them away—that was awesome.

Annee: Are you talking about the Yuppie Eradication Project?

Carmen: Damn right! Local activists got so angry at how the neighborhood was changing and how many people were getting kicked out that they started putting up all these posters telling people to slash tires and key cars that looked expensive. It was really fucking awesome. I mean—they didn't hurt anybody—just their fancy cars.

Claudia: Those posters were really cool. I think a lot of cars got trashed—it was great. Most of us in the neighborhood don't even own cars and the ones who do have old junkers they fixed up. All of a sudden there are BMWs and giant expensive SUVs all over the place. It was so offensive. Then they put up posters that were slamming the new la de da fancy restaurants—they were really funny and were so anti-yuppie.

Rita: I totally agree. The posters were funny but they were also helpful because they explained what was going on in the Mission—all the changes that were happening—they encouraged everyone to fight back.

The first round of posters encouraged the destruction of expensive cars that began to pepper the neighborhood. Slashing tires, scratching paint, and breaking windshields of yuppie cars were promoted. Posters aimed at newly opened restaurants were quite clever and seethed with indignation at how the neighborhood was changing. For example, one poster read "Neighborhood enemy number one is Beauty Bar. At the northeast corner of Mission and 19th, Yuppies Paul Devitt and Aaron Buhrz spent over $100,000 taking over the liquor license and renovating this place to look like Barbie's Malibu Beach House. Beauty Bar is a chain with other versions of this blight in New York City, and soon in LA. *Beauty Bar must be destroyed.*"[12] Another poster fumed "Blowfish Sushi, on Bryant and 20th, brings rich pigs to the Mission, and offers nothing to working and poor people here. It's a nest of cell-phone yuppies and upper middle-class privilege. *The Mission will be a better place when Blowfish Sushi has been blown out of the water.*" These posters echo the resentment that Rita, Claudia, and Carmen expressed at the destruction of their community and at their own displacement. Long-term Mission residents were systematically uprooted from their homes, families, churches, and schools. As an anti-poverty activist and resident of a neighborhood also undergoing dramatic change, I appreciated the anti-gentrification message and the call for direct action. Although I am vehemently opposed to violence, I must admit I was secretly delighted by the Yuppie Eradication Project's promotion of damage to cars; all those Land Rovers, BMWs, and hulking Lexus SUV's were the epitome of yuppie consumerism. I mean, really, who needs a Land Rover in San Francisco? In addition, the owners of the targeted high-end vehicles had insurance to cover the damage. At no time did members of the Yuppie Eradication Project advocate violence toward individuals, and destruction of restaurants rarely, if ever, occurred. At the height of the Yuppie Eradication Project, numerous Latinx families were being driven from their neighborhood. Unfortunately, this form of activism, while ideologically satisfying, did little to prevent the destruction of this Latinix enclave.

GENTRIFICATION ON THE FAULT LINE

The voices of the homeless mothers and of the local activists speak volumes about race, class, and gender inequality in San Francisco and the changing social topography of the city. As more people relocated to San Francisco to work in white-collar professions, the divide between rich and poor widened further. New residents were highly educated, many at elite universities throughout the country. Large numbers of newer employees, particularly in the financial, high tech, and dot-com industries, were young white men. In addition, there was a smaller influx of super-rich venture capitalists who were fast becoming millionaires and even billionaires. These highly privileged white men dramatically changed the nature and spirit of the city. Oxygen bars, overpriced restaurants, hipster clubs, chain stores, and expensive specialty shops opened up throughout the city. Funky neighborhoods like the Lower Haight, Haight Ashbury, and Hayes Valley, lost their edge and were becoming more expensive, and less accepting of the eccentric residents who gave those neighborhoods their charm to begin with. Traditional working-class neighborhoods like Excelsior, the Fillmore, the Tenderloin, and Western Addition all became prohibitively expensive. Throughout San Francisco, rents became excessive and it was common for potential renters to try and bribe landlords with gifts. There was an unrelenting frenzy in the home-buying market. People frequently made bids significantly higher than the asking price on a home. In fact, it was not unusual for someone to offer $50,000 to $60,000 more than the condo or apartment was listed for. Political activists, artists, musicians, and writers could no longer afford to work part-time and devote their lives to social justice or to their art. Blue-collar jobs disappeared and were replaced by service economy jobs that did not pay a living wage. Poverty increased and inequality became more highly gendered and racialized. Latinxs and African Americans suffered the most severe economic disenfranchisement. Low-income parents of color could no longer work two and three jobs and survive on minimum wage. Over 73 percent of low-income renters in the city were paying more than 50 percent of their income on housing. Many families became fractured and the burden of survival typically fell to women, many of whom were already single mothers. By the end of the decade, San Francisco lost 10 percent its Latinix population (Mirabel 2009). Between the historical exodus of African American families, the recent departure of Latinix families, and the uprooting of artists and activists, San Francisco was becoming frighteningly homogenous and utterly insipid. Urban development privileged a large class of young white male elites who enjoyed unprecedented access to the city's neighborhoods and resources. Regrettably, these social structural changes in the economy and the housing market conspired to force impoverished families, who could not afford to leave the city, into homelessness. Widespread macro-economic shifts that have rocked San Francisco, particularly during the 1990s, have created new types of race, class, and gender oppression in the form of homeless women and children of color. Corresponding shifts occurred throughout urban America, and similar examples of race, class, and gender inequality can be found in cities across the country. These economic transformations continued steadily over the next two decades and have exacerbated the gap between rich and poor (Collins and Bilge 2016).

NOTES

1. "The Best City on Earth" was the slogan of Channel Two News (KPIX) from 1994 to 1998. The entire slogan was "The Best Place for News in The Best City on Earth." After growing up with a mother who believed that New York City was undoubtedly the center of the universe, this slogan always made me chuckle.

2. The U.S. Bureau of the Census uses the term Hispanic or Hispanic origin to denote people who originate from Spanish-speaking countries. I only use this term when referring to data collected by the U.S. government. I prefer the term Latinix because it is a more accurate reflection of Latin American ancestry. In addition, politicized Latinixs typically reject the term Hispanic because it was constructed by the Census Bureau solely for the purpose of more manageable data collection and does not reflect their self-identification. Finally, I use Latinix (not Latina/o) because it is gender neutral and nonbinary, and is therefore more inclusive.

3. Section 8 housing refers to a combined federal and local voucher program run by the Housing Authority to help low-income families pay their rent. The program covers the difference between the market cost of rent (with a federally set local cap) and 30 percent of the tenant's income.

4. Throughout the book I use the real names of shelters, residential motels, and public locations in the city, because doing so does not compromise the anonymity of homeless families participating in my research. In addition, identifying particular landmarks and street names provides context for readers familiar with San Francisco.

5. Stratified housing includes low-income, moderate-income, and above moderate-income units. Stratified housing is meant to avoid the pitfalls of low-income housing projects that segregated the poorest families with the least resources together, isolating them completely from economically diverse families.

6. The theme that families would not become homeless in the recent past recurs throughout the book. However, the reasons given for this phenomenon differ and are articulated in each chapter. For example, the focus in this chapter is on the role of urban development, low wages, and the lack of affordable housing. In later chapters the focus will be on the impact of domestic violence, welfare reform, and the loss of social support networks. Ultimately, all of these social problems combined have contributed to the recent rise of homeless families.

7. Mayor Willie Brown was the first African American mayor of San Francisco and served from January 1996 to January 2004. During his term in office Mayor Brown actively courted large-scale development projects and welcomed the booming dot-com industry to San Francisco. His term in office is characterized by expanding urban and real estate development and the beautification of the city. Although he proffered a discourse of compassion for the homeless, more homeless street people were ticketed for quality-of-life violations during his term than under the previous mayor, Frank Jordan, who espoused a hard line toward the homeless. Mayor Brown was notorious for his dapper personal style and expensive hat collection. The expression "Da Mayor," initially a term of endearment in the African American community, ultimately became a term of derision for some.

8. The Franciscan is a filthy and dilapidated hotel in the Bayview-Hunter's Point section of San Francisco and is home to many destitute families and individuals.

9. Owner move-ins allows the new owner of a building to evict the current tenants if she/he/they reside in the building for three years following the eviction. At the conclusion of the

three-year period the owner can return the unit to the rental market and charge higher market rate rents. However, loopholes in local housing laws and a lack of enforcement resulted in landlords evicting tenants after purchasing new properties, jacking up the rents, and returning units to the rental market at increased rates before the three-year time period expired (Alejandrino 2000; Mirabel 2009). This practice contributed to widespread evictions throughout San Francisco during the 1990s.

10. Kaiser Permanente is an integrated managed care consortium hospital.

11. San Francisco is characterized by a variety of micro-climates. The Mission District is outside of the famous fog zone that characterizes many other parts of the city and is often quite sunny and warm.

12. The Beauty Bar currently has establishments in ten cities, including Las Vegas and is characterized on yelp.com as "hipster, dive-y."

Chapter Two

Home is Where the [Broken] Heart is

My life is a living hell. My childhood was a nightmare. I lived in six foster homes by the time I turned eighteen. I was beaten in every one of them and two of my foster brothers raped me. I got pregnant at nineteen and my boyfriend beat the shit out of me for five years. I finally got away from him but now I'm homeless. My life is a living hell.—Cindy

THE NEW HOMELESS

Throughout the 1980s there was a dramatic rise in homelessness among single adults in the United States.[1] As a result, there has been an enormous amount of research on homeless street people over the last thirty years. A large majority of this work is survey research documenting rates and causes of homelessness (Burt 1992; Jencks 1994; Rossi 1989; Whitbeck and Hoyt 1999). Although these data reveal important information about the prevalence of poverty and homelessness, they do not depict the brutalizing conditions suffered by the poor. The ethnographic research examining the daily struggles of the homeless focused primarily on single adult males living on the streets (Dordick 1997; Rossi 1989; Snow and Anderson 1993; Wasserman and Clair 2009) and more recently, work among homeless recyclers in San Francisco (Gowen 2000 2010). Ethnographic research examining homeless women is just beginning to emerge. With the publication of their book, *Hard Lives, Mean Streets: Violence in the Lives of Homeless Women*, Jasinksi et al. (2010) document the survival strategies of homeless women subsisting on the streets. The book poignantly depicts the experiences of homeless women, many of whom have long histories of physical and sexual abuse prior to becoming homeless. These women continue to be beleaguered by physical and sexual violence as they negotiate the urban environment. This book is an exceptional piece of scholarship and broadens our knowledge about gender differences among homeless street people.

Beginning in the 1990s women and their children began to join the ranks of the homeless in unprecedented numbers. Shockingly, the percentage of women and children comprising the urban homeless population increased from 9 percent in 1987 to 34 percent in 1997 to a staggering 40 percent in 2001 (Burt 1992; Burt, et al. 1999; U.S. Conference of Mayors 2001). The percentage of homeless families currently hovers around 40 percent (Bassuk at al. 2014; National Alliance to End Homelessness 2018). As a result of the changing landscape of homelessness, research on homeless families began to proliferate. Initial research examining homeless families focused on causes of familial homelessness (Kozol 1988; Masten et al. 1997; Seltser and Miller 1993; Shinn and Weitzman 1996), life in homeless shelters (Arrighi 1997; Bassuk 1986; Liebow 1993; Kozol 1988), and developmental and educational deficits of homeless children (Bassuk and Gallagher 1990; Memmott and Young 1993). More recently, scholars have begun to examine the long-term socio-emotional and economic effects of homelessness on women and their children (Annooshian 2005; Buckner 2008; Guarino, Rubin, and Bassuk 2007; Bassuk 2010; Gerson 2007; Huntington, Buckner, and Bassuk 2008; Shinn et al. 2008). In order to truly understand the lived experiences of homeless families, we must first identify who they are.

A large majority of homeless families (84 percent) are headed by single women (U.S. Department of Housing and Urban Development 2007, 2018). The typical homeless family is a mother with two to three children under six years old (Bassuk 2010; U.S. Department of Housing and Urban Development 2009). In 2006 there were 1.5 million homeless children; approximately one in fifty kids. The figure rose to 1.6 million in 2010. Currently, more than 2.5 million children live in homeless families. In fact, one in thirty children is now homeless. Among those, 42 percent are under the age of six. Racial disparities among homeless families are staggering. Forty-seven percent of African American children experience homelessness. In 2010, one out of every 141 individuals in black families stayed in a homeless shelter compared to one in 990 for white families; a rate seven times higher for African Americans (Institute for Children, Poverty & Homelessness 2012; National Center for Children in Poverty 2009). Most homeless mothers have not completed high school, have frayed social support networks, limited work experience, and lack marketable job skills. Homeless families live in a perpetual state of chaos and uncertainty. As a result, homeless women have high rates of chronic illness, unemployment, and often lose their kids to the foster care system. In addition, homeless mothers have approximately three times the rate of Post-Traumatic Stress Disorder (PTSD), four times the rate of depression, and twice the rate of substance abuse than their non-homeless counterparts. Similarly, homeless children suffer from high rates of developmental deficits and learning disabilities, asthma, anxiety, and a variety of other physical and emotional problems (Bassuk et al. 1996; Bassuk 2010; Bassuk 2007; Guarino and Bassuk 2010; Hayes et al. 2013). We can see by these data that familial homelessness is both gendered and racialized. Deconstructing the appalling conditions under which homeless women and children live, and the violence endemic to their lives, is essential if we are to understand how social structural conditions impact their individual experiences.

FAMILY VIOLENCE

Intimate partner and community violence is an unrelenting presence in the lives of many homeless women and children. Impoverished communities are fraught with public acts of violence. It is not unusual for low-income urban residents to observe gang- and drug-related violence in their daily lives. Witnessing various displays of intimate partner violence in public spaces is common. Observing drug use, prostitution, hyper masculinity, and a general disregard for life is an assault on one's humanity. African Americans have also historically been persecuted by social structural violence. Slavery, indentured servitude, economic inequality, and the use of violence as a form of social control are part of the fabric of American culture. Latinixs have experienced similar types of racial oppression in the form of forced deportation, union busting, exploitive migrant farm labor and low wage service-sector work, and anti-immigration legislation. Although all residents in poverty-stricken neighborhoods are exposed to a relentless onslaught of violence, it is the women and children who are typically the recipients of violence by family members and intimate partners. According to Shirley A. Hill (2005) historical and contemporary racial inequality stripped black and Latino men of their economic resources and power, which resulted in them directing their rage against women. Other scholars have also documented the ways in which disenfranchised men of color exert their masculinity by physically and sexually abusing their intimate partners (Anderson 1999; Bourgois 1996; Majors and Billson 1992). In his extraordinary ethnography of crack dealers in East Harlem, Bourgois painfully detailed the practice of gang-raping neighborhood girls as initiation into the drug network and ultimately into manhood. Bourgois argues that sexual violence against women prevalent in impoverished neighborhoods like East Harlem is a reflection of the guy's internalized worthlessness.[2]

Undoubtedly, the violence of poverty affects family life in profound ways. For example, rates of domestic violence and childhood sexual abuse are excessively high for poor women of color. In fact, rates of intimate partner abuse are five times higher among the poor. Since African American women and Latinas have higher poverty rates than white women and are

more likely to become homeless, they are more likely to be victims of domestic violence. Some research estimates that black females are 25 percent
more likely than white females to be battered by intimate partners (Hill
2005). In addition, 60 percent of welfare recipients have a history of domestic violence (Scott, London, and Myers 2002). Although domestic violence
and childhood sexual abuse exists in all social classes and among all racial
ethnic groups, it is more prevalent in low-income communities of color.
Race, class, and gender discrimination intersect and result in communities
plagued by inadequate educational opportunities, high rates of unemployment, excessive crime, and poor physical and mental health. In fact, exposure
to family violence in the context of chronic poverty and racism creates emotional and behavioral problems in children (Gewirtz 2007 and Edleson 2007).
In addition, women who have been sexually abused as children are more
likely to be revictimized by sexual assault as adults (Wesley 2009; West,
Williams, and Siegel 2000). These abysmal living conditions create high
levels of stress and are associated with high rates of domestic violence and
sexual assault (Hill 2005). For homeless families these stressors are mag-
nified by the added chaos of finding safe and permanent housing. In a society
in which achievement is measured by wealth and power, low-income men
are demoralized by an emasculating social structure. One way for disempowered men to assert their dominance is through violence toward women. Racism and economic inequality foster physical and sexual violence, which is
highly gendered.

While there is a substantial body of scholarship on domestic violence,
much less is known about the specific relationship between domestic violence and family homelessness. Research that examines domestic violence as
a cause of homelessness among mothers and their children reveals that many
women and children become homeless as a result of family violence (Brandwein 1999; Bassuk 2010; Browne and Bassuk 1997; Davis 1999; Davis and
Kraham 1995). Women frequently stay in abusive relationships for several
years before fleeing their homes in terror (Davis 1999). Women who go to
battered women's shelters can no longer stand the abuse and are essentially
choosing to stop it by becoming homeless. While homeless and battered
women's shelters provide women with a safe haven from domestic violence
they are temporary and rarely provide help for more than three months. Low-
income women, with few alternatives, are forced further onto the margins of
society by a callous patriarchal system.

Although this research examines violence as a cause of homelessness, the
majority of research on the interconnection between family violence and
homelessness does not posit a causal relationship. Rather, most of the studies
document an association between gendered violence and homelessness
among women. Exposure to prolonged physical and sexual violence is widespread among homeless mothers and is well documented by the literature.

For example, Jasinski et al. (2010) found that one in four homeless women were either victims of childhood sexual abuse or violence from an adult intimate partner.[3] A longitudinal study conducted by the National Center on Family Homelessness found that 92 percent of homeless mothers experienced some form of severe physical or sexual abuse by a family member or intimate partner (Bassuk et al. 2014). In addition, 43 percent of homeless women reported that they were sexually abused by the time they were twelve, usually by multiple attackers (Bassuk et al. 1996, 2014). More recent research on homeless families confirms the prevalence of violent victimization as an antecedent to homelessness. Hayes et al. (2013) found that 93 percent of homeless mothers experienced at least one traumatic event and 81 percent experienced multiple traumatic events. The most common trauma was physical violence and/or sexual abuse and was experienced by 79 percent of respondents in childhood, 82 percent in adulthood, and 91 percent in both adulthood and childhood. Seventy percent of the women reported being physically assaulted by a family member or someone they knew and 50 percent reported being sexually assaulted. In a study of family violence that did not include sexual abuse, Anooshian (2005) found that 88 percent of homeless mothers were physically abused and 63 percent were assaulted twenty or more times. In addition, 71 percent of the mothers in her sample were victims of violence as children. Although these data do not stipulate a causal relationship, they convincingly illustrate that for many homeless women violence that begins in childhood often continues well into adulthood (Guarino and Bassuk 2010; Bassuk 2010). What these data cannot communicate however, is the horrific conditions under which these women have been forced to live. Whether recipients of physical or sexual violence or both, homeless mothers have entered the seventh circle of hell.[4] Unfortunately, extricating themselves from a violent family background or a battering partner does not free them from the inferno. Being homeless is inherently dangerous and results in continued exposure to community and interpersonal violence further increasing a family's vulnerability and trauma (Guarino, Rubin, and Bassuk 2007). Because of the persistence of interpersonal violence, homeless mothers can become emotionally paralyzed, and often have difficulty navigating the minutia of their everyday lives. Given the implications of these data, it is essential to document the extreme physical and sexual violence experienced by homeless women to give meaning to their experiences and to construct social policy that reflects the reality of those experiences.

THE VIOLENCE OF POVERTY

Chapter 1 detailed the experiences of families who became homeless as a result of historical and contemporary macroeconomic shifts. These individuals came from impoverished backgrounds but they did not suffer from significant family dysfunction. Respondents who became homeless due to a loss of housing, low wages, and exorbitant rents did not have histories of physical or sexual abuse, nor did they suffer from drug or alcohol addiction. In addition, the majority of the family members introduced in chapter 1 held jobs throughout most of their adult lives. Despite the difficulties faced by these families, they are the ones who were the most likely to eventually find permanent housing. Unlike those respondents, the persistently homeless women in this chapter have long histories of exposure to and experience with physical and sexual violence. These women are often overwhelmed by drug and alcohol abuse, physical and mental health problems, long-term unemployment, and chronic homelessness. Many of the women you will meet in this chapter continue to be victimized by emotional, physical, and sexual abuse, have lost children to the foster care system, and some have even periodically turned to prostitution. Sadly, some of these women also physically abuse their own children, perpetuating a seemingly never-ending cycle of violence. Despite the inexorable obstacles that these women and their children face, they all struggle to remain active agents in their own lives.

Early on in my fieldwork, I was picking up kids from foster care and residential motels and taking them to the Beach House. One evening I was returning Deborah, a Latina teenager, to her residential motel in the Tenderloin, when a fight broke out in the hallway. Two men, who were obviously wasted, were screaming at each other. Spit and sweat were flying as their anger escalated. I quietly urged Deborah to open the door to her room more quickly as I was getting a little uncomfortable with the level of rage emanating from the men. She was very calm and took what seemed like an eternity to find her key. Suddenly one of the men took out a gun. Although I was not concerned about being shot (the men were at the far end of the hallway) I was terrified that Deborah and I would witness someone being shot. I whispered to her to hurry up and open the door. Deborah still seemed fairly nonchalant. I, on the other hand, could feel the adrenaline coursing through my body. I was horrified at the thought of seeing someone shot and knew I would be permanently traumatized by seeing that level of violence. When we got inside her hotel room, I asked Deborah why she took so long to find the key and didn't seem compelled to open the door and get us to safety more quickly. Deborah told me that she wasn't really scared because she had seen someone get shot in her neighborhood two years earlier and that violence was a part of her everyday life. Deborah told me the following:

I seen violence my whole life Annee, it doesn't hardly affect me no more. My pops beat the crap out of my moms since I was a little kid. The only time I got some peace was when he took off. But you know, my moms had other boyfriends since my dad left and most of them beat her too. That's why I ain't got no boyfriend. I don't want anyone beating on me—but that is just the way it is around here. I seen men hitting on their women all the time. So I figure it's better to be on my own. There are drug dealers and gangs, pimps and hookers, everywhere you look. When I was little I remember walking over crack vials on my way to school. Now I walk over needles too. When I was fourteen, I saw a kid in my neighborhood get shot. It really scared me—I had nightmares for a long time. But then after a while I just stopped thinking about it. I can't do nothin' about it—so I just tried to forget about it. Plus I see so much violence everyday it just doesn't bother me no more. I figure if I see someone else get shot it won't be as bad as the first time anyway.

Deborah's story is reflective of the everyday public acts of violence endemic to impoverished communities. At sixteen, Deborah, like most of the kids in my research, had already spent a lifetime witnessing interpersonal violence. When I told Deborah that I was afraid of seeing someone get shot, and that I thought it would emotionally scar me, she giggled and told me to "toughen up." For several months after the experience, Deborah loved to tease me about how I needed to be more street tough. She and some of the other girls would try to teach me how to walk and talk more like a "gangsta." Although Deborah satirized the experience by teasing me, she also used it as a pretext to discuss her painful life with me. We had many long discussions over the next year about poverty and violence. Although the fight in the hallway was peacefully resolved, it was an extremely profound experience for me. This was my first visceral on-the-ground experience of how insidious poverty and violence really are. I knew that if I witnessed someone get murdered I would never get over it. Deborah, on the other hand, perceived it to be just another episode of violence in a life filled with hostility, and numbed herself to the pain. Her experience reinforces the idea that public acts of violence are commonplace and eventually become unremarkable. Several months after this experience I had two more encounters that highlighted the inherent violence endemic to poverty.

James was a single father with an infant daughter when he came to Home Away. His girlfriend couldn't handle being a mother, so she left them as soon as she gave birth. James was twenty-eight and had recently lost his job because he had no access to child care. James was staying at a residential motel in the Tenderloin. James shared a tiny bed with his infant daughter Aubrey. One evening he awoke to a strange sound emanating from Aubrey's mouth. When James turned over he was sickened to discover that she was sucking on a used condom that was left in the bed by the previous tenant. The anguish in James's face when he recounted this story was unbearable. Although James's daughter will never remember this experience, it is indelibly burned into his memory. Someone could argue that although repulsive, this experience was not violent. I would however, vehemently disagree. Aubrey could have choked to death on the condom or contracted a sexually transmitted disease. As a father, James felt physically assaulted by this experience. He was helpless to protect Aubrey from the everyday ravages of poverty and it mortified him. The next day James checked out of the motel and left town. Jeanie and I were deeply sickened by what happened to Aubrey and the pain of this experience lingered with us both. Unlike the majority of families who utilize Home Away programs, James was a single white father. Although we often identify white men as the unmarked and privileged category when we talk about intersectionality theory, James was not in a privileged position. James and Aubrey were denied admission into any of the family shelters. When they became homeless, it was standard policy to keep single men out of family shelters, even if they had children. The policy was meant to protect children from sexual predators. However, this policy disadvantaged homeless men with children. In addition, just because an adult male is accompanied by a woman, it does not mean that he is not a sexual predator. Sexual abuse perpetrated by fathers, stepfathers, and other male relatives is widespread even when a woman is present in the home. Protecting children in homeless shelters from exploitation is an admirable goal. However, systematically denying single fathers' entry into family shelters is not the answer. In this case, James's whiteness did nothing to benefit him, and his gender was in fact a disadvantage. James's story provides an excellent example of why we must examine the intersection of race, class, and gender inequality in the context of specific experiences. It is clearly not the case that being a white male automatically results in access to privilege in every situation.

After several months in the field, I began spending more time with homeless kids staying at the Hamilton Family Shelter. I showed up once per week to pick up the Beach House kids. When I arrived, I gave the shelter staff the list of kids who were slated to go that week. Sometimes, a kid scheduled to go to the Beach House wouldn't show up. When that happened I would allow another kid to go in her/his/their place. The first time this happened there was a little girl who was about five years old who desperately wanted to go to the Beach House. She was jumping up and down begging me to let her go. I checked with her mom Keisha, who was happy to let Jacinta go. When I told Jacinta she could go she jumped into my arms, wrapped her arms around my neck, and with a flirtatious twinkle in her eyes said "give me some sugar baby," and began to kiss me on the mouth using her tongue. I was completely caught off guard and was utterly astonished by her response. In that moment I knew Jacinta had been a victim of sexual abuse and I did not want to call attention to her wildly inappropriate behavior. I immediately slid my hand between our faces, gently pushed her face away from mine, and softly put her down. Needless to say I was completely freaked out! Jacinta was only five years old and she had already learned to use her sexuality to express gratitude. I was overwhelmed with a variety of emotions, but I had a carload of kids to take to the beach. So off we went. When we got to the Beach House the kids wanted to go swimming. Since Jacinta was so young she needed help changing into one of the bathing suits. When she took off her shirt I saw that she had cigarette burn scars on her back. I was now completely horrified and filled with an overwhelming sense of despair. I had to muster every ounce of inner strength to keep myself from becoming hysterical. I stuffed my feelings down hard and managed not to cry. The last thing I wanted to do was to scare Jacinta—she was at the Beach House to escape the painful reality of her life, not to be reminded of it. I helped her get into her bathing suit and off we all went—into the ocean. We jumped the waves, rode bikes, ate pizza, and all the kids had a wonderful day. I, however, could not get the picture of Jacinta trying to kiss me or the image of her cigarette scars out of my head.

I felt assaulted by the violence in this little girl's life. I was so angry at the pain Jacinta was subjected to that when I returned her to her mother, I wanted to grab her by the throat and shake her until she dropped. I no longer had a structural analysis of poverty, I had only anger. I was so disturbed by Jacinta trying to kiss me that it took me over a month to discuss it with Jeanie. When we did eventually talk about it I explained to Jeanie that I knew the literature on sexual abuse and was aware that victims of sexual abuse can become overly sexualized at an early age. However, I was totally unprepared to see it expressed in a five-year-old. I also never expected it to be directed at me. Despite the fact that Jacinta was only five, I actually felt violated in some odd way. The experience embarrassed me. I also told Jeanie about the cigarette burn scars and how much rage I felt toward Keisha. Jeanie encouraged me to take a step back, take a deep breath, and to feel compassion for Keisha. Jeanie reminded me that Jacinta's mom was a victim of habitual physical and sexual violence. In her hippie way, Jeanie exuded love for a woman who she saw as being damaged by her own abuse. She reminded me that at one time, Keisha was also an innocent child. Jeanie and I did not share a common discursive strategy. Jeanie spoke in loving, flowery, artistic, and often circular verbiage. I, on the other hand, spoke the discourse of academic sociology. Despite the vastly different ways we articulated ourselves, we both agreed that this was an example of the complicated relationship between social structure and individual agency. Poverty is a violent and powerful force in people's lives. While people do make choices, those choices, and their consequences, are constrained by their social structural location. The abysmal conditions under which Keisha lived impinged on her behavior as a mother. Keisha was so overburdened by her own pain she sometimes expressed it through violence toward Jacinta. While Jeanie and I hated the physical violence Jacinta suffered at the hands of Keisha, we understood how the overwhelming inhumanity and devastation of her life led her there. Racism, poverty, and gendered violence became organizing principles in Keisha's life and then got passed down to her daughter. Thankfully, Keisha participated in counseling and parenting classes to learn to cope with the pain of her existence. Keisha wanted be a better mother and did not want to hurt Jacinta. Ultimately, Keisha became an active agent in her life and tried to overcome the powerful social structural forces of poverty.

My experiences with Deborah, James and Aubrey, and Keisha and Jacinta were life-altering. As a sociologist specializing in family poverty, domestic violence, and race, class, and gender inequality, I was thoroughly versed in the academic literature on these subjects. I had even published my own research on family poverty and race, class, and gender inequality. However, my early research was based primarily on national survey data. This was my first experience doing long-term ethnographic research. Seeing the effects of poverty and violence on individuals' lives first-hand allowed me to empathize with them from deep in my gut. I gained a new level of insight into the unrelenting presence of violence in the public and private lives of the urban poor. As a result of these experiences and the ones that followed over the next four years, I incorporated social change and political activism into all of my teaching, research, and community work.

STANDING AT THE GATES OF HELL

During the course of my fieldwork it became clear that there were two types of homeless families in San Francisco: families that experienced brief spells of homelessness and families that were chronically homeless.[5] Families that had short-lived stints of homelessness often experienced a precipitating crisis that led directly to their homelessness. For some families the loss of a job or housing was a frequent cause of their homelessness. For other families the onset of a serious illness, whether of a parent or child, was another. In general, these families were able to find housing and rarely returned to the family shelters or to Home Away. These families typically included two parents, both of whom had graduated from high school, and had solid work histories. Members of these families did not have extensive histories of physical or sexual abuse, nor were they likely to suffer from mental health problems. The majority of these homeless families simply needed help getting back on their feet. For example, Allen and Kathryn came to Home Away after losing their apartment and everything they owned in a fire. Kathryn had recently given birth to their daughter Phoebe. Allen was a trained chef and had an excellent job in an upscale restaurant. Kathryn planned on staying home until her daughter was in pre-school, when she would return to work cutting hair. After the fire they showed up at the Hamilton Family Shelter.

Initially, when Kathryn and Allen first arrived at the shelter they were told that Allen could not stay there if he continued to work. According to Hamilton's rules, residents must return to the shelter by 8:00 pm. Anyone who arrives after the curfew is denied entry. This policy was intended to maintain stability and prevent residents from coming in late and disturbing sleeping children. However, this rigid mandate would have prevented Allen from working late nights at the restaurant, and would have forced him to choose between losing his job and sleeping on the streets. Either choice would have necessarily prolonged his homelessness. This rule embodies the inflexible structure of homeless family shelters, which is often experienced by clients as yet another form of tyranny. After we vigorously advocated with the staff on Allen's behalf, they finally agreed to allow him to continue working and return late to the shelter. They lived there for three months while Allen worked and saved up enough money for an apartment. Once their finances were in order, Allen, Kathryn, and Phoebe moved into an apartment and did not become homeless again. Despite the turmoil in their lives and the initial setback they encountered at the shelter, Allen and Kathryn were able to draw on their emotional resources and overcome their homelessness. To be sure, Allen and Kathryn witnessed acts of aggressive parenting at the shelter, and drug abuse and street violence in the neighborhood. However, whatever brutality they observed as they traversed through their homeless experience was fleeting, and did not result in permanent emotional damage. Neither Allen nor Kathryn had personal experiences with familial or community violence and were generally well-adjusted. As a result they were extremely adaptive and able to cope with the chaos of their unfortunate circumstances. Throughout the course of my fieldwork, there were other homeless families that came and went, experiencing only brief intervals of violence and homelessness. These families were more emotionally and physically intact, and had the inner resources to survive their crises without completely imploding.

THE SEVENTH CIRCLE OF HELL

Alternatively, there was a hard-core group of chronically homeless families in San Francisco that cycled in and out of homelessness over the course of several years. These families were most likely to be single-mother families with children under the age of six. In addition, these women had prolonged exposure to physical and sexual violence. Many of the mothers suffered from depression, had significant health problems, and struggled with drug and alcohol addiction.[6] Children in these families also had serious physical and developmental difficulties. In addition, these kids often had serious emotional and behavioral problems. The longer I spent in the field, the more I learned about the emotional, physical, and sexual violence that characterized the lives of these women and their children. For chronically homeless mothers, life is bleak and filled with anguish. Women courageously told me their stories, no matter how painful. Homeless mothers were no longer willing to remain invisible; they desperately wanted to be heard. Barb, a white mother of two, cried through chipped teeth, a sallow complexion, and a face scarred with the violence of her life, when she said:

Being homeless is hard, it's just hard, it's too hard. No one cares about me or what I been through. I been beaten down my whole life. My daddy used to get drunk and beat me when I was little. Then when I was about twelve he started to molest me. At first he would just touch me and stuff and then he made me touch him. I tried to tell my mom but she acted like I made it up. I think she acted like she didn't believe me because she was afraid of him—he beat her when he got drunk too. When I got into high school he started to rape me. I hated it but what could I do? I couldn't run away, where could I go? I just started drinking and drugging, you know as an escape. I got in with a bad crowd at school and started messing around with lots of boys. I knew it was a bad idea but I hated myself so much. I think I wanted to hurt myself. Even though it wasn't my fault what my daddy was doing to me—I felt like it was— he made me feel that way—like I wanted him to rape me. So I just took lots of drugs and slept around. My parents knew I was taking drugs and fucking around and they started giving me a hard time. I hated them—it was their fault I was so fucked up to begin with. We were always fighting and screaming at each other. One day I couldn't take it anymore and I punched my mother right in the face. Things got ugly and they kicked me out. I was seventeen. I had no money and no place to go. I started having sex for money. At first it was disgusting but after a while I got used to it. I took whatever drugs I could find and that helped. I got beat up all the time too, and raped. I hated living on the streets. After about a year I couldn't take it anymore so I begged my aunt to let me move in with her. My aunt is a Christian. She said I could come live with her but I had to get my life together. No more drugs and no more sex. I moved in with her and started a twelve-step program at her church and got clean. After a while I got a job at McDonald's. I gave my aunt a little bit of money every week and saved a little bit. I felt really good about myself. I was working and being responsible. For the first time in my life I had some peace. I even started to respect myself. I lived with her for almost two years. Things were pretty good. Then I met Jason. He seemed like such a great guy. He had steady work and treated me real good. We started dating and then I got pregnant. He said he loved me and was ready to have a kid so we got married and moved in together. At first it was great—like a fairy tale. He was so nice to me and we were a family. But then he started to criticize everything I did. He would get angry for no reason and then he started hitting me. At first it wasn't too bad and he always apologized after and was really nice for a few weeks. After Shannon was born he got jealous and started to whale on me. I told him I was going to move back in with my aunt if he didn't stop beating me. That scared him so he stopped for a while. Then my aunt died and that was it. He knew I had no place to go and he got real mean. He beat the crap out of me and he raped me too. I felt like I was living my childhood all over again, only this time I couldn't escape because I had Shannon. When Shannon was two I got pregnant again and I was trapped. I lived with Jason for eight more years. I kept trying to leave him—I even went to a shelter a couple of times—but I kept going back. I had no money and no place to go. I started using again. He was so mean—he broke my nose and some of my teeth. Once he even broke my arm. One day he chocked me so hard I passed out and I had a big red ring around my neck. That was it. I grabbed my kids and left. I went to a battered women's shelter and stayed there for a few months. Now we live in the Franciscan and I am on welfare. I can't work—I got no one to take care of my kids but even if I could I can't hold on to a job. I am so fucked up—so tired—I can't concentrate, I have nightmares, and I get super depressed. Sometimes I can't even get out of bed, and I still do drugs. I have been beaten down my whole life and I just can't take it anymore.

Barb's choice to live with her aunt and then get married illustrates her desire to exert autonomy over her life. She wanted to experience a loving family; first with her aunt and then with Jason. Unfortunately, her choice to marry Jason made her more vulnerable to violence and ultimately served to reproduce her poverty. As a result of the physical and sexual violence Barb suffered throughout her life, she and her children became homeless.

Jalesa, an African American woman, had a similarly violent childhood. Jalesa's mother was a drug addict and was periodically incarcerated. Jalesa lived with relatives when she was a baby but eventually ended up in foster care. Jalesa had a long history of drug abuse and intimate partner violence. Jalesa had several health problems associated with poverty. In addition, Jalesa struggled with depression and sometimes thought about suicide. Despite the circumstances of her life, and her lack of formal education, Jalesa was exceptionally self-reflexive. She understood the impact of poverty and social structural inequality on her own life. Jalesa explained to me:

I had a horrible childhood Annee. I lived with my grandmother when I was a baby but she got sick when I was five and couldn't take care of me. I went to live with my aunt and my two cousins and stayed there until I was eleven. We lived in Bayview-Hunters Point. It was a scary place to live. There were gangs and drugs and all kinds of nasty violence. Men were always beating their women in public. I grew up with violence as part of my life. And of course, my aunt was crazy and she drank too much. She worked as a maid cleaning office buildings so she was never around at night. She always had some boyfriend that would live with us. Some of the boyfriends were nice to us but mostly they beat us. One boyfriend molested me and my cousin when she was at work. That was a pretty bad scene but when I went to foster care things got worse. The first foster house I lived in had seven kids. We never had enough food and we were always hungry. The older kids would beat up on the younger kids—it was a free for all—total chaos. There was all kind of sexual abuse going on too. I hated that place. I went to another foster family after that but it wasn't much better. I never went to a doctor when I was a kid—if I got sick we went to the emergency room. Now I have all kinds of health problems. I didn't go to a dentist until I was an adult. That's why my teeth are so nasty. All of these experiences fucked me up big time Annee. Being poor sucks—it's all violence and pain. It really is a vicious circle. I got beat as a kid and then I got beat as an adult. When you grow up the way I did you don't care about yourself. You'll have sex with anyone, take drugs, turn tricks—whatever. I swore I would never treat my kids the way I was treated—but you do. The stress of your life just builds up and you take it out on your kids. I'm not proud that I hit my kids. I don't want to, but sometimes life is just too stressful. My kids are always sick and Malik has a learning disability. Sometimes I just need them to leave me alone. Why do you think I am so depressed now? Who wouldn't turn to drugs, who wouldn't want to die, after living my life? Sometimes I get so depressed I can't even move. I just get overwhelmed. How can I be expected to work, to find a place to live, pay rent? Sometimes I can barely breathe.

Jalesa's analysis of the impact of social structural inequality on her own life is dead-on. Jalesa is cognizant that the violence she suffered as a child has essentially destroyed her adult life. Jalesa is self-reflective enough to recognize that race, class, and gender inequality have limited her life chances and those of her children.

Camila's childhood was also fraught with physical and sexual violence. Camila, a Chicana, was raped by two boys in her neighborhood when she was fourteen. They threatened to kill her if she told anyone, so she remained silent. Previously outgoing, Camila became depressed and withdrawn. She was terrified to go outside and stopped going to school. Camila began to have flashbacks of her rape and would eventually be diagnosed with PTSD. Like many victims of sexual violence, Camila turned to drugs to numb her pain. Eventually Camila met Ricardo, who turned her on to heroin and got her pregnant. By the time I met Camila she had been struggling with heroin addiction for ten years and had lost her daughter to foster care. When we met, Camila was in a residential drug treatment center and was working diligently to regain custody of her daughter. Camila had been clean for six months and was about to be released from the treatment center. Camila was astoundingly optimistic about her future and about getting her daughter back. When we spoke Camila told me:

I am being released in three weeks and I am so excited. My case worker found me a place to live in the tenderloin. It is one of those transitional housing places which is really good because they have strict rules and they don't allow any drugs. The rooms are pretty nice and it is very clean. I think I'll feel safe there. She is helping me find a job too. If I stay clean and keep a job for one year I'll get Blanca back.

When I asked Camila if she was worried about being in the Tenderloin, surrounded by drugs and violence, she said:

> No. I am not worried. I know I can stay clean this time. I want my baby back and will do whatever it takes. Blanca needs me and I am not going to let her down.

I, on the other hand, was not so optimistic. Despite her desire to stay clean and get her daughter back from foster care, the odds were not in Camila's favor. Although she was given fairly long-term, stable housing, it was ultimately temporary. Camila's only job prospects were in the service economy and would most likely pay minimum wage. Camila's salary and her welfare benefits would not be enough to lift her above the poverty level. In addition, Camila's housing unit was surrounded by pimps, prostitutes, gang members, drug dealers, and discarded drug paraphernalia. Although Camila was determined to exert her agency and turn her life around, the social structural constraints were monumental. After being released from treatment Camila found a job cleaning bed pans at a local hospital. She worked steadily and stayed clean for eight months. After a misunderstanding with her boss, Camila got fired. The stress of losing her job pushed Camila over the edge. Feeling that all her hard work was pointless, Camila started using drugs again, got kicked out of her transitional housing, started having sex for money, and lost her daughter to foster care forever.

HELL ON EARTH

All of the stories, so eloquently expressed by homeless family members, corroborate the research literature on poverty and interpersonal violence. Understandably, early exposure to community and family violence does often continue well into adulthood. Like respondents depicted in prior research, women in this book who have endured physical and sexual violence as children have high rates of drug and alcohol abuse, chronic illness, depression, and are victims of intimate partner violence. In addition, their children are often placed in foster care, and are at risk for chronic illness and developmental disabilities. During my four years in the field, I spent countless hours listening to excruciating narratives of violence and degradation that were similar to those you just read. These accounts irrefutably illustrate that for many women and their children, becoming homeless is a direct result of family violence and poverty. In addition, these poignant narratives advance our understanding of the interlocking nature of race, gender, and class oppression. Women, and in some cases men, are oppressed because of their poverty, gender, and race-ethnicity. As we saw with James, being a homeless father in the context of a family shelter was in fact a disadvantage. However, as a white man James had more options as he struggled to overcome his homelessness. White men have higher rates of employment and are systematically paid more than men or women of color. In addition, because of the gendered nature of parenting in American society, it is likely that James will find a partner to help care for his daughter. Furthermore, if James does find a partner he does not have the added burden of being victimized by domestic violence. Despite his dreadful circumstances, James does have race, class, and gender privilege when compared to his female counterparts. We can clearly see by this example that race, class, and gender are shifting categories of oppression and that individuals do not react uniformly to social structural constraints. Although at first glance it might seem that homeless fathers are more disadvantaged than homeless mothers, the reality is that they are not. Women, on the other hand, are more subjugated by social structural inequality. For women, minimizing one form of oppression will still leave them subjugated in equally dehumanizing ways. For example, finding stable housing and a living wage job might mitigate their class oppression, but it would still leave women vulnerable to the violence of patriarchy. As we know, women are infinitely more likely to be victims of intimate partner violence than men, regardless of class. Yet we also know that rates of domestic violence are highest among low-income African American women and Latinas (Sokoloff and Dupont 2005) and in impoverished neighborhoods (Copp et al. 2015). In addition, middle-class and affluent women who do experience intimate partner violence have access to more resources to cope with their trauma. Clearly, race and class inequality result in the most severe violence being experienced by the most disenfranchised citizens. We can see how race, class, and gender are fundamental organizing categories of society. Examining the physical and sexual violence associated with poverty reveals that race, class, and gender are indeed social practices, institutions, and social structural arrangements. These practices, institutions, and arrangements structure the lives of homeless families forcing them through the gates of hell, landing them smack in the center of the seventh circle of Dante's Inferno.

NOTES

1. Some of the text contained in this chapter is reprinted by permission from Copyright Clearance Center: Wiley Blackwell, Sociological Forum, *Our Lives Matter: The Racialized Violence of Poverty Among Homeless Mothers of Color*, Anne R. Roschelle, 2017

2. It is not just low-income men of color who engage in sexual violence toward women. College fraternities, athletic teams, and the military are also notorious for their exaggerated expressions of masculinity and brotherhood which is habitually expressed via sexual abuse and rape of women (Yancy, Martin, and Hummer 1998). The 2015 documentary, *The Hunting Ground* (Dick and Ziering 2015) provides a detailed account of sexual violence perpetrated against women by athletes and fraternity brothers at several colleges and universities. In his book *Missoula: Rape and the Justice System in a College Town*, John Krakauer examines the

lives of five rape victims at the University of Montana and documents how hundreds of students' reports of sexual assault made between 2008 and 2012 went uninvestigated. A federal lawsuit was filed against the Defense Department in February 2012, claiming that the military is "rife with sexual abuse" and promotes a culture that fails to prevent rape and sexual assault among the troops (Parker 2012, A18). Clearly, in patriarchal communities and organizations in which hyper-masculinity is celebrated, it is not only low-income men of color who perpetrate violence against women.

3. Jasinski et al., focused on homeless women living on the streets and in homeless shelters. Although some of their respondents were mothers, the majority of them were living without their children. Nonetheless, the physical and sexual violence experienced by these women in childhood and adulthood supports the contention that violence is a precursor to homeless among women.

4. This is a reference to the fourteenth-century poem *The Divine Comedy* written by Dante Alighieri. The seventh circle of hell is violence.

5. These findings are consistent with other research that has distinguished between transitional homelessness (single episodes of homelessness), episodic homelessness (infrequent episodes of homelessness), and chronic homelessness (long-term and/or multiple homelessness) Culhane and Metraux 2008; Jasininski et al 2010).

6. For most of the women in my study, drug and alcohol addiction were not the causes of their homelessness but rather an effect of poverty and violence. Other researchers have demonstrated that many homeless individuals begin using drugs or increase their drug use after becoming homeless (Arnold 2004; Conley 1996; Hedden et al. 2015). In addition, a large number of people in the general population, many white and middle-class engage in illicit drug use and do not become homeless (Wasserman and Claire 2010.) In fact, in 2014 the National Survey on Drug Use and Health (NSDH) found that 27 million people age twelve and older, or approximately 1 in 10 Americans, reported using an illicit drug during the last month. In addition, 4.3 million people age twelve and older reported using nonmedical prescription pain relievers. The tendency to blame familial homelessness on drug use is more reflective of uninformed stereotypes than of reality.

Chapter Three

The Unraveling Social Safety Net

I think it is shameful how poor people are treated in this country. We have a bunch of rich white men in charge who don't understand what it is like to be homeless. They said they were going to change the welfare system so people who really need it can get it. All they did was make it harder. They put in all these rules to trip us up and then when we mess up they take away our benefits. I am homeless with two kids. That's pretty much as bad as it gets. I need welfare to survive. I constantly feel like my life is unraveling.—Mariana

WELFARE REFORM

For decades, poor women, many of whom were victims of domestic violence, relied on welfare to survive.[1] However, that is no longer the case. Throughout the 1980s and 1990s a pervasive discourse swept the nation that vilified impoverished black and Latina mothers as pathologically lazy and welfare-dependent. Conservative politicians and policy analysts initiated this discourse to promote their racialized anti-welfare agenda (Mead 1992; Murray 1984). Even Bill Clinton, a political moderate, jumped on the bandwagon during his presidential campaign when he pledged "the end of welfare as we know it." President Clinton made good on his campaign promise and in 1996 he passed the Personal Responsibility and Work Opportunity Reconciliation Act (PRWORA), ushering in an era of draconian welfare reform. The underlying ideology of this radical reform was to eliminate welfare dependency, promote heterosexual marriage, and require poor women to go to work. The new federal legislation put a maximum five-year lifetime cap on welfare receipt, although some states chose to implement a more punitive two-year cap. Despite more than twenty years of research indicating that the majority of welfare mothers are not long-term recipients but rather cycle on and off as their family and work lives necessitate (Bane and Ellwood 1994; Edin and

Lein 1997; Ellwood 1988; Gottschalk, McLanahan, and Sandefur 1994), the underlying assumption of the reform was that women of color are lazy and don't want to work. While it is true that there has been a small subsection of women who were long-term welfare recipients, it was not because they are lazy. Long-term welfare recipients are the most disenfranchised members of the population and come from persistently poor families. They typically have young children, little to no work experience, physical and mental health problems, high rates of family violence, children with chronic illness, and less than a high school degree (Taylor and Barush 2004). Not surprisingly, homeless mothers possess many of these same attributes (Bassuk, et al. 1996; Hicks-Coolidge, Burnside-Eaton, and Peters 2003). Women with these traits are highly likely to be sanctioned by case managers, have high rates of intermittent workforce participation, and use up their five-year lifetime allotment fairly quickly (Hays 2003; Turner and Main 2001; Zedlewski and Loprest, 2001).

In addition to the five-year lifetime cap, the new legislation also imposed excessive sanctions for women who do not comply with the requirements of the legislation.[2] In California, legislators opted for partial family sanctions in which only adults are penalized for failing to comply with welfare requirements. Partial family sanctions mean that only the parent's portion of cash benefits is eliminated, and children still receive their assistance.[3] Partial family sanctions are meant to be less punitive, presumably protecting children from destitution. In order to understand the consequences of being sanctioned, we must first understand who welfare recipients are. Approximately one-third of welfare recipients are African Americans, one-quarter are Latina, and over one-half are white. Ninety percent of welfare recipients are single mothers, over 50 percent of them have a child younger than six, and over one-quarter of recipients have a child under two. About 30 percent of welfare mothers have a disability and approximately 25 percent have at least one child with a chronic health problem or disability. Forty percent of Temporary Aid to Needy Families (TANF) recipients have a high school diploma and only about 3 percent have a college degree (Committee on Ways and Means U.S. House of Representatives 2008).[4] In addition, 60 percent of welfare recipients have a history of domestic violence (Scott, London, and Myers 2002). Welfare mothers and their children represent the most vulnerable members of society, and for them sanctions can be devastating.

Research illustrates that women who are sanctioned have more children, more economic hardships, more chronic physical and mental health problems, lower levels of education, are more likely to be long-term welfare recipients, and are more likely to end up homeless than non-sanctioned women (Cherlin et al 2002; Kalil, Seefeldt, and Wang 2002). Once sanctioned, women have a greater risk of food insecurity, child hunger, hospitalization, utility shutoff, and eviction. In addition, sanctioned welfare leavers are less likely to find work after being sanctioned. Women who are able to obtain work are often paid less than non-sanctioned welfare leavers (Goldberg and Schott 2000). Oftentimes, women who are sanctioned are forced to resort to selling their possessions, panhandling, and sometimes engaging in criminal behavior (Cherlin et al. 2002; Kalil, Seefeldt, and Wang 2002; Reichman, Teitler, and Curtis 2005). Even more alarming is that fact that sanctioned mothers experience higher levels of severe economic deprivation, including eviction and homelessness, than their non-sanctioned counterparts. In an extensive study of the hardships associated with being sanctioned, Reichman, Teitler, and Curtis (2005) found that sanctioned mothers face an increased risk for eviction or homelessness. In fact, women who reported eviction or homelessness at a first interview experienced an almost fivefold increase in the likelihood of becoming homeless or evicted at the second interview three years later.

Given the racialized discourse that portrays black women as chronically dependent welfare queens, it is not surprising that African American women are significantly more likely to be sanctioned by their caseworkers than white women (Casey 2010). Caseworkers have ultimate discretion regarding who they sanction and why. Research indicates that case workers often fail to distinguish between procedural violations and willful substantive violations. In addition, case workers tend to apply sanction rules narrowly and are skeptical of "good cause" exception claims (Lens 2008).[5] Although sanctions are intended to provide women with disincentives for refusing to work, it turns out that a majority of sanctions are for missed appointments and for not filing paperwork (Cherlin et al. 2002).[6] For homeless women who are also victims of domestic violence, the relentless imposition of sanctions has been disastrous.[7] Many victims of domestic violence are sanctioned and lose their benefits as a result of their partners' harassment, stalking behavior, emotional abuse, unreliable parenting, and physical violence (Brandwein and Filiano 2000; Brush 2006; George 2006; Lyon 2000; Raphael 2000; Riger and Staggs, 2004; Scott, London, Myers 2002; Staggs and Riger 2005; Talyor and Barusch 2004; Tolman and Raphael 2000). Rigorously imposing sanctions was an integral component of welfare reform. Although sanctions were touted as a way to simply enforce work requirements, I would argue that they were in fact meant to punish poor women of color for their perceived indolence. Whether intended or not, the consequences of this legislation have been dire for countless women who have been forced off the welfare rolls, into the arms of abusive men, and ultimately onto the streets.

WELFARE SANCTIONS

Unintentional Slip-Ups

Prior to the passage of the PRWORA, severely impoverished women could rely indefinitely on welfare to survive. Because the new legislation is meant to eliminate welfare dependency, and promote work, it includes stringent sanctions for recipients who fail to comply with the requirements. In addition, the legislation is intended to promote abstinence and heterosexual marriage, discourage abortion, and reduce non-marital births among poor women. Paradoxically, while women are being sanctioned for failure to comply with regulations, states are being rewarded for curtailing "illegitimacy" and reducing the number of abortions in their jurisdiction. The federal legislation set aside $50 million per year to subsidize state abstinence education programs. In addition, $100 million is shared annually by the five states that have the best record of reducing non-marital births without increasing their abortion rates. Not surprisingly, the reform does not include funding for birth control or family planning education (Hays 2003). Regrettably, it does include a family cap which excludes benefits to any children born to mothers who are already recipients of TANF (Personal Responsibility and Work Opportunity Reconciliation Act 1996). These state-level rewards and punishments reflect the ideological viewpoint of policy makers that poor women are out-of-control breeders in need of restraint. Under the new legislation, women are disciplined for not complying with a multitude of regulations. Unfortunately, research on welfare reform indicates that homeless welfare recipients are particularly disadvantaged and find it exceedingly difficult to comply with the requirements of the PRWORA. The research also indicates that welfare recipients are frequently sanctioned by caseworkers for missed appointments and not filing paperwork. This research is supported by the women in my sample. Many of the women I spoke to got sanctioned for failing to show up for meetings and for misunderstanding program regulations. Although caseworkers recognized the myriad problems plaguing homeless mothers, they often seemed unsympathetic. One common difficulty that exacerbated homeless women's ability to attend meetings was the health problems of their children. Many homeless kids in my research suffered from a variety of physical and emotional disabilities. As a result, mothers had to frequently pick up their kids early from school, keep them out of school, and spend endless hours in hospital emergency rooms. In addition, homeless kids with "behavioral" problems often got in trouble at school requiring mothers to continually visit the principal's office.[8] Troubles with children were often exacerbated by the ever-present violence in these women's lives. These troubles often led to women being sanctioned by case workers for being late and for missing appointments. The following conversation between Alma, Rendisha, and Shirley captures the inherent absurdity of welfare reform sanctions that ignore the realities of poor women's lives.

Alma: I got sanctioned because I missed a meeting with my caseworker. I had to go to school to pick up Eduardo. He got sick, you know he has bad asthma. The school nurse told me to take him to the hospital. So we got on the bus and went to the emergency room. We were there for six hours. I don't have a cell phone. If I had one I could have called and told her where I was but she probably wouldn't care—that bitch hates me. She doesn't care about how much pain I've had or how rough my life has been.

Rendisha: I hear ya sista. My caseworker is a bitch too. I missed an appointment and she sanctioned me for six months. What the fuck? My kid was sick too and I had to take him to the hospital. You know they kick us out of the shelter all day, so what am I supposed to do? Bring a sick kid to my caseworker's office? Yeah right. I'd probably get sanctioned for that.

Shirley: I missed an appointment once because I was too afraid to leave my hotel room. My ex was looking for me and I didn't want him to find out where I was living. He beat the shit out of me for years and it took all my strength to leave the bastard. If he finds me I'm afraid he'll kill me—I gotta lay low. I told my caseworker he was looking for me but she didn't give a shit. All she cared about was some stupid appointment I missed. I got so pissed off I told her to fuck off and that was it—she kicked me off.

Rendisha: I know other families at the shelter who lost their welfare too. This new system is really harsh—they just want to kick everyone off. They sanction you for the stupidest things—one lady got called to school to pick up her kid for fighting and missed her meeting—she got kicked off. Another lady was late and the bitch sanctioned her. These caseworkers—they fuckin' hate us.

Alma: I know—they're so rude and mean. Who needs that shit? We get enough of it from our men; we don't need it from them too.

Alma, Rendisha, and Shirley all became homeless as a result of intimate partner violence. All three of them were severely battered, and despite the prospect of becoming homeless, they found the strength to leave. Although this conversation is not specifically about domestic violence, it serves as the backdrop of their lives. Being sanctioned for missed meetings due to the exigencies of their lives reflects the administrative violence perpetrated against them by a callous state bureaucracy.[9] Compared to the heinous violence depicted in the previous chapter, this might seem a bit hyperbolic. However, given the physical, emotional, and economic deficits these women shoulder, the labyrinthine welfare system is simply one more burden for them to bear.

Consistently meeting with caseworkers is only one example of the administrative expectations required of welfare recipients. In addition, they are required to attend orientation meetings, workshops, and job training programs. These requirements are particularly difficult for homeless mothers. Women living in shelters are required to vacate the shelters by 9:00am. Women with young children have no access to daytime child care and cannot bring their kids to these meetings. Women living outside of shelters often spend their days navigating San Francisco in search of shelter beds, soup kitchens, and a myriad of social services dispersed throughout the city. Residents of seedy motels also utilize the soup kitchens for themselves and their children because they lack cooking facilities in their rooms. Because soup kitchens typically provide meals during work hours, homeless folks must oftentimes choose between eating, working (Snow and Anderson 1993), and attending mandated meetings. Regardless of their individual circumstances, homeless women in my sample struggled desperately to comply with the requirements of the newly implemented welfare reform. Many women felt they were treated unfairly, that caseworkers were unsympathetic to the realities of their lives, and that some were purposefully vindictive. Women were being systematically expunged from the welfare rolls for minor infractions, compounding the violence of their lives.

A Maze of Confusion

In addition to being sanctioned for missed meetings, mothers were penalized for a variety of seemingly trivial violations of CalWORKs.[10] In fact, the very structure of the welfare legislation systematically ensured their failure. Numerous women were unable to comply with the morass of regulations contained in the reform and were therefore denied benefits. Others qualified but had difficulty maintaining their assistance. Women with less than a high school education found it particularly difficult to understand the complex requirements of the new legislation and were less likely than more educated women to appeal sanctions (see, for example, Zedlewski and Loprest 2001). Income limits, reporting changes in household composition, income, and criminal justice status, child care provisions for single- and two-parent families, limits on property and resources, rules about car ownership, use of electronic benefits cards (EBC), immunization requirements, mandatory school attendance for children, and the understanding of exactly what constitutes acceptable participation in CalWORKs programs was utterly confusing.

For many women complying with the exceedingly complex legislation became a Sisyphean task.

> Annee: Last time we talked you mentioned how hard it was to follow the rules of the new welfare reform. Can you tell me more about that?

> Mariana: O.K. sure. Well you know they added all these new rules we have to follow. If we don't we lose our money.

> Annee: Do you remember what they call it when they take away your benefits?

> Mariana: Oh yeah, sanctions.

> Annee: Where did you find out about the new rules and about the sanctions?

> Mariana: At my orientation meeting. But it was so confusing. There were two women in charge of the meeting—but they kept talking over each other. We were there a long time and everyone was asking all these questions. It was very confusing. There was all this stuff about Medi-Cal and food stamps and a card that is like an ATM card but is how they pay us our benefits. They told us we had to name the father of our kids or we couldn't get welfare. They also said we had to report any income and tell them if we owned a car . . . I don't know, it was so crazy.

> Annee: Did they talk about finding a job?

> Marian: Oh yeah, they said we have to look for work for a certain number of hours every week and if we don't we get sanctioned. But I couldn't remember exactly what kind of work counted. Also, there was some stuff about what to do if we were in school but I couldn't really follow it. Plus, there were all these exceptions to the rules that I wasn't sure had anything to do with me. It was way too much information and I kind of just spaced out after a while.

> Annee: Did you meet with your GAIN caseworker after the meeting? Was she able to answer all your questions?

> Mariana: We did meet but she seemed to be in a hurry. There were lots of other women waiting to see her. She did help me understand some of the stuff about work but I was still pretty confused.

Annee: Do you think being confused is why you got sanctioned last month?

Mariana: Hell to the yes! I got sanctioned twice already. I am trying really hard to follow the rules but there are so many of them—and they are really confusing. I just can't keep up. That's the reason I asked you to help me. You're so smart—I'm really glad you're helping me figure all this out.

Annee: I don't know about that Mari, I went to a few of those orientation meetings with moms from Home Away so I could help them understand the new regulations. Wow, they are really confusing. I'm still a little confused, but I have a manual from Social Services and I just keeping looking up the rules. Hopefully, we can figure things out together and can keep you from getting sanctioned again.

The CalWORKs legislation and the concomitant welfare-to-work programs called Greater Avenues to Independence (GAIN) contain an absurd number of requirements. As part of my advocacy while in the field, I accompanied several women to their CalWORKs orientation meetings. My role was to help explain what was expected of them. Although the caseworkers were optimistic about the new reform and were well-intentioned, they too seemed confused by the endless requirements. Each rule had countless restrictions and exceptions which further complicated things. For example, applicants are required to receive a home visit by the Department of Social Services (DPSS) within five days of their return appointment. If applicants do not agree, they are denied CalWORKs benefits. Exceptions to this rule include living in a domestic violence or homeless shelter or a sober living facility. Verbal or written verification from the facility is required. If applicants are homeless they must prove it, if they cannot, they can sign an affidavit attesting to their homelessness. Applicants who work thirty-two or more hours per week during normal work hours are exempt. Written verification of work hours is of course required from an employer. Applicants living with a non-relative who refuses to allow a home visit are exempt, if they provide an affidavit from the non-relative indicating they will not allow a home visit. In this case DPSS refers the applicant to the fraud investigation unit. There are several good cause exemptions as well, all requiring notes and affidavits which are decided on a case-by-case basis. This incessant demand for affidavits and supporting documents infantilizes, and ultimately demoralizes, welfare recipients. Once the home visit is agreed upon DPSS does a walk through in every room of your home, unless the room belongs to someone who is not part of the family applying for benefits. DPSS does not tell applicants what day or the exact time they plan to show up. Ironically, applicants are told that the home visit should not interfere with their job, training, or educational activities. However, unless applicants have a nine-to-five job, they are not exempt from the home visit. If an applicant misses three (unscheduled) home visits she is denied benefits. This is only one example of one requirement necessary to *qualify* for CalWORKs. Regulations regarding participation in the program also seem purposefully convoluted and mean-spirited. It seems to me the very structure of the legislation is meant to torment and punish so-called lazy, overly sexualized women of color and poor white women.

During the course of the first CalWORKs orientation I attended, case-workers went through each component of the reform. By the third hour I was bleary-eyed and totally confused. With all my education and well-developed coping skills, I became confused and angry, and I began to shut down. However, in the fourth hour, I perked up when the caseworker began to discuss the welfare-to-work requirements contained in GAIN. This information was central to successfully navigating the new reform. I learned that if you are a single parent you must participate in welfare-to-work activities thirty-two hours per week, unless you are excused. In families with two parents, the participation requirement is thirty-five hours per week, with one parent completing at least twenty hours per week. In all families, twenty hours must be devoted to "core" work activities including on-the-job training, county apprenticeships, unpaid work experience, community service, job searches, and vocational training. The remaining work hours can be devoted to "non-core" activities such as studying for a GED, Adult Education, and English as a Second Language classes. Mental health, substance abuse, and domestic violence services can count toward the total number of work-related hours required—of course these must always be documented. There are numerous exemptions, including caring for a first child under twelve months old, or any later child under six months old. If applicants do not qualify for any of the exemptions they can apply under the good cause exemption. There are also several good cause exemptions, but they are applied at the discretion of each caseworker (Los Angeles Coalition to End Hunger and Homelessness 2005). Working as an unpaid apprentice or doing community service seems to be more about exploiting the labor of welfare recipients than training them for work in the paid labor market. By far, the most infuriating aspect of the welfare-to-work portion of the orientation was the discussion of the benefits of working. In addition to increased self-esteem and self-sufficiency, case-workers informed the group that they could save money and start a retirement account! Yes, a retirement account! With a smile on her face, the caseworker discussed the possibility of starting a 401K. I almost fell off my chair. The jobs that these women were eligible for were the lowest-paying jobs in the service economy. Most of the jobs did not pay a living wage, did not include benefits, and would certainly not provide self-sufficiency. Many women would be unable to secure employment, and the ones who did find work, would be joining the ranks of the working poor. In fact, 40 percent of former welfare recipients were still not employed by 2002. Of the 60 percent of former welfare recipients who were employed, only half made enough money to extricate their families from poverty (Hays 2003). Retirement benefits? Really? I understand the desire to motivate low-income women to embrace the Puritan work ethic, but this was preposterous. These examples scarcely evoke just how convoluted and complex the PRWORA really is.

Failure to Comply

Even when women did understand the legislation they often had a hard time complying with it. For example, in order to be eligible for TANF, parents need to provide proof that their children have been properly immunized. In California, parents have an initial thirty-day period to provide documentation upon approval of Medi-Cal. There is an extension of this time period for another thirty days if the parent can prove she does not have to access to medical care or she provides a sworn statement that immunization is against her religious beliefs. However, if the parent does not provide this proof then all aid to adults is cut off until verification is provided (Los Angles Coalition to End Hunger and Homelessness 2005). Providing evidence of children's immunization records is a daunting task for homeless women who migrate between homeless shelters, residential motels, park benches, and friends' couches. As homeless women in San Francisco move between temporary residences it is extremely difficult to keep track of medical, financial, and school records. As Aisha, commented:

> When I applied for welfare last year they told me I had to give them copies of Trey and Lakisha's immunization records. I told my case worker that when we were living at Hamilton [family shelter] I kept all my stuff under my bed in a garbage bag. One night someone ripped off my bag. They took everything I owned, including all of my kids' doctors notes. When I explained this to my caseworker she said she was sorry for me but that I still needed to get copies of the records. Even after I told her that we had gotten the shots at different clinics she didn't seem to care. She just kept saying I needed to show proof that my kids were immunized. We've moved around so many times I can't remember where my kids got their shots. I mean give me a break I'm fuckin' homeless. After trying to figure it out for two months I just gave up. I guess I better figure it out soon cuz Lakisha starts school next year and they probably won't let her in if I can't prove she got her shots. I am so frustrated—no one will help me.

This frustration was expressed by several women who had similar stories of lost or stolen health and school records and their inability to qualify for welfare as a result. Women who are homeless are often in a perpetual state of chaos. Frequent moves, stressful living conditions, interpersonal violence, and relentless uncertainty often result in the loss of personal records, family photos, toys, clothing, and other items. When women cannot find the documentation necessary to receive welfare benefits, they often become overwhelmed and give up. Thus the very structure of the welfare system itself pushes homeless women further onto the margins of society.

As previously stated, women were often confused by the complexities and requirements of the new legislation. For example, homeless women in my study were extremely confused by the CalWORKs felony drug provision. This provision denied women convicted of a drug felony after 1997 child care, CalWORKs aid, or other supportive services such as substance abuse rehabilitation. Many women were unaware that even if they were dropped from the welfare rolls for a felony drug conviction, their children would still qualify for cash assistance. In addition, many homeless women in San Francisco did not realize that if their drug convictions were not for the sale or manufacture of drugs, they might still qualify for TANF (Los Angles Coalition to End Hunger and Homelessness 2005). It was difficult for some women in my study to differentiate between the particularities contained in the CalWORKs legislation and their continued eligibility for assistance. Janet expressed this confusion when she told me:

> I can't get welfare anymore cuz I got busted with drugs. After I got busted I stopped going to see my caseworker. What's the point? That bitch would have sanctioned me anyway. It was bad enough I got arrested; I didn't need to be humiliated by her too.

When I explained to Janet that she would only be sanctioned if she were convicted of a drug felony she expressed confusion:

> I got caught with a little weed—that ain't no felony. Shit, I fucked up. My friend told me that if I got caught with any drugs they would kick me off. My caseworker never explained this to me. She is always rushing me out of her office and I get really confused about all the new rules. When I ask her for help she gets pissed off. Man I can't keep all this shit straight it's so fuckin' complicated.

Similarly, Lydia explained:

> I liked the old welfare better. There are so many new rules that I have a hard time remembering all of them. Last year I got convicted of a felony for smoking crack. I was told by my caseworker that I would be kicked off welfare forever. How the fuck can they do that? How am I supposed to survive? I told her, my kids and me will starve. I mean shit we are already homeless now they are going to let us starve to death too?

When I asked Lydia if her caseworker explained that her two sons would still be eligible for cash assistance and she might still be eligible for food stamps, she replied:

> To be honest she never got a chance. I was so pissed off that I started scream-
> ing at her and when I refused to calm down the security guard came and kicked
> me out of the office. I was so angry I never went back. Now that we are staying
> at the shelter we get breakfast and dinner every day but I don't know what the
> hell we'll do when we have to leave the shelter.

Neither Janet nor Lydia understood the complexities of the CalWORKs legislation with regard to drug convictions. Like many other women in my research, they did not understand that they might still be eligible for some services or that they could appeal their sanctions under the good cause provision. This finding was extremely common among the homeless women I interviewed. Many were confused about the myriad requirements of the new TANF legislation and would often simply give up rather than fight for rights they were unsure they were entitled to. For homeless women in San Francisco the social welfare system is just another form of abuse they are forced to endure. Institutionalized indifference to homeless women's humanity is shared by impoverished mothers throughout the country, who are harassed by the stringent requirements of the reform legislation. Unbelievably, about one-quarter of welfare recipients nationally are enduring sanctions for failing to comply with the byzantine regulations of the welfare reform (Hays 2003).

Administrative Violence

For some homeless women, complying with the complex regulations was exacerbated by severe physical and emotional trauma, which interfered with their ability to find and keep work. For example, many persistently homeless women in my sample suffered from stress, severe anxiety, depression, anger, and sleep disorders. Many women also had significant health problems such as diabetes, respiratory illnesses, and circulatory diseases. These health problems often kept women out of the paid labor market altogether or made it difficult for them to keep stable jobs as they were often fired when they called in sick. Under the new welfare legislation, eligibility requirements for State Disability Insurance (SDI), Temporary Workers Compensation, and Social Security Disability (SSI) were tightened. As a result women in my study with significant health problems were often denied disability compensation and were required to work. Although the horrific conditions these homeless women faced kept them from successfully fulfilling welfare-to-work requirements they paled in comparison to the problems of their battered counterparts.

For homeless women who were also victims of domestic violence, employment barriers were more severe and were exacerbated by post-traumatic stress disorder and a variety of physical problems related to years of bodily violence. I met several women who were ravaged physically and psychologically by years of poverty and violence. For example Myrna told me:

> I can't work anymore. My body is trashed. My back aches, my jaw hurts and I get headaches from all the times I've taken a beating over the years.

Similarly, Melinda said:

> How am I supposed to get a job? My body is totally fucked up I am in hella pain. Not to mention I'm afraid of the dark and can only sleep a few hours a night. I have really bad dreams and sometimes I wake up screaming thinking I'm being beaten in my sleep. I can't concentrate for very long and I'm afraid of everything.

Several women in my study were wracked with pain, were missing teeth, had broken bones that were never set, were fraught with anxiety, and looked significantly older than their years. These women were often sanctioned for their inability to comply with the new welfare requirements. The ones who managed to avoid being sanctioned were fast approaching their five-year lifetime cap since they simply couldn't work. These women are clearly not success stories despite the fact that they are included in the data documenting the 50 percent reduction in the welfare caseload.

WELFARE-TO-WORK: ADMINISTRATIVE VIOLENCE

There were many women in my sample who were physically capable of working. However, men engaged in a variety of inventive tactics to sabotage women's training and employment responsibilities. One common tactic utilized by violent men was to harass women at their workplace which often got them fired. Several women told me stories of their intimate partners tracking them down at work and threatening them and their co-workers. Nilda's experience with this type of workplace harassment was typical:

> After years of getting the shit kicked out of me I finally got the nerve to leave—even though it meant going on welfare and living in a family shelter for a while. Since my kids are in school, I knew I could get a job. I've worked on and off over the years so I wasn't too worried about finding something. My caseworker helped me find a job and I started working at one of the hospital cafeterias. It wasn't the most exciting job but I liked the people I worked with and I felt good about myself. I was proud that I left my ex and that I was working. I really started to believe that things would finally be O.K. for me

and my kids. After about four months Diego showed up at work. I am not sure how he found me but he did. He would wait outside for me and as soon as he saw me he would start screaming at me. Sometimes he would threaten to kill me and sometimes he would just scream curses at me. Sometimes he would beg me to come home. A few times he actually came into the cafeteria and start screaming at me. One time when my supervisor asked him to leave he told him to mind his own business or he would beat the shit out of him too. My supervisor called security but Diego ran out when he saw him pick up the phone. My supervisor told me if Diego came back he would have to fire me. He told me he felt bad about that but he couldn't help it—Diego was scaring the customers and my co-workers. Sometimes Diego wouldn't come around for a few weeks and then he would show up again. After a few months my supervisor fired me. That really sucked—but what made it worse was that my caseworker sanctioned me for getting fired! What the fuck is that? I get fired for getting threatened at work. At least I was trying. After that I got really depressed and started hanging out in the park during the day when the shelter closed. I mean what the fuck's the point of looking for a job if I'm just gonna get fired once Diego shows up again?

Similarly Shonda told me that:

I got a job and then my asshole boyfriend found out where it was. He would call me at work all the time and my boss got really pissed off. Then he started showing up at my job and got me fired. I found another job after that and he did the same thing. Finally, I stopped looking for work because I was terrified that he would hunt me down and kill me.

After leaving her abusive husband Anita got a job as a secretary in an office. Her husband repeatedly called her at work, threatening and terrorizing her. Initially Anita's boss was very supportive and tried to advise her. However, she eventually lost patience with the situation and told Anita that if she couldn't get her husband under control she would have to find another job. When Anita's husband showed up at work and carved up the office door Anita was immediately fired. As Anita said to me:

That bastard got his way—I had to move back home after I lost my job—I got kicked off welfare for getting fired. I only stayed with him for 6 months. He started beating me so badly again that I ended up in the hospital. I took the kids and got the hell out. I'm meeting with another caseworker to get my benefits back and am looking for another job—but I am terrified he'll figure out where I am and come after me again.

Many battered homeless women in my sample shared similar stories of being hunted down at work and threatened by current and former intimate partners. These tactics instilled tremendous fear in homeless women who were already hanging on by a thread. I witnessed the emotional unraveling of women who had become newly confident after their decisions to leave violent men. I saw numerous women become utterly paralyzed by their fear. These women stopped looking for work, fell off the welfare rolls, and in some cases turned to drugs and alcohol to numb their pain. Other women persevered—reapplying for welfare benefits and looking for new jobs—over and over again, until they too became overwhelmed by the violence in their lives. When I asked the women in my research if they were aware of the Family Violence Option (FVO) contained in the reform, they had no idea what I was referring to.[11] Clearly, these homeless and battered welfare recipients were not apprised of the possibility of being exempt from the work requirements at their initial CalWORKs training or by their caseworkers and ultimately fell through the cracks.

Another way in which violent men controlled their intimate partners was by preventing them from attending school, training programs, and job interviews. A common strategy was to keep women up all night so that they would be too exhausted to succeed at their interviews and in their classes. Another more insidious tactic was to beat up their partners so that they would have bruises and cuts and be too embarrassed to be seen in public. Some men beat their partners because they were terrified they would meet other men at school or work and leave them forever. Some men became enraged at the thought of their partners succeeding without them and felt the need to punish them physically. These behaviors are well documented in the research literature (Baker, Cook, and Norris 2003; Brush 2006; George 2006; Lyon 2000; Raphael 2000; Riger and Staggs 2004; Scott, London, Myers 2002; Staggs and Riger 2005; Talyor and Barusch 2004; Tolman and Raphael 2000) and were widespread in my study as well. Women told me horror stories of their partners beating them to prevent them from going to work or school. Rochelle's story is typical of many women in my sample:

> I been homeless for over a year. It's such a struggle to get out of bed every day. But as bad as it is being homeless is still better than being with Gus. My kids are suffering too but at least they don't have to watch me get my ass beat anymore. He is one crazy motherfucker. When he used to stay at my apartment he would get mad every time I tried to find a job. I kept telling him I needed to work or I would get kicked off welfare. He didn't care. If had a job interview he would smack me around and punch me in the face—he'd give me a black eye or a fat lip. Sometimes he made me have sex with him—he raped me. Then he would say something like no one's gonna give you a job with an ugly puss like that. He didn't want me to work because he wanted to control everything I did. I couldn't get a job because he beat me so bad. Since I never made it to my interviews I got sanctioned, lost my apartment, and now I'm living at the shelter. I feel so beat down I can barely get up in the morning—I can't imagine looking for a job—I feel like shit.

When I first met Marta, her husband Ricardo was incarcerated. She and her daughter had been homeless for several years, moving between shelters and residential motels throughout the city. After several months at Home Away Marta began a training program at a vocational school and her daughter Olivia was reenrolled in school after a two-year absence. They were both doing exceptionally well. For almost a year Marta was complying with all of the TANF requirements. She never missed any of her required appointments, had a good relationship with her caseworker, and was doing well in school. Eventually Ricardo was released on parole and moved into the residential motel with Marta and Olivia. Immediately upon Ricardo's return, the domestic violence resumed and Marta's life began to unravel. Ricardo did not want Marta to continue in her vocational training and tried to force her to take drugs with him. When Marta refused he became extremely violent:

> Ricardo was so angry that I was doing well. He didn't want me to better myself—he wanted me to hang out with him in the hotel room and smoke crack all day. When I talked to him about how well I was doing in school he made fun of me and called me stupid. He kept accusing me of being a whore and fucking the men at school. Sometimes he would wait for me after school and drag me home. He was so jealous of nothing—I never cheated on him—but he didn't believe me. He kept picking fights with me and accusing me of cheating. We would stay up all night fighting. I was so tired after those fights that I started being late for school. I got in trouble at school for being late and then I couldn't keep up with all the work. Ricardo would get drunk and want to have sex and he kept me up all night. If I said no he hit me. After a while I just couldn't take it anymore. I was too tired! I stopped going to school and my welfare got cut off. Then I got really depressed—so I started using again and now I am back to where I started—nowhere and on drugs.

Many women told me similar stories of unfounded fits of jealousy that resulted in extremely violent abuse and the subsequent loss of their welfare benefits. Numerous women who left their violent partners were stalked, harassed, and threatened at school and work, resulting in the loss of their welfare benefits. Women who left their abusive partners lived in constant fear that their abusers would retaliate against them for leaving. Given that the majority of women who are killed by their batterers are killed once they leave (U.S. Department of Justice 1991), this fear was totally justified. Many women felt that the government had completely abandoned them. Homeless women often expressed outrage at a sexist society in which men were allowed to continuously harm them and in which there were no social safety nets to protect them.

THE WELFARE STATE AND THE REPRODUCTION OF RACE, CLASS, AND GENDER INEQUALITY

Over the course of my four-year ethnography I met many women who stayed in abusive relationships for several years before finally choosing to leave. These women felt stymied by the new welfare legislation which they felt necessitated their staying in violent homes so they could survive. By the time I met these women they could no longer stand the abuse and essentially made the choice to stop it by becoming homeless. Despite their fear, some of the homeless women in my research felt compelled to maintain contact with their abusers for minimal financial help as they cycled through jobs or lost benefits as a result of sanctions. Other women cut off all contact with former abusive partners. Regardless, all the battered homeless women in my sample struggled desperately to comply with the requirements of the newly implemented welfare reform. These women felt themselves being systematically forced further onto the margins of society by a patriarchal system that, in their opinion, feigned concern for women and children. Battered homeless women understood in a deeply visceral way that the intent of welfare reform was to punish them, not make them self-sufficient. Despite the inclusion of the Family Violence Option and good cause exemptions included in the CalWORKs legislation, battered homeless women in San Francisco were frequently sanctioned by caseworkers for failing to comply with a variety of welfare-to-work requirements. Similarly, women who were not victims of domestic violence also had difficulty complying with the myriad requirements of the legislation. Many women felt they were treated harshly by an unforgiving welfare state. Homeless mothers also expressed their disgust with caseworkers who showed no empathy for their tragic lives and treated them with disdain. Exempting battered homeless women from participating in welfare-to-work activities exists in principle but for many women in my study, does not exist in reality. These women are being purged from the welfare rolls as a result of the violence in their lives. The vacuous claim by policy makers that the PRWORA is a resounding success because the welfare rolls have been decreased by half is offensive to battered homeless women in San Francisco, who may no longer be receiving TANF, but are certainly not thriving.

For decades, welfare was the one social safety net poor women could rely on to survive. However, during the 1980s and 1990s a vitriolic debate on welfare reform swept the nation. Despite evidence to the contrary, there was a pervasive view that poor women of color were welfare-dependent and had additional children to obtain more benefits. Poor women of color were vilified as lazy and sexually promiscuous. Essentially, the legislation was predicated on stereotypic racialized notions of class and gender. The purpose of the reform was to eliminate welfare dependency, discourage abortion, promote abstinence and heterosexual marriage, and force poor women into the labor market. As a result, radical welfare legislation containing sweeping reforms was passed. This legislation systematically marginalized an already disenfranchised population. Although poor white women have been victimized by this legislation, black women and Latinas have suffered further. Women of color are more likely to be poor and are more likely to be victims of community and intimate partner violence (Copp et al. 2015; Richie 2012; Sokoloff and Dupont 2005). The five-year lifetime limit on welfare receipt is disastrous for women of color who, because of institutional racism, use up their allotment more quickly. Similarly, women of color are also more likely to be sanctioned than white women (Casey 2010), embedding them in the lowest recesses of the social structure. This is particularly true for women who come from the most economically disadvantaged backgrounds. Excessively poor women have very little education and lack the cultural capital of their more educated and less economically deprived counterparts. Subsequently, these women are less likely to leave abusive relationships and have less access to therapeutic resources. It is true that battered women's shelters and community domestic violence services are available to all women. However, access to therapists and long-term treatment is more available to women who are less destitute. Low-income women with consistent work experience and a high school education are better equipped to navigate the system and find long-term help. Ironically, class differences exist even among welfare recipients. Of course affluent and middle-class women are the most likely to have access to the best resources, and possess the cultural capital necessary to obtain those resources. Race, class, and gender intersect under the tyranny of the welfare state, which further recreates socially structured race, class, and gender inequality. Despite being severely disenfranchised, homeless women exert their agency as they attempt to traverse the morass of the welfare state. Sadly, they are often overwhelmed by the racist, sexist, and classist social structure that forces them onto the margins of society. Clearly, the social safety net that once existed is no longer viable for homeless women and their children.

NOTES

1. Some of the text contained in this chapter is reprinted by permission from Copyright Clearance Center: Springer, Gender Issues, *Welfare Indignities: Homeless Women, Domestic Violence and Welfare Reform in San Francisco*, Anne R. Roschelle, 2008

2. The PRWORA included sanctions for people who do not comply with the welfare-to-work requirements. California legislators imposed partial family sanctions (as opposed to full family sanctions) that only penalize the abled-bodied adult who fails to comply with welfare-to-work requirements. Partial family sanctions mean that children of a single parent will still receive their cash benefits even if that parent is sanctioned so the family loses only that adult's share of the CalWORKs cash grant. The sanctioned individual develops a compliance plan with her/his/their caseworker and once she/he/they meet the terms of that plan cash assistance is

restored. If an individual is sanctioned a second time, cash benefits are rescinded for three months or until she/he/they comply fully with program requirements or whichever comes first. If there is a third sanction, assistance is withheld for six months or until the adult complies with the regulations, whichever comes first (Ong & Houston 2005). Reasons for sanctions include failure to comply with welfare-to-work activities which include but are not limited to the following: Welfare recipients are expected to spend 32 hours per week in job-related activities for single parents and 35 hours per week for two-parent families. Welfare recipients must spend at least 20 of those 32 hours in "core" job-related activities such as looking for a job, doing community service, on-the-job training, county apprenticeships, etc. "Non-core"-related activities include adult basic education, mental health counseling, substance abuse programs, studying for the GED, vocational training, and domestic violence services. In addition, welfare recipients may be sanctioned for failure to provide caseworkers with immunization and school records, for their children's truancy, and for losing a job even if they are fired. Finally, welfare recipients in California are expected to provide a quarterly report (QR-7) that indicates any changes in residence, the number of people living in the household, changes in income, and any criminal justice–related problems. This report must be handed in every three months even if there are no changes in the recipients' status. In order for welfare recipients to avoid sanctions for failure to comply with any CalWORKs requirements or to challenge being sanctioned, they must demonstrate good cause for their behavior. This provision in the legislation requires that welfare recipients convince their caseworkers that their reasons for non-compliance were justified (Los Angles Coalition to End Hunger and Homelessness 2005). The good cause provision provides caseworkers with discretion in how each case is processed. Although sanctions were included in the previous welfare legislation know as Aid to Families with Dependent Children (AFDC), they were imposed less frequently and with less vehemence.

3. California currently has a staggering number of child-only CalWORKs cases in which the parents no longer receive benefits. According to MaCurdy, Mancuso, and O'Brien-Strain (2000) the rise in child-only cases, in which parents no longer receive benefits, is a direct result of CalWORKs policy, particularly sanctions. The rise in child-only cases can also be attributed to adults who have exceeded their five-year lifetime cap. The number of parents who have "timed-out" increased from zero in 1997, to 5,300 in 2003, and skyrocketed to 40,000 in 2005, as parents reached their lifetime limits (Similanick 2006).

4. Temporary Aid to Needy Families (TANF) replaced Aid to Families with Dependent Children (AFDC) in the reform legislation.

5. Good cause exceptions allow for exemptions from specific welfare-to-work requirements if a recipient can show good cause for not participating.

6. In a recent article, Shaw, Horton, and Moreno (2008–09) argue that some welfare recipients actively refuse to comply with certain sanctions as an act of resistance and that that the barriers thesis is overstated. In my four-year ethnography I *never* encountered women who refused to comply as a way of exerting their agency. Rather, the women in my research were often desperate to comply and frustrated when they were unable to.

7. Approximately 60 percent of welfare mothers have been victims of domestic violence in the past and 15 to 34 percent of welfare recipients are current victims of domestic violence (Hays 2003; Lyon 2000; Tolman and Raphael 2000). For many battered women intimate partner abuse was the cause of their initial welfare receipt (Brandwein 1999; Davis 1999; Meier, 1997).

8. For a critique of how homeless kids' behavior is typically misinterpreted as problematic, see Roschelle and Kaufman (2004).

9. I would like to thank my good friend and colleague Karl Bryant for suggesting the phrase "administrative violence."

10. The California Work Opportunity and Responsibility to Kids (CalWORKs) was created by the California State Legislature in 1997 as a response to the 1996 Personal Responsibility and Work Opportunity Reconciliation Act (PRWORA) and is essentially the states version of Temporary Aid to Needy Families (TANF). Subsequently, throughout the book I use Cal-WORKs, TANF, and welfare reform interchangeably.

11. The Family Violence Option (FVO), also known as the Wellstone/Murray Amendment, gives each state the option to grant work requirement waivers to women who are victims of

domestic violence. Each participating state is allowed to exempt 20 percent of their overall caseload from the five-year lifetime cap without losing their federal funding. Forty-two states and the District of Columbia have at least some provisions for victims of domestic violence. However, research has shown that welfare applicants may receive little or no information about the availability of the FVO (Hearn 2000). In addition, some women do not want to disclose their abuse to welfare officials, welfare officials are sometimes non-responsive to claims of domestic violence, and welfare officials are often hostile to the needs of victims of domestic violence (George 2006; Hearn 2000; Levin 2001; Pearson, Griswold, and Thoennes, 2001; Postmus 2004). In fact, one study found that, of the abused women who applied for the FVO, only one-third actually received it (Hearn 2000).

Chapter Four

The Tattered Web of Kinship

When I was growing up people took care of each other. It didn't matter if you were blood-related or not, if you needed help, kinfolk stepped in. Now you are on your own.—Effie

EXTENDED KINSHIP NETWORKS

Extended kinship networks have historically played an important role in racial ethnic families.[1] These networks are characterized by frequent interaction, close affective bonds, and exchanges of goods and services among family and nonfamily members. Extended kinship networks are often referred to as informal social support networks because they customarily include both family and friends. Network members rarely differentiate between blood relatives, relatives acquired through marriage, or fictive kin[2] (Roschelle 1997; Stack, 1974). Networks are characterized by mutual aid and can be either emotional or instrumental (Litwak 1960; Sussman 1965). Emotional or expressive aid includes offering general daily advice and providing emotional support during times of crises or stress. Instrumental aid includes assistance with child care, grocery shopping, and household labor. Instrumental help can also include monetary exchanges, intra-household division of expenses, and exchanges of goods and services such as food stamps, clothing, and furniture. Finally, economic help includes housing network members who are in danger of becoming homeless. An essential component of network participation is exchange reciprocity. Each member of an extended kinship network is expected to provide help when asked. If a network member receives help but does not reciprocate, she will be dropped from the network. Historically, extended kinship networks have been a common element of racial ethnic family life, particularly among low-income women of color, who relied on exchange networks to survive in an economically hostile world (McAdoo 1980; Roschelle 1997; Stack 1973). In addition to ensuring economic survival, extended kingship networks also reflected important cultural norms endemic to African American and Latinix families. Caring for other people's children has historically been a significant role for African American women. During and after slavery, informal adoption of children by non-biological mothers, what Patricia Hill Collins (1990) terms *other mothers*, was common and represented the cultural value placed on cooperative child care traditionally found in African culture. Similarly, Latinas placed important cultural meaning on participation in extended kinship networks and on mothering. In Latinix culture, the term "familism" refers to putting the needs of the extended family above the needs of the individual. An essential expression of familism is through the custom of *compadrazgo* (god parenthood), in which non–biologically related individuals become part of the extended family. This custom dates back to pre-Colombian conquest. Because of their role in child care, women form the core of the extended family network. Both *comadres* (god mothers) and *other mothers* are highly revered members of their communities who acquire cultural meaning from their network participation. Tragically, these thriving networks began to unravel during the 1980s.

NO MORE KIN

During the 1980s and 1990s researchers began to reexamine the prevalence of extended kinship networks among racial ethnic families. Both ethnographers and survey researchers discovered that the extensive web of kinship networks that once characterized low-income families of color were eroding (Menjivar 2000; Roschelle 1997). There are many socioeconomic factors that are responsible for the erosion of social support networks traditionally found in racial ethnic communities. During the early 1980s poverty escalated and there was a tremendous influx of drugs (particularly crack) into minority neighborhoods. As illustrated in chapter 1, increasing unemployment and subsequent economic hardships occurred as a result of the deindustrialization of the inner city. In addition, the migration of the middle class out of the inner cities and persistent residential segregation resulted in increasing social isolation of these communities. Consequently, there was a disturbing rise in violent crime and street homelessness. During the first three years of the Reagan administration there were drastic cutbacks in Medicaid, maternal and child health programs, Aid to Families with Dependent Children (AFDC), food stamps, funds for day care, and child nutrition programs (Sidel 1986). Far-reaching reductions in social services continued throughout the 1980s. During the 1990s, the gap between rich and poor continued to widen, making it harder for low-income women to participate in their networks (Roschelle 1999). In addition, a segmented labor market in which women were segregated into the lowest-paying jobs in the occupational structure has contributed to women's economic disenfranchisement (Reskin and Hartmann 1986) and restricted their ability to participate in exchange networks. The decline in extended kinship networks represents a significant erosion of an historical safety net and has forced many women to rely on institutional forms of social support.[3] Nonetheless, due to the historical significance of extended networks in racial ethnic communities, policy makers consistently assert that thriving kin and non-kin social support networks continue to characterize minority family life. Policy recommendations based on these underlying assumptions have led to the implementation of harmful social policy.

EXTENDED KINSHIP NETWORKS AND WELFARE REFORM

In the second year of my fieldwork, President Clinton passed the most profound piece of welfare legislation since Franklin Delano Roosevelt's New Deal. The underlying ideology of this sweeping reform was to eliminate welfare dependency, promote marriage, and require poor women to go to work. In addition to pejorative stereotypes about women of color, the legislation was predicated on the belief that poor women would rely on an extended network of family and friends for their survival. In 1997, I published my book *No More Kin: Exploring Race, Class, and Gender in Family Networks*. A major finding of this research was that extended kinship networks traditionally found in low-income Puerto Rican, Chicana/o, and African American families were eroding as a result of economic oppression. I argued that due to increasing residential segregation, drug-related gun violence, and severe economic deprivation that characterized the Reagan era, extended social support networks traditionally found in communities of color were not as prevalent as they were in the past. As the welfare debate raged on, I wrote: "The vitriolic debate on welfare reform currently sweeping the nation assumes that if institutional mechanisms of social support are eliminated, impoverished families will simply rely on an extensive web of kinship networks for their survival. The implementation of social policy that presupposes the availability of familial safety nets in minority communities could have disastrous consequences for individuals that do not have access to extended kin networks." Little did I know how accurate that statement would become!

Listening to policy makers propagandize about the utility of extended social support networks among impoverished racial ethnic families was particularly offensive. For decades, the public discourse on extended kinship networks was that "pathological" elements inherent in minority cultures were responsible for deviant family structures. Black families were depicted as being matriarchal, disorganized, and ultimately dysfunctional, whereas Latinx families were characterized as rigidly patriarchal (Bermúdez 1955; Heller 1966; Lewis 1965; Moynihan 1965; Rainwater 1966). Extended households and elaborate social support networks among racial ethnic families were seen as deviations from the norm of the middle-class, white nuclear family. For politicians to suddenly extol the virtues of kinship networks as a way to dismantle the welfare system was cynical and repugnant. When I began my fieldwork, I did not intend to examine the relationship between unraveling kinship networks and familial homelessness. I was eager to start a new project that was unrelated to my previous work. However, the loss of extended networks was unmistakably on the minds of homeless men and women. Throughout my time in the field, respondents frequently lamented the loss of kinship networks that in the past, would have buffered them from becoming homeless. Over the course of my research, I saw first-hand the devastating effects welfare reform had on families who became homeless when their social support networks were shredded beyond repair.

EXTENDED KINSHIP NETWORKS AND HOMELESSNESS

The literature on homeless families indicates that there is in fact a relationship between the loss of extended kinship networks and the rise in family homelessness. Early research that examined this relationship indicated that homeless families have fragile or unreliable networks and that homeless families have less social support than their housed counterparts (Bassuk et al. 1996; National Center for Children in Poverty 2010; Letiecq, Anderson, and Koblinsky 1998). In addition, some research found that homeless individuals are socially isolated and have limited contact with family members (North and Smith 1983). The research that did find homeless families with access to social support networks discovered that network members did not provide economic resources to those families (Toohey, Shinn, and Weitzman 2004). These findings are extremely disturbing since economic resources and social supports are a critical factor in preventing low-income women from becoming homeless (Bassuk et al. 1996; Guarino, Rubin, and Bassuk 2007).

In order to determine whether or not homeless families are socially isolated, more recent research examines access to social support networks and types of help available. Much of this research indicates that homeless mothers are not in fact socially isolated and have contact with extended kinship networks. In one study, women reported having a mother, grandmother, close friend, or relative living in the same city. Many of the women were in close contact with members of their exchange network and had even lived with them prior to becoming homeless (Toohey, Shinn, and Weitzman 2004). Similarly, Tucker et al. (2009) found that homeless mothers were in contact with extended kin and non-kin network members, and often received emotional support. Nonetheless, homeless women indicated that members of their extended kinship network did not have room to house them and would refuse to let them reside with them even for a short time (Toohey, Shinn, and Weitzman 2004). These finding are consistent with earlier research that found that a major reason mothers gave for being homeless was that they could not stay with family or friends. Homeless women believed that network members were too poor to provide resources and that their homes were too small to house them and their children (Maurin, Russell, and Memmott 1989). Impoverished single mothers do not become homeless as a result of social isolation, but rather, because members of their exchange networks are too poor to provide financial help or housing. Even when network members can provide limited housing, homeless families have to be careful not to overstay their welcome (Toohey, Shinn, and Weitzman 2004).

These findings indicate that homeless families can no longer rely on an extended network of family and friends for economic resources or housing. The days of doubling up with relatives and couch surfing are over.[4] Kin and fictive kin now run the risk of being evicted from their own housing if caught concealing relatives or friends. In San Francisco, where the housing market is insanely tight, landlords and representatives of the Housing Authority expel tenants who violate occupancy restrictions or housing policies. Welfare recipients have the added burden of being evicted from subsidized housing and sanctioned if caught sheltering friends or family. In addition to the sanctions outlined in chapter 3, the PRWORA also includes sanctions for a variety of housing-related infractions. Welfare recipients may be sanctioned for the presence of drugs found in subsidized housing (even if the drugs do not belong to the welfare recipient) and failure to comply with subsidized housing requirements. Because welfare recipients in California are required to provide a quarterly report that indicates any changes in residence or the number of people living in their household, the structure of welfare itself prevents families from taking in extended kinship members in need of housing. In addition, subsidized housing projects often have stringent rules requiring the eviction of any tenants who live with a family member convicted of a drug-related felony or who exceed occupancy restrictions. Unfortunately, when single mothers cannot double up with friends or relatives, they are forced to move to residential motels, family shelters, and substandard apartments in violent neighborhoods.

Regardless of whether homeless families became homeless as a result of urban development, gentrification, low wages, exorbitant rents, domestic violence, or welfare sanctions, they all had one thing in common; the lack of thriving extended kinship networks upon which they could rely. Throughout my fieldwork, homeless families repeatedly discussed the lack of financial help available from family and close friends. Women in San Francisco were in contact with their extended kinship networks were not socially isolated and received emotional support. However, because network members were also typically impoverished, they were rarely able to provide economic support or housing. For some homeless families, there also seemed to be a cultural shift in people's attitudes toward network participation that was connected to economic disenfranchisement. As a result of the drug trade and increasing gun violence, particularly in housing projects, the role of community mothering was vanishing.

MACROSTRUCTURAL SHIFTS AND EXTENDED KINSHIP NETWORKS

Macroeconomic shifts and concomitant urban development in San Francisco have contributed directly to the unraveling of extended kinship networks. As a woman in her mid-forties, Effie had fond memories of the extended kinship networks that characterized her childhood and early married life. She lovingly reminisced about how women in her housing project were revered for their role as *other mothers*. All the women in the community were responsible for each other's children. Children in the community knew that if they misbehaved in public, they would likely be disciplined by whatever mother happed to observe their errant behavior. In addition, those children could expect that their own mothers would be apprised of what transpired and they would absolutely be punished again. During the crack epidemic of the 1980s the public expression of *other mothering* began to decline. Drive-by shootings and drug-related violence became rampant. Gang members asserted their dominance and showed little respect for *other mothers*. As a result, many women began to retreat into their own apartments and started to mind their own business. As Effie so eloquently stated:

> When I was growing up things were different. We knew all of our neighbors and we took care of each other. All the women kept an eye out for each other's kids. If someone acted up on the playground or anywhere else in public they got whooped. It didn't matter if it was their own mother who caught them or someone else's mother—they got whooped. Then that lady would call their mother and they would get whooped again. Discipline was very important in those days and women were in charge of handing out that discipline. You didn't sass older women, you didn't cuss, you showed older women respect. Mothers were very important in our community. Whenever you needed help someone in your kin group would help. If you needed some food, or clothing, or a place to stay while you got back on your feet, you could always rely on kin. It didn't matter if you were blood-related or not, if you needed help, kinfolk stepped in. Now you are on your own. This makes me very sad. You know black women have always been important for the survival of our people.

When I asked Effie if the loss of extended kinship networks was partly responsible for her and Jeremiah becoming homeless, she responded by saying:

> Totally! You know we lost our housing when they kicked us out of Hayes Valley. But I really believe that if this happened twenty years ago we would not have become homeless. Me and Jeremiah and the kids would have gone to stay with cousins or aunties or neighbors. In those day kinfolk took you in. It didn't matter how long you needed to stay—you were always welcome. No one would turn their back on family. No one was homeless. I mean, there were always one or two homeless men hanging around but they were crazy and most of them were addicts. But there were no homeless families back then.

When I asked Effie what she thought had changed over the last twenty years, she replied:

> I don't know. Things are just different now. People are scared of each other, they don't know their neighbors. All these gang bangers hanging around with guns, selling drugs, they're crazy scary. They don't have respect for their elders and believe me if you get in their face they'll just gun you right down in the street. You see the news, people gettin' shot left and right. Also, it seems like times are harder now. Poor people just seem to keep getting poorer and are hanging on by a thread. How can you help your kinfolk if you don't have anything? Plus, it is impossible to stay with family now. All the housing projects are so strict. If you get caught letting someone stay with you that is not on your lease you get kicked out. It's the same with Section 8 housing. If the landlord finds out you have extra people in the apartment you get evicted. Then instead of one homeless family there are two. I could never ask anyone to risk losing their own housing to take me and Jeremiah and the kids in. It just wouldn't be right. And to be honest, no one in their right mind would take us in.

Jeremiah concurred with Effie's analysis of the more recent loss of extended kinship networks. He added:

> Back in the day, when I was coming up, folks took care of each other. People shared their homes with you if you needed a place to stay. I remember when my auntie's husband died and she couldn't afford to keep her apartment. She moved in with us for about six months with my two cousins. We all lived together until she got back on her feet and could move out. We weren't worried the landlord would kick us out. Family took in family that was just how we lived. Now, you can't do that—no way. If you have extra folks living with you and the landlord or your caseworker finds out, everyone gets kicked out. It just aint right.

Effie and Jeremiah were in constant contact with their extended kinship network. Effie in particular had lots of kin and fictive kin in her life. However, given their economic circumstances, Effie's network members could only provide her with emotional support. This emotional support was vital to Effie and it helped her cope with becoming homeless. Unfortunately, due to their inability to provide Effie with economic aid, network members could do nothing to prevent her from becoming homeless. The inability of network members to provide resources to kin and fictive kin was also common among Latinix respondents. For example, members of Adela's extended network were always available to provide emotional support and advice, but could not provide economic resources, or a place to stay. Even though Adela was in her early twenties, she was aware of the tradition of *compadrazgo* that character- ized Mexican culture. She told me that her *abeula* (grandmother) regaled her with stories of *comadres* who took in struggling family and community members in Mexico and in San Francisco. Adela said:

> I grew up hearing stories of important women in the community who took in friends and family when they couldn't take care of themselves or their chil- dren. My *abeula* knew lots of *Mexicanas* who gave food and clothing to people when they needed it and took care of their children when they were at work or got sick. She also told me that if a mother couldn't take care of her kids, a neighbor or relative would always help—would give them a place to live for as long as they needed it. You would never let anyone from your community become homeless, especially a mother and her children. That is fuckin' shameful. *Abeula* was proud that it was women who kept *la familia* alive. My *mami* [mom] also told me stories about friends who lived with aunts and cousins when things at home were bad. Sometimes it was only for a few weeks, but she told me about her cousin Elsa who moved in with her mom's best friend and lived with her for three years. Everyone was poor but they all took care of each other. No one went hungry and no one ever lived on the streets—never. But it is not like that anymore. Now everyone is just hanging on trying to survive. It is disgraceful how things have changed. My sister lives in San Francisco and we are very close. I talk to her all the time and she is very caring. She gives me advice and helps me look for work, but she works two shitty jobs and can't help take care of my kids. She doesn't have any money either so she can't buy us food or clothing, diapers, nothing. I know she would let me and my kids live with her but she would get kicked out of her apartment if we got caught. Then she would be homeless too. Her landlady doesn't care if we are living on the streets or in a shelter, as long as we don't stay in her apartment. She's a heartless bitch!

Similar stories were related to me by other Latina respondents as well. For women in the Mission District, rampant gentrification accelerated the shredding of their already unraveling networks. As Rita previously articulat- ed, many long-term Latinix families from the Mission District were forced to move out of the Bay Area. There has, in fact, been a considerable exodus of families moving from the Mission to places like Stockton, Tracy, and Lodi, in the Central Valley. This migration has impacted Rita in significant ways:

After me and Nestor and Ceci got evicted I decided to stay in the city. We got into Hamilton and have been there for two months. I am not sure what will happen when our three months are up but I can't think about that now. It is very lonely in the city because so many of our family and friends moved to the Central Valley. I didn't want to go because I have a job here. I can't afford a car and it is two hours away. If we moved to Stockton or Lodi I couldn't keep my job. There is no way in hell I'm gonna move to the Central Valley and become a farm worker. Are you fuckin' kidding me? I was born here, I am not an immigrant. As shitty as my job is, it is a million times better than farm work. No fucking way I am bending over in a hundred degree weather picking vegetables for ten hours a day. I guess there are other jobs up there—but no way I'm moving there. I grew up in San Francisco; it is my home—plus who wants to live out in those horrible towns. Have you ever been out there Annee? It is awful. Totally flat and ugly. I am glad we didn't leave, but it is hella lonely. When I lived with my family on Guerrero, we knew everyone in the neighborhood. It was a tight community and we all looked out for each other. It isn't really like that anymore. I mean, it was already different from when I was a kid. You know, when I was growing up everyone looked out for each other. People took you in if you had a baby and couldn't afford a place to live or if you lost your job. If someone in the family got sick you would go live with your *abuela* or with a family friend. No one would ever become homeless, no way. Women were always in charge of the family and the community—they were admired and respected. That is our history. But things started to change, even before the *gringos* moved in and we became homeless. Some kids in the neighborhood started to join gangs and sell drugs. People were afraid of getting shot and started to mind their own business. Adults in the community were no longer respected and women stopped looking out for other people's kids. Landlords started to evict families for having relatives stay with them without permission. It wasn't really like when I was a kid anymore. But, still, we did have a feeling of community and we mostly knew our neighbors. Even if people couldn't help you out with a place to stay or food or whatever, they always had a kind word and a smile. You could always get advice about your troubles. Once those computer *gringos* moved in, forget it. They never smiled or said hello, I guess they were just too cool for us poor Mexicans. It all happened so fast, more and more people were forced to move away and we never saw some of them again. They destroyed our neighborhood, our community. But even before they moved in, things had changed and you couldn't rely on your family to take you in anymore. Everyone was just too poor.

Historically, African American women and Latinas formed the backbone of their communities. Extended kinship networks represented both an economic survival strategy and a cultural practice that accorded women respect. As a result of the seismic structural upheaval that rocked San Francisco, families of color could no longer rely on their social support networks to mitigate against the devastating effects of poverty. Despite their adherence to cultural norms valuing familism and *other mothering*, the constraints of a hostile economic system prevents racial ethnic families from participating in ex-

change networks. Consequently women of color are oppressed both culturally and economically: they are unable to live by the values essential to their
cultural survival because of racial discrimination and economic disenfranchisement. In addition, the lack of available social support networks reflects
gender discrimination, since women of color have traditionally derived
prominence from their role as kin keepers. Unfortunately, women who are
struggling to keep their families afloat can no longer rely on an extended
network of kin or fictive kin for their survival.

POVERTY, COMMUNITY VIOLENCE, AND
EXTENDED KINSHIP NETWORKS

Macroeconomic shifts and urban development have clearly contributed to the
fraying of extensive social support networks. Further exacerbating the unraveling of these networks is an increase in community violence. In fact, the
theme of neighborhood violence was common during the course of my fieldwork. I met many families who felt under siege by the gang, drug, and gun
violence that had infiltrated their neighborhoods and destroyed previously
thriving kinship networks. Even Effie and Jeremiah, who represented the
older generation of respondents, commented on increased community violence when they were discussing the loss of their networks earlier. Another
intact family actually chose to become homeless as a result of the violence
that inundated their neighborhood. José and Elisa and their two children lived
in Section 8 housing in Excelsior. They were frightened by the violence in
their community and its impact on their family and friends. One evening
when the family was sitting down to dinner, three bullets shot through their
window, narrowly missing Elisa. Terrified and hysterical, they gathered their
belongings and left their home. When I met José and Elisa, José told me the
following:

> We were eating dinner and there was a drive by shooting on my street. All of a
> sudden we heard rapid gun fire, bam, bam, bam, bam, bam. The kids immedi-
> ately dove onto the floor. We taught them that because there are lots of shoot-
> ings in the neighborhood. This time three bullets flew through our window and
> almost killed my wife. The kids and Elisa were hysterical. When it was over
> we could see where the bullets went into the wall. That was it, I had enough.
> How can anyone be expected to live with that kind of violence? We packed
> our stuff and left. We stayed with Elisa's best friend who lives on Polk Street
> but she made us leave early the next morning. If she gets caught with another
> family living in her apartment her landlord will kick her out and she will lose
> her welfare benefits. We were glad she could take us in for one night. Polk
> Street is pretty nasty and there are street prostitutes all over the place. At least
> you don't have to worry about getting shot. Shit, I can't believe this is happen-
> ing to us.

When I asked José if he had any other family in the Bay Area he could stay with, he told me that he and Elisa had lots of family in San Francisco, but none of them could help out with housing or financial resources. In fact, like many other homeless families I met, his extensive social support network could only provide emotional support. Network members could not lend money, provide child care, or provide housing support. Like others in my research, José lamented the loss of these historical, culturally based networks. José was familiar with the historical role of *compadrazgo* and his family had participated in thriving networks in San Francisco when he was a child. He absolutely attributed his homelessness to poverty, violence, and the erosion of traditional kinship networks previously common in San Francisco's Latinix communities.

POVERTY, INTERPERSONAL VIOLENCE, AND EXTENDED KINSHIP NETWORKS

In addition to community violence, interpersonal violence also undermined participation in extended networks among homeless women in San Francisco. As I illustrated in chapter 2, being homeless is inherently dangerous and results in continued exposure to community and interpersonal violence, further increasing a family's vulnerability and trauma (Guarino, Rubin, and Bassuk 2007). Because of the unrelenting persistence of intimate partner violence, homeless mothers can become emotionally paralyzed, and often have difficulty navigating the minutia of their everyday lives. In addition, family relationships are destabilized by the presence of domestic violence. Consequently, battered homeless women typically have the most severely frayed extended kinship networks. Some of these networks are eroded after years of violent partners isolating women from family and friends. Others are destroyed by the very parents who perpetrated physical, emotional, and sexual violence on their own children.

In chapter 2 we met Keisha, who was in counseling and taking parenting classes to learn how to raise Jacinta without abusing her. Keisha initially became homeless when she left her partner who had battered her for years. When I met Keisha, she no longer had family or friends upon whom she could rely. She told me that:

> I got no one to turn to for help Annee. My family is so f'd up I don't talk to them anymore. My father was violent as all hell and he beat up my mother and me and my sister. My mother was so beaten down by him she could barely move. One time he beat her so hard he broke her jaw and busted open her head. My sister called the cops and they hauled him off. The cops said he violated his parole and he went back to prison. I didn't care, I hated him anyway. After that my mom just gave up and hit the pipe—you know—started

smoking crack. She had no money so sometimes she turned tricks just to get high. I don't want to say she was a crack ho cuz she is my mom . . . but . . . she was a crack ho. You should have seen her, all skinny and wasted looking. It was bad. There was always nasty men coming and going, looking at me and my sister all funny, like they wanted to have sex with us. Sometimes they would try and grab us but we were always able to get away cuz we were fast and they were so high. A lot of times we would stay outside just to avoid them, but we had to go home sometime. Imagine growing up like that? Its f'd up! My older sister tried to take care of us but she was still in high school. How she gonna take care of a little sister? We were hella tight but she passed a few years ago. After Latasha passed I got so depressed I didn't have the energy to make any new friends. Plus, I don't trust no one anymore. No one's gonna care about me like Latasha did—who can I trust? Living like this, it makes you mean. I was even so angry at my mom that I stopped talking to her like 10 years ago. I think she got off the pipe, but I don't know where she lives or if she is even alive. I haven't seen my father since they hauled his ass off that night. My whole life has been shit. I got no money, I got no family, and I'm so f'ing angry. I swore I would be a better mother to Jacinta—but I been hard on her. Sometimes when she was bad I hurt her. My ex-Jerome used to beat both of us. He burned Jacinta with cigarettes and that's when I left. It broke my heart—I wanted to protect her better than my mother protected me—but I couldn't—I was too beaten down. Since I been at the shelter I'm taking classes on how to be a better parent. I don't want her life to be like mine, filled with pain and endless anger. That's why I left Jerome—to keep us safe.

Keisha's story was fairly typical among the chronically homeless women in my research. Many of the women who experienced lifelong exposure to violence, drug abuse, and sexual assault were extremely guarded and had trouble making friends. The more resilient women often had extended kindship networks that they could turn to for emotional support. However, women like Keisha, alone in the world, with no access to kin support, often reproduce the violence they suffered by engaging in self-destructive behavior and by directing their anger toward their own children. Fortunately, Keisha ultimately recognized her detrimental behavior and actively chose to overcome it.

In chapter 2 we also met Barb, a lifelong victim of physical and sexual abuse. Barb found refuge in the home of her aunt until she married Jason. After Jason began to abuse Barb, her aunt died and she could no longer rely on her for sanctuary. As a result of Jason's increasingly dangerous behavior toward Barb, she finally left him and chose to become homeless. Barb ended up in the Wagon Wheel; a bleak, filthy, and dangerous motel. Because Barb's father raped her and her mother allowed it to happen, she had not spoken to either of them in years. Barb's hatred of her parents was visceral. Barb told me that being homeless was preferable to the violent home life she was forced to endure. Barb and I had endless conversations about her lack of social support. In addition to having no family upon which she could rely,

Barb had no close friends. She had difficulty trusting anyone and suffered from severe emotional trauma. Given the chaotic nature of her life, Barb never really had the opportunity to create enduring friendships. Essentially, the violence that characterized Barb's life prevented her from developing any network ties at all. Subsequently, Barb and her kids were on their own. The pain of Barb's existence and her social isolation was profound.

> Barb: I aint got no one except my kids, Annee. Shannon and Justin are the only things keeping me alive. My life is so painful. You know—My father raped me, my mother didn't do a fuckin' thing to stop it and then I married Jason, who beat the crap out of me. All my life I've been raped and beaten. I can hardly get out of bed anymore. I got nothing. No friends, no family, nothing—except my kids. When my aunt was alive I lived with her for two years. That was the only time I had any peace. The only time I ever felt like I was loved. She helped me get clean and keep a job. Without her I would have been homeless years ago. I miss her.

> Annee: Do you think if you had other family members to rely on you might not be homeless?

> Barb: I don't know. It's hard to imagine anyone would want to help me—I'm so fucked up and I have two kids. I guess if I had a close friend or someone from my family who loved me they would let me stay with them even for just a little while. Maybe help me out with some food or a little money. Maybe even babysit once in a while. Yeah—I guess if I had a family that could help me I wouldn't be homeless—they would take care of me and the kids. Maybe they could even help me get a job. I could work at Micky D's again if I had someone to watch Justin and Shannon.

> Annee: You have mentioned to me several times that you don't have any friends. Why do you think that is Barb?

> Barb: When I was still living at home I was terrified that someone would find out that my parents were abusive. Then when my father started to rape me I freaked out. I hung out with a really bad crowd—but they weren't really my friends. We just did drugs together. I was trying to numb the pain of my fucked-up life. I didn't want to get close to anyone. Sometimes I think about those kids and I wonder if some of them were going through the same shit I was. I did have one girlfriend from work before I got married. Her name was Nina and we became really good friends. We talked about everything. Once I got married though, things changed. Jason didn't really like her anymore and gave me shit whenever I went out with her. He was jealous of our friendship and he wouldn't let me go out with her. Once he started beating me, she couldn't handle it and

sort of dropped out of sight. It was really sad—she was the only real friend I had back then. The only other person I got close to was Jason and when he started beating me, I think that made me even more closed off— like if I get too close to someone they're just gonna hurt me or leave me— so I figured I was better off alone. But being alone sucks. I don't have anyone who I can talk to about my life—to give me advice and help me figure out how to make things better. I'm so tired. I wish I had some real girlfriends to talk to. Since I been going to Home Away there are a couple of mothers I hang with. We try to support each other with what we are going through. It does help that someone else understands what I been through but a lot of times we don't see each other that much. Like when I don't have money for the bus to go to the Club House and then I don't see them for a while. Sometimes when I do go there the mothers I am friends with don't show up. Sometimes they don't have bus fare and sometimes they're meeting with case workers or teachers or taking their kids to appointments. It just depends. The worst is when I make friends with someone and after a couple of months they disappear. They go to shelters or move out of the city and if you don't have a beeper there is no way to keep in touch. It makes me feel even more alone.

Except for the two years Barb lived with her aunt, her entire life has been one of violence and degradation. However, Barb was not merely a passive receptacle of her social structural position. She did exert agency in the decisions that she made for herself and for her children. However, it is clear that her decisions were influenced by that social structural position, and that her agency was limited in profound ways. The unrelenting family violence Barb experienced shaped her choices and made her wary of getting close to any-one. As a result, Barb did not have any close women friends to rely on for instrumental support. The only emotional support Barb received was from the friendships she made with other homeless women. Although these friend-ships were vital, they were with ultimately precarious. After years of physical and sexual abuse, Barb chose to disassociate herself from her parents. Al-though her parents might have been able to provide some economic help, this decision seemed quite rational. Her parents were the source of enormous pain and it was better for Barb's mental health to disentangle herself from their grip. Some people might argue that Barb should put aside her past experi-ences and have been willing to ask her parents for help. However, there is no guarantee that they would have helped her financially, and those same people would be the first to condemn Barb for endangering her children by allowing her rapist father access to them.

As Barb and Keisha's stories illustrate, some homeless women initially had network support to draw on, but maintaining that support became diffi-cult as intimate partners escalated their violent behavior and/or as loved ones died. As a result of their abusive upbringings, both women had difficulty making lasting friendships and their ability to form extensive kin and fictive kin networks was stymied. During the first year of my fieldwork, as I was getting to know Barb and Keisha, my husband and I split up. My rent was exorbitant and my salary was fairly low for San Francisco. I was paid monthly and after paying my bills and buying food, I ran out of cash by the third week of each month. Since I had been a graduate student for many years I was skilled at eating cheaply. I could make dried beans, potatoes, rice, pasta, and other modestly priced food last till the end of the month. In addition, I did not have any children to support. However, I would often run out of fruits and fresh vegetables before the month was over. Periodically, my friend Karen would show up with fresh produce. Ironically, I was now living my own research. Karen's behavior was evidence that further supported the findings of my book *No More Kin*. My research revealed that middle-class white women were the most frequent participants of instrumental exchange in extended social support networks. In subsequent qualitative research I found this to be true among a sample of Puerto Rican women in upstate New York as well.[5] I theorized that this was because middle-class women actually have economic resources to share. It became clear that low-income women, traditionally associated with kinship networks, simply had nothing left to share. As I was receiving instrumental and emotional support from my fictive kinship network, Barb was left to fend for herself. In fact, as will be revealed in chapter 5, Barb was sometimes forced to prostitute herself in order to survive.

WELFARE REFORM, HOUSING, AND EXTENDED KINSHIP NETWORKS

In addition to macroeconomic shifts, community, and interpersonal violence, extended kinship networks have been further eroded by welfare reform. Although the popular justification for the reform was to help poor women find work, the underlying ideology was to promote abstinence and heterosexual marriage, discourage abortion, decrease non-marital births, and to punish poor women for their lack of motivation. A fundamental assumption of the PRWORA was that poor women would simply rely on an extended network of kin and fictive kin for their survival. I find this assumption particularly distasteful. For decades policy makers argued that extended kinship networks endemic to low-income racial ethnic families were inherently pathological, caused poverty, and were at odds with normative (i.e., middle-class white) nuclear family structure. For politicians to suddenly laud the virtues of kinship networks as a way to dismantle the welfare system was cynical and ultimately shameful. Predicating welfare reform on the belief that family and friends would pick up the slack left by the state has been disastrous for homeless women in San Francisco. Given the already precarious nature of their extended kinship networks, welfare reform has further isolated homeless families, anchoring them securely at the outskirts of society.

The claim that poor women could rely on their extended kinship networks for assistance is particularly problematic when it comes to housing. Most homeless families are unable to double up with relatives due to housing restrictions and fear of eviction. Although I did meet some homeless mothers who periodically stayed with friends or relatives, it was typically for less than a month. Friends and relatives of homeless respondents (many of whom were also welfare recipients) ran the risk of being evicted from their own low-income housing if caught. As the housing market got increasingly tighter, landlords and representatives of the Housing Authority were more likely to kick out tenants who violated occupancy restrictions. As a result, family and friends who might otherwise be willing to provide shelter could not. Historically, a major function of kinship networks was to take in family members who became homeless. In San Francisco, during the 1990s, relying on an extensive kinship network to provide housing was no longer viable for homeless welfare recipients. Women expressed frustration that although family members wanted to provide housing for them, they couldn't. In addition, caseworkers saw doubling up as a violation of welfare reform and threatened to sanction recipients who "illegally" housed anyone. This inflexible attitude among the gatekeepers of welfare illustrates how the legislation itself fostered homelessness among poor families. As family members were forced to move to residential motels, family shelters, and sometimes out of San Francisco, the already fragile networks often completely disintegrated.

In chapter 3 Alma, Rendisha, and Shirley, all victims of intimate partner violence, discussed their experiences with the welfare state. Despite being in abusive relationships, Alma, Rendisha, and Shirley were not isolated from their kinship networks. Miraculously, all three women were able to maintain stable connections with family and friends. However, none of their network members could provide them with housing. The following conversation between Alma, Rendisha, and Shirley captures the inability of network members to house them because they themselves would risk becoming homeless:

Annee: Do any of you have friends or family members in San Francisco that you can stay with?

Alma: Not me.

Rendisha: Me either.

Shirley: Nope.

Annee: Can you tell me why?

Alma: I got a bunch of cousins in the city but they all live in public housing. They want to help me and Eduardo but they can't. If they let us stay with them and we get caught they will end up in the shelter with me.

Annee: Why is that?

Alma: (Laughing) Really? Why you asking me that? You know. I guess you just want me to say it right?

Annee: (Laughing) You know me so well. Of course I know why—but it's important to hear it from you.

Alma: Yeah yeah, I know. Well it's like this—they got all these strict rules in public housing about how long people who don't live there can come and stay. If I stayed too long with my cousins and the housing authority found out—they might get kicked out.

Rendisha: My best friend from growing up still lives in the city and we help each other out best we can. Sometimes we watch each other's kids. A couple of times I did her laundry at Home Away. I did stay with her for two nights when I first left Marvin but I couldn't stay any longer. She lives in her own apartment in The Point [Bayview Hunters Point], not the projects, but if her caseworker finds out she has someone staying there and she doesn't report it—well you know Annee—those bitches are always trying to trick us up and get us off welfare. Away, her landlord would kick her out if he found out we were living with her.

Shirley: It's the same for me. I stay in touch with family and friends but they can't give me a place to live. Everyone I know is poor and they are barely hanging on themselves. Plus, as Alma and Rendy just said—if anyone lets us live with them they will get thrown out of their apartments, either because of the Housing Authority, heartless caseworkers, or nasty landlords. None of us want to be the reason our family or friends get evicted. It's not worth taking the chance, so we go to the shelter and hope we can get into transitional housing.

People living in public housing are allowed to have overnight guests. However, that does not include someone who stays for extended periods of time and does not have her/his/their own address. Those individuals must be added to the lease as a member of the household. If a person stays for an extended period of time and is not added to the lease, that is cause for eviction. This policy also has implications for welfare recipients who must report any changes in household composition every three months and might lose benefits if they are perceived as having extra rental income. In addition, if an apartment is deemed to be at capacity by the Housing Authority, adding another tenant could mean problems for that family. Although families living in private rental units could conceivably hide extra household members from caseworkers to avoid a change in their income status, they still risk eviction if the landlord finds out. Here we see the structure of welfare reform, public housing policy, and a tight rental market conspiring to disenfranchise homeless women and their children despite the existence of extended kin networks.

DECLINING NETWORKS AND RACE, CLASS, AND GENDER INEQUALITY

It should now be clear that many homeless women, not victimized by family violence, do in fact maintain contact with members of their kin and non-kin networks. Women often received emotional support in times of crisis. However, because homeless families come from impoverished backgrounds, their networks are devoid of economic resources, making instrumental support impossible. Throughout my research, women of color expressed concern over the inability of their social support networks to provide instrumental support. There was a general feeling that extended networks were important to the cultural survival of the community but had become unavailable, particularly among women who were victims of sexual abuse. Many of these women expressed sadness that something as important as extended kinship networks had disintegrated as a result of economic oppression. Because women traditionally comprise the core of the extended kinship network and gain status as network participants, homeless women were particularly upset that their customary role of culture bearers was now unavailable. In the past, network participation represented a form of privilege among otherwise disenfranchised women. The shifting categories of gendered and racialized economic inequality, family violence, and welfare policy prevented women from experiencing important elements of their cultural heritage. In their attempt to recreated frayed social support networks, homeless women often turned to institutional forms of social support and to other homeless families in their struggle for survival while others were left to fend for themselves.

NOTES

1. Some of the text contained in this chapter is reprinted by permission from Copyright Clearance Center: John Wiley and Sons, "Our Lives Matter: The Racialized Violence of Poverty among Homeless Mothers of Color," *Sociological Forum*, vol. 32, S1. Anne R. Roschelle, 2017.

2. Fictive kin refers to non–biologically related members of an extended kinship network who are considered to be family.

3. Although much of the research on extended kinship networks has documented the decline in network participation, particularly among low-income women of color, there is some recent work that suggests that certain types of exchange behavior still persists. Gerstel and Sarkasian (2008) and Sarkasian and Gerstel (2004) find that white families are more likely to provide emotional support and substantial financial help to network members than women of color. African American and Latinx families, on the other hand, are more likely to exchange household work, child care, and transportation help. This research suggests that economic inequality explains the differences in types of help given and received in exchange networks. Because African American and Latinxs typically have less income and have higher rates of poverty, they are less likely than whites to provide financial help and are more likely to provide help with household tasks (Gerstel and Sarkasian 2008; Sarkasian and Gerstel 2004). Although providing network members with child care, housework, and transportation may enable disenfranchised women to work in the paid labor market, it is not sufficient to prevent them from becoming homeless. Therefore, it is imperative to examine the specific relationship between social support networks and familial homelessness.

4. Couch surfing refers to staying on someone's couch for a short period of time before moving to another person's couch in another home. Couch surfing implies repeated movement between homes.

5. See Roschelle, Anne R. 2002. "The Tattered Web of Kinship: Black White Differences in Social Support in a Puerto Rican Community." In *The New Politics of Race: From DuBois to the 21st Century*, edited by Marlese Durr, 113–35. Westport, CT: Praeger.

Chapter Five

Life's a Bitch

The Everyday Struggle for Survival

I came to San Francisco with my three kids to stay with my sister after my house in Oregon burned down. What a mistake that was. The bitch kicked us out after two weeks and now we are homeless. At least I can rely on Home Away and the friends I've made there to help us survive in this heartless city.—Pamela

SURVIVAL STRATEGIES

Being homeless is an extremely chaotic existence. Homeless individuals are forced to find ways to survive the unpredictable and often dangerous streets of urban America. Not surprisingly, there is a large body of research that examines the survival strategies used by homeless people living on the streets. Much of this research focuses on homeless men and identifies panhandling, recycling, petty theft, hustling, drug dealing, participation in the informal economy, day labor, selling blood plasma, and identity work, among common survival strategies used (Gowen 2000 2010; Rosenthal 1994; Snow and Anderson 1993; Snow and Mulcahy 2001; Wasserman and Clair 2010). Similar survival strategies are also are found among homeless women who live on the street and are unencumbered by children (Jasinski et al. 2010; Passaro 1996). Of course, homelessness, like most aspects of society, is highly gendered (Meanwell 2012; Passaro 1996). Therefore, homeless women must also contend with physical and sexual victimization as they attempt to survive the streets. In fact, homeless women are more likely to be victims of crime (Lee and Schreck 2005; Huey 2010) and are more likely to experience physical violence and sexual victimization than homeless men

(Evans and Forsyth 2004; Jansinksi et al. 2010; Wenzel, Leake, and Gelberg 2001). Not surprisingly, the longer women remain on the streets the more likely they are to be exploited (Geissler et al. 1995; Wenzel, Koegel and Gelberg 2000).

Like men, women also rely on panhandling, petty theft, drug dealing, and shoplifting for economic gain. Given their potential vulnerability, homeless women also engage in unique survival strategies to avoid being physically or sexually victimized. However, those strategies are limited by gender inequality (Gilfus 2006; Jasinski 2010). In their research, Huey and Berndt (2008) identified four types of gender performances women used to safely navigate city streets in Scotland, Canada, and the United States. They found that some women used overt femininity to obtain emotional or material resources, while others adopted a masculine persona to appear more aggressive and less vulnerable. Some women attempted to become invisible by appearing genderless, while others tried to "pass" as lesbians so men would ignore them. Each type of gender presentation had dangers and benefits associated with them depending upon the situational context (Huey and Berndt 2008). Clearly, these survival strategies were an attempt by homeless women to exert their agency and control their inherently dangerous surroundings.

In addition to gender performance, homeless women also engage in a variety of economic survival strategies including panhandling, trading sex for housing, food, drugs, or money. Unfortunately, these types of economic subsistence strategies put women at risk of being victims of physical or sexual assault (Wenzel, Koegel, and Gelberg 2000; Wenzel, Leake, and Gelberg 2015). As a result of their limited access to legitimate economic subsistence, some homeless women resort to street prostitution (Jasinski et al. 2010; Simmons and Whitbeck 1991; Whitebeck and Simmons 1993). Although some feminists argue that sex work is empowering, research illustrates that there is an "almost unimaginable level of violence in street prostitution" (Gilfus 2006, 13). In fact, street prostitution represents a culture in which the violent victimization of women is coupled with economic marginality (Gilfus 2006). In addition, a majority of homeless women who engage in street prostitution are victims of childhood violence and sexual assault, which contributes to an utter lack of self-worth. Subsequently, chronic childhood physical and sexual abuse increases the likelihood that homeless women will survive the streets by engaging in prostitution and/or exchanging sex for housing, food, and other resources (Gilfus 2006; Wesley 2009; Wesley and Wright 2005). Panhandling, prostitution, and sexualized bartering are less common among homeless women with children than among homeless women living on the streets. Women with children are more likely to be housed in shelters, residential motels, or transitional housing (Burt et al. 2001). Shelters and transitional housing units often have strict rules about "appropriate" behavior and require homeless families to be in for the night fairly early. Nonetheless, there were some homeless mothers in my sample, living in residential motels, who engaged in sexualized bartering and prostitution. These women were ravaged by years of familial physical and sexual abuse and were heartbreakingly damaged. For these women, their sexualized bodies were the only form of survival they could rely upon. This is not surprising given that women who are sexually abused or victims of incest as children are at serious risk for re-victimization as adults (Russell 1986; West, Williams, and Siegel 2000; Wyatt, Guthrie, and Notgrass 1992) whether in their intimate partner relationships or in their attempts at survival. In addition to these individualized economic survival strategies, homeless women with children also attempted to recreate extended social support networks among their homeless compatriots.

Most sociologists now agree that extended kinship and social support networks have been steadily eroding since the 1980s. This has been found in both quantitative (Eggebeen 1992; Eggebeen and Hogan 1990; Hofferth 1984; Hogan, Eggebeen, and Clogg 1993; Miner 1995; Miner and Uhlenberg 1997; Raley 1995; Roschelle 1997) and qualitative research (Menjivar 2000; Roschelle 2002). As I demonstrated in chapter 4, homeless women who came from chronically violent family backgrounds were unable to maintain stable relationships with kin or fictive kin. Women from less-damaged families did have extended kinship networks, but members were too impoverished to provide economic resources or housing. For homeless mothers in San Francisco, social support network members could only provide (much needed) emotional support. The question now becomes: what has replaced these historically and culturally vital networks among impoverished families?

In an ethnographic study of evicted tenants in high-poverty urban neighborhoods, Matthew Desmond (2012) identifies what he calls disposable ties. He illustrates that evicted families often relied upon new acquaintances rather than on kin or fictive kin. Both African American and white evicted tenants quickly formed and used new network ties by accelerating their intimacy with virtual strangers. Once these disposable ties were formed, a variety of resources flowed through them. According to Desmond (2012) disposable ties were characterized by accelerated intimacy, an unusually high amount of time spent together, reciprocal or semi-reciprocal exchange, and an extremely short life span. Despite knowing acquaintances for short periods of time and essentially being strangers, evicted tenants became fast friends and often moved in together immediately. In addition, they pooled their money to buy food and household items, disciplined each other's kids, and exchanged food stamps,[1] employment information, drugs, and sometimes sex. Some new acquaintances even participated in illegal activities together. Because these evicted tenants were tied together by their chaotic circumstances and were practically strangers, their ties were extremely fragile. In fact, the "strategy of forming, using, and burning disposable ties allowed families caught in a desperate situation to make it from one day to the next, but also bred instability and fostered misgivings between peers" (Desmond 2012, 1296). As a result these brittle ties were typically fraught with turmoil and were short-lived. Homeless families in San Francisco, devoid of extended kinship networks, also created disposable ties with new acquaintances. Similar to the networks Desmond (2012) identified, these networks were also characterized by immediate intimacy, lots of time spent together, exchange reciprocity, and turbulence. In addition, given the pressures of homelessness, these networks were extremely unstable and rarely lasted for more than a month or two. Nonetheless, they represent an attempt by homeless mothers to exert their agency by replacing diminished familial support networks in order to survive.

When disposable ties fail, homeless women rely on institutional forms of social support. It is estimated that approximately half of all homeless people stay in shelters at some point in their homeless odyssey and that a majority of homeless individuals utilize soup kitchens, drop-in centers, and other social service agencies (Burt et al. 2001; Lee et al. 2011; Meanwell 2010). Subsequently, there is a large body of research that examines the social service infrastructure, including the interactions between service providers and the homeless, the expansion of the shelter industry, and the quasi institutionalization of the homeless population (Meanwell 2010; Williams 2003). Some research indicates that homeless clients often feel infantilized, disrespected, and trivialized by shelter staff and other service providers. In addition, shelter residents often feel that their experiences and ideas are discounted (Hoffman and Coffey 2008; Lyon-Callo 2000). Some homeless individuals even reported negative interactions with volunteers working for faith-based food providers who incessantly proselytized them (Sager and Stephens 2005). Given the power imbalance between homeless service providers and their homeless clients, it is not surprising to find that in some shelters residents felt that staff actively prevented friendships from developing between residents in an attempt to control their behavior. This research has provided much-needed insight into the ways in which homeless service agencies operate, how they treat homeless clients, and how they are perceived by the homeless (for an extensive review of this literature, see Meanwell 2012). What is missing from this literature is an examination of how homeless families use these institutional supports to replace extended kin networks and whether or not they are successful. Homeless families in my research often turned to institutional forms of social support to replace their disintegrating kin networks. However, they were often frustrated by what they perceived as representatives of an unfeeling poverty industry more concerned with fast-tracking them through the system then with attending to their needs.

NAVIGATING THE STREETS:
PANHANDLING, PAWNSHOPS, AND CRAFTS

Although the chronically homeless families in my research were housed in shelters, transitional housing, or residential motels, some of them engaged in street-level survival strategies common among the homeless street population. A few women with very young children would panhandle in the Haight and on Market Street during the day when the shelters were closed. When I asked them about their panhandling experiences several women told me that they were desperate for cash and had no other way to obtain it. Some women were no longer receiving TANF as they had been sanctioned by caseworkers and had no more cash assistance. Although they still received partial-cash assistance for their children and food stamps, it wasn't enough to make ends meet. Other women were simply trying to supplement their inadequate welfare benefits. In addition, some of the women commented that, because they were kicked out of the shelters during the day and had small children to tote around, they had no place to go and might as well make good use of their time on the streets. For example, Nicole, a twenty-three-year-old African American woman with a three-year-old daughter told me:

> Sometimes I panhandle down on Market Street. I don't do it in the Haight because it is too close to the shelter and if someone sees me they might tell the staff and then I would probably get kicked out. I take Jasmine with me because I don't have anyone to take care of her during the day. I'm not proud of it but what else can I do? I need to find a way to get some extra cash. I only started begging when I got kicked off welfare. My caseworker said it was because I missed too many meetings with her and was always late. I don't understand how she can be so mean. Now I am forced to ask strangers for money. Some of them are very nice, but a lot of them tell me to get a job or yell at me for panhandling with my daughter—they tell me I'm a bad mother and should be ashamed of myself. Imagine how that makes me feel. At least I'm not so desperate that I would ever become a street whore.

Lucia, a Guatemalan immigrant with two children, told me a similar story:

> My kids are eight and eleven so they are in school during the day. After they get on the bus to go to school I have nowhere to go and nothing to do. It's not like I can hang out in a café all day and drink coffee and read. I tried that a few times but I got kicked out. I like to read and it is always warm inside—but I kept getting kicked out. I guess the people that work in the cafés could tell I was poor or something. I don't know—I'm not dirty like the people living on the streets, but my clothes are ratty and I look kind of hard—you know from being poor all my life and then homeless—it gives you an emptiness—a kind of look that only hard living can give you. Plus, I am always struggling with money. I get welfare but it isn't enough to survive. The shelter feeds us breakfast and dinner but I have to go all day without eating. So one day I

decided to hit the streets and panhandle. You know I have to do whatever I can to take care of myself and my kids. I made a few bucks so I kept doing it. I am very polite and friendly so I think people feel sorry for me. Sometimes though, it is kind of dangerous. Once a homeless man knocked me down and stole my money. Another time some teenage kids made me give them my money. They threatened to beat me up if I didn't give it to them. And this was during the day—not even at night. It's not really safe for women to be alone on the street with money—thank the good lord me and my kids are in a shelter. I would be terrified if I had to live on the streets, especially at night. Can you imagine how scary that would be—getting beat up and raped and stuff? After the teenagers stole my money I got too scared to keep panhandling. Now I come to Home Away during the day and have a good meal, do my laundry, and I even get to read as much as I want. I could use the cash—but it really isn't worth the danger. Plus, I want be around to take care of my kids—not dead in an alley somewhere.

Panhandling was not a common survival strategy among the homeless families in my research. Women with school-aged children often spent their days looking for work to fulfill the new welfare-to-work requirements. Recent welfare recipients and women with children under five spent their days traversing the city going to orientation workshops, job training programs, Cal-WORKs meetings, substance abuse meetings, meetings with caseworkers, and meetings with teachers. Women living in residential motels spent their days going to soup kitchens, looking for shelter beds, and other social services dispersed throughout the city. The women who did panhandle were often ostracized by passersby and harassed by people they encountered on the streets. The gendered nature of street survival created an added burden of potential victimization that limited mothers' ability to earn extra cash. Because homeless mothers had access to other forms of economic support not available to homeless street women, most of them did not panhandle for extended periods of time. Ultimately, homeless mothers felt vulnerable on the streets and did not want to be victimized further.

A common survival strategy among homeless families was to sell personal items to pawn shops. Several respondents pawned whatever possessions they could find. Unfortunately, selling items to a pawnshop is a finite survival strategy, as homeless families usually have very little to sell, and what they do have is gone quickly. The following conversation between Carlos and Isabela provides insight into the short-term gains of pawning goods. It should also be noted that both Carlos and Isabela had long work histories before Carlos got injured on the job and was fired. Therefore, they actually had something of value to sell, unlike most of the families I worked with.

Annee: Can you tell me some of the ways you made money when you first became homeless?

Isabela: We hawked whatever we have to hawk.

Carlos: Everything is in the pawn shop right now.

Isabela: Everything that we own is in the pawn shop.

Carlos: One of the TVs we still have. But everything else is gone.

Isabela: We pawned all of his expensive Swiss army watches, I mean, like $500.00 watches, for like $20.00, just to get a meal for the night.

Carlos: I also had a ring that belonged to my father and some tools that I pawned.

Annee: So what are you going to do when all your stuff runs out?

Isabela: Well, it has run out already. Now we're at the end.

Carlos: Don't forget Isabela, we still have the T.V.

Isabela: Oh yeah.

Carlos: I guess that's next. I hate to do it but we have no choice, we need the money. We need to buy food for our family.

Annee: So what will you do after you pawn the T.V.?

Carlos: I guess we'll just go hungry.

Isabela: Yeah, we'll just go hungry. But we sure won't sell our bodies. That's one thing we'll never do. We'd rather starve than do that. And selling drugs is out of the question. We both had drug problems years ago so we can't take the risk of using again, or getting arrested. You know, we have children. The deal is you either starve or you come here [Home Away]. You know, I wish they were open every day. I wish, you know, they were open for us every day because like it's really hard the days they're closed, when we're not to be able to come here.

Although pawning personal belongings is not dangerous, it is extremely demoralizing. Most homeless individuals who pawn things never have enough money to purchase them back. Commemorative family items, work tools, gifts, jewelry, and things people worked hard for are lost forever. Once again, we see that the most destitute among us are overwhelmed by an inequitable social structure that continually marginalizes them. Given that women and people of color are systematically paid less than white men in the labor market, and are therefore more likely to be poor, they have less items of value they can pawn.

One of the most gut-wrenching stories of street survival I encountered was Tiffany and her daughter Steph. Tiffany was a white woman in her mid-forties, who, after a lifetime of domestic violence, drug and alcohol abuse, and chain smoking, looked well over sixty. Her daughter was eighteen, so neither Tiffany, nor Steph, who had no children, was entitled to any PRWO-RA assistance. In addition, because Steph was over eighteen, they were ineligible to stay in a family shelter. Tiffany did receive Supplemental Security Income (SSI) for being disabled, after her ex-husband beat her nearly to death and she suffered permanent bodily injuries. Tiffany's SSI was used to pay for a hotel room they shared at the Franciscan. When I met her, Steph had advanced bone cancer and was confined to a wheelchair. In order to help pay for Steph's medication Tiffany sold homemade hemp bracelets to tourists on the corner of Powell and Market Streets by the cable car turnaround. Tiffany spent all day sitting on that corner making and selling bracelets. They were very simple macramé style with small beads embedded in each one. She sold them for three to five dollars per bracelet, depending upon how long it took her to make them. I would periodically hang out with Tiffany as she sold her wares. It was devastatingly painful to watch her interactions with tourists, business people, and local teenagers. The bracelets were not exactly art and some of them were dirty and pretty scraggily-looking. She was mocked and scowled at by some people and ignored by others. Every once in a while a kind tourist would buy a bracelet because they felt sorry for her. Some days she would make eight or ten bucks, but most days she didn't sell any bracelets. On the days that Steph, who looked pitiful in her wheelchair, accompanied her, Tiffany would usually sell a few more. Given the futility of trying to earn money this way to purchase expensive medicine, I wondered why Tiffany bothered. She told me:

> My daughter is sick and in so much pain. The cancer is all over her body, deep in her bones. I have to do something to help her—I can't just let her die in agony. She's my child—I'm desperate to help her.

Imagine the indignity of selling a few dollars' worth of bracelets to purchase cancer and pain medication for your daughter in a country as wealthy as the United States. Even in the face of such devastating economic inequality, Tiffany exerted her agency in the only way she knew how. Given her social structural position, however, her attempts at actively overcoming her marginality proved ineffective. Tiffany never made enough money to purchase any medicine, yet she persisted. Tiffany's devotion to her daughter was unwavering. Even now, all these years later, as the debate about the Affordable Care Act rages on and Trump and the Republicans attempt to dismantle it, I think of Tiffany, who tried desperately to comfort her daughter and of Steph, who remained in utter agony until the day she died. Tiffany and Steph's life illustrates how the confluence of gender and class inequality shaped their existence in interactive process. Tiffany, a victim of violent abuse by her husband, was unable to work as a result of his physical brutality. Her inability to work meant she did not have health insurance. Although Tiffany was fraught with a host of illnesses related to her poverty and abuse, they were nothing in comparison to her daughter's aggressive bone cancer. If Tiffany had access to good medical care, perhaps doctors would have caught Steph's cancer before it spread throughout her body. Even if Steph's cancer was terminal, with good health insurance, she would have had access to drugs and palliative care that would have eased the excruciating pain she was forced to endure in the bleak confines of the Franciscan Motel.

NAVIGATING THE STREETS:
SEXUAL BARTERING AND PROSTITUTION

Although a majority of the homeless mothers I encountered did not engage in sexual bartering or prostitution as survival strategies, some women did resort to using their bodies to subsist. As predicted by the research literature the women who did engage in sexualized survival strategies were shattered by years of familial violence and sexual abuse. These women were profoundly emotionally damaged by their horrific lived experiences. For battered women, their sexualized bodies were the only form of survival upon which they could rely. In addition, their sense of self-worth was shattered. Even so, the majority of women who did engage in sexual survival strategies did not participate in street prostitution. During the four years I spent with homeless families in San Francisco, I only met seven women who sold sex for money. Many more traded sex for housing, food, and clothing. The main reason for the limited reliance on prostitution was that the majority of women in my sample lived in family shelters and transitional housing. Shelters and transitional housing have very strict rules about when family members must be in for the night; usually by 8:00–9:00 pm. Since most prostitution occurs late at night, this was typically not an option for mothers. In addition, if single mothers leave their children alone in these housing situations, they are promptly kicked out. Further, transitional housing opportunities were rare, and once a family scored an apartment (or room) they were very conscientious about following the rules so as not to jeopardize their lodging.

The majority of sexualized bartering comprised exchanging sex for housing. Several women I met who lived in residential motels lived with men who they "hooked up" with specifically to get off the streets. These women had become homeless and were either waiting for shelter beds or a motel room.

While they were navigating the social service system, they met men who offered to give them a place to stay in exchange for a sexual relationship. What is unique about these exchanges is that the men agreed to let their children live with them, creating instant families. In most cases homeless mothers saw these exchanges as legitimate survival strategies, not much different from marriage. In chapter 2 we met Deborah, who lived in a residential motel in the Tenderloin with her mother Luz. When Deborah was a teenager, Luz became homeless after a lifelong struggle with depression and drug addiction, caused by childhood sexual abuse. After living on the streets for a couple of weeks, Luz met Eduardo in line for food at Glide Memorial Church. They started talking and found common ground in their ethnic heritage. Both Luz and Eduardo's families had migrated from Central America to the United States before they were born. Both were raised in violent impoverished homes in California. Eduardo's father was an abusive alcoholic who systematically beat Eduardo and his brother. Luz, who grew up in the Central Valley, was repeatedly raped by her uncle from the age of thirteen until she moved to San Francisco when she turned eighteen. Luz perceived her arrangement with Eduardo as a strategic relationship that was not that different from marriage. Luz conveyed the following:

> When I met Eduardo, Deborah and I were on the streets for about two weeks. We were confused about how to find shelter and were sort of wandering around. No one seemed to be able to help us. At night we huddled up in an alley near the U.N Plaza. There were a lot of homeless people there so we hung out with some women to stay safe. Sometimes we also went there to eat—you know that's where those hippies from Food Not Bombs provide meals. I didn't really like their food though because it never had any meat— they were always serving vegetarian soup, which kind of pissed me off. I mean—I'm Latina—we eat meat! Plus, they were a little too self-righteous about animal rights for my taste. Who cares about animals when you are freaking homeless? Someone mentioned the soup kitchen at Glide so we started to go there. One day when I was in line this guy started to flirt with me. He was pretty charming and seemed nice enough. I kept running in to him and one day he told me he had a motel room and that if Deborah and I wanted to come live with him we could. He was pretty clear that I would have to have sex with him. He said I could be his girlfriend. At first I told him no, it seemed kind of slutty, I hardly knew the guy. But after a few more nights on the street I decided to take him up on his offer. I needed to get me and Deborah off the streets. It was cold and we were scared. And anyway—it wasn't like I was selling my ass to a bunch of different strangers. I mean—it's not much different from marriage is it?

The idea that marriage was ultimately an exchange of sex for resources was echoed by Myrna and Melinda, two Latina victims of domestic violence we briefly met in chapter 3. As you may recall, both women were besieged with physical pain, were missing teeth, had broken bones that were never set, were suffering from post-traumatic stress disorder, and looked considerably older than their years Their experiences with intimate partner violence provides the context for their views on sexual bartering and marriage:

Myrna: If I could find a dude to live with and get out of the shelter I totally would. I don't have to be in love to live with someone. Anyway—being in love doesn't mean you won't get beat up. So what the hell—why not fuck a guy you don't like? I've been doing that my whole life whether I wanted to or not!

Melinda: Yeah—I hear ya. When I was younger and not so beat up, I moved in with a couple of dudes over the years to get off the streets and have a roof over my head. I didn't feel any shame in that—I was just trying to survive. Anyway, it's not any different from marriage. Women are basically prostitutes when it comes to marriage. You do what you are told or you get beat—how is that different from how a pimp treats you? Besides, men just think they are in charge. We have ways of doing what we want and having our freedom, they just don't realize it. They think they run our lives, but they don't; even when they're beating the shit out of us. Plus, I would do anything to get my kids out of this nasty shelter—we hate it here.

Myrna: Right on. It's all about survival. But look at us—we both look like shit, our bodies are killing us, and we look so old, so hard. Who would want to fuck us now? Maybe for a quick fuck in an alley—but who would want to live with us now? I wish I could find someone to take me in. I'd do it in a heartbeat. And yeah, Melinda is right, men just see us as punching bags and fuck machines. I was married and it was brutal—but I protected my kids and saw my friends, in between beatings I did what I wanted. You know, there really ain't no difference between marriage and moving in with a guy who wants to get laid. They use us, but we get what we need—like a place for our kids to live.

After a lifetime of abuse, Luz, Myrna, and Melinda had bleak prospects for healthy relationships. Their willingness to use whatever sexuality they had left in exchange for a dilapidated motel room might seem self-destructive and irrational. However, these mothers were desperate to find secure housing for their kids and themselves. Given their limited opportunities for stable housing, using their sexuality as a survival strategy is completely rational. In addition, their willingness to sexualize their bodies for residential security is, in their minds, an act of resistance to patriarchal domination. By using their sexuality as a commodity, they are in control of their bodies and their housing situation; they get what they need. However, this resistance strategy typically has the unintended consequence of reinforcing women's disenfranchised position, miring them further in unhealthy, often violent, relationships with men. For these women, sexual bartering is the result of structural inequality that creates barriers to independence. Racial discrimination, economic disenfranchisement, and gender inequality all contribute to a lack of opportunities for homeless women in San Francisco.

Although prostituting oneself was not common among women in my research, some women did utilize this survival strategy. As previously stated, the women who worked as street prostitutes were the most severely abused women I met. I got to know Barb and Jalesa intimately over a three-year period. They spent countless hours at the Club House while their kids went to the Beach House and participated in the After-School Educational Program. Barb and Jalesa trusted me with their kids and with their stories. Sitting on the back porch smoking (them, not me), Barb and Jalesa repeatedly opened up to me, exposing the brutal realities of their lives.

In chapter 2, both Barb and Jalesa gave detailed accounts of their childhood sexual abuse. Barb was raped by her father and later by her husband Jason. Jalesa was molested by her mother's boyfriend and then raped in foster care. In addition to her two kids, Jalesa had an adult son, Zion, who she hadn't seen since he was put into foster care years earlier. Both women expressed a primal lack of self-worth and neither had social support networks to rely on. Jalesa hadn't seen Zion since he was put into foster care. As a result, Jalesa and Barb took a lot of drugs and slept around. Jalesa disclosed that she "turned tricks" as a teenager while living in foster care. Jalesa and Barb each turned to prostitution as a way to survive economically. As Barb said:

> I know I've said this before, but my life is hard. I been beaten down so low I can't go any lower. So yeah, I sell my ass on the street. Me and the kids, we live in the Covered Wagon Hotel. It is a total dump and we are crammed into this tiny room. We have one bed for all three of us to sleep on. The ceiling leaks over our bed. I keep asking them to fix it. But they just ignore me. There are cockroaches crawling all over the place, there are fat rats everywhere, I mean it is just disgusting. They keep telling me the exterminators are coming in, but they never do. This is the third month now they said they were coming in. They're supposed to be there today and I know it won't happen. There are beer cans, liquor bottles, crack vials, and hypodermic needles down the stairs. The conditions are so fucking bad. The bed that we have in the room is tore up. I mean, like from crack addicts hiding their dope or whatever, you know, I don't know what it's from but the bed is all tore up. We don't get clean sheets, we don't get towels. I literally had to take the bedding back because it had stains all over it. I almost puked up when I saw how nasty it was. When we moved in there, I had to clean the room myself. That's the conditions in that dump, that's the conditions in my life. I have to pay for the room somehow.

Plus, I don't have money for food or clothes or school supplies—for nothing. So, I turn tricks. It is so nasty, I hate it, I get beat up all the time, but what else can I do? I need the money. How else can I survive?

When I asked Barb how it made her feel to prostitute herself, she replied:

How do you think it makes me feel? Like shit, like I'm less then human—but I already feel that way. I hate it, I hate myself. Who wants to stick some nasty dude's dick in their mouth? Sometimes I just wanna die so I get high to block the pain. I try not to get high too much because I don't want the kids to see me like that. But sometimes I need to get high. To be honest, I am amazed that men still pay to fuck me—I look like a beaten down old hag. Look at me. I hardly got any teeth; my face is all tore up. But they don't care. Men are disgusting. I hate them and I hate myself. But I have to take care of my kids and I can't do nothing else. Some days I can't even get out of bed. What kind of job am I gonna get? I fuck men for money, that's what I can do, I got no other choice. All I got is my body so I fuck men to survive.

One night I went out dancing with some friends in the South of Market Neighborhood (SOMA). The club was a few doors down from the Covered Wagon. As we were leaving I ran into Barb, who was on her way home from working the streets. She seemed embarrassed when she first saw me so I gave her a big hug and introduced her to my friends. That put her at ease and she hung out and chatted with us for about twenty minutes. We talked about the DJ and how much fun we had. Barb commented on how weird it was to see a bunch of yuppies, hipsters, and working stiffs in her neighborhood out clubbing at 2:00 am. We talked about how SOMA was rapidly gentrifying and she wondered whether she would still have a place to live in a few years. The juxtaposition of middle-class interlopers with prostitutes, transients, junkies, and the homeless was not lost on Barb. I was not absolved of Barb's critique. By our mere presence, my friends and I were implicated in the dismantling of yet another affordable neighborhood. In fact, when I recently tried to find out if the Covered Wagon was still in business, I found a hotel review by Henry Swanson (2008), who indicated that they were running ads on Craigslist to attract students and tourists in what he described as a rat-infested SRO. In his review, Swanson condescendingly mentions that the hotel has arrangements with some of the local homeless service groups and puts transitioning homeless people up in the hotel. In a decidedly snarky tone, he goes on to say that he is all for housing the homeless and doesn't mind sharing space with any considerate adult but that he's met enough homeless people to know that "the sad fact of the matter is, when you get into any place that houses homeless people, you inevitably see a big jump in irresponsible and inconsiderate behavior thanks to the heavy drinking-and-drugging lifestyle that goes hand in hand with homelessness. This is obviously reflected in the grossness of the bathrooms in this case" (2008, 2). Ironically, the club we just left was filled with "drinking-and-drugging" young, white, privileged professionals, and the bathroom was vile. Ultimately a rat-infested hotel with backed-up toilets is the fault of slumlords who neglect these dilapidated SROs in favor of maximizing their profit, not the impoverished residents who are forced to reside there. Swanson ends his review on an upbeat note when he says that these types of hotels are becoming "more pleasant" and "attract a higher caliber of tenant" as the city gentrifies!

Jalesa worked as a street prostitute in the Mission District on the corner of Capp and 20th Street. This high-crime corner was, and still is, notorious for prostitution and drug dealing, despite being in a residential neighborhood. As a result of being systematically raped while in foster care and throughout her adult life, Jalesa also saw prostitution as her only way to earn money. Similar to Barb, Jalesa articulated that if she was going to be abused by men, she might as well benefit from it. You may recall that when talking about her upbringing in chapter 2 Jalesa said:

> All of these experiences fucked me up big time Annee. Being poor sucks—it's all violence and pain. It really is a vicious circle. I got beat as a kid and then I got beat as an adult. When you grow up the way I did you don't care about yourself. You'll have sex with anyone, take drugs, turn tricks—whatever. Why do you think I am so depressed now? Who wouldn't turn to drugs, who wouldn't want to die, after living my life? Sometimes I get so depressed I can't even move. I just get overwhelmed. How can I be expected to work, to find a place to live, pay rent? Sometimes I can barely breathe.

She went on to say:

> The only skill I have is sex. I got nothing else to offer this world, except my kids and I'm not too optimistic about them. I go out at night and come home late and they're alone. I'm depressed and angry; I do drugs, what kind of a life is that for kids? But what else can I do? If I don't work the streets we have no money. I need money to pay the rent and buy food. The kids get breakfast and lunch in school but I have to feed them dinner. I go to the food bank and get food, but it's all canned, nothing fresh. I need to buy some fruit and vegetables for them. Forget about clothes or school supplies—I am barely hanging on. So, I hit the street and have sex with disgusting men I don't know. They are mean and violent, I get beat up all the time, but what can I do? When you grow up poor you gotta do what you gotta do to survive. For women like me, the world is fucking cruel. There ain't no other way to say it Annee, but life's a bitch!

Culture of poverty theorists point to the behavior of women like Luz, Myrna, Melinda, Barb, and Jalesa to promote their ideology of pathology. Proponents of this perspective argue that poor women of color are out-of-control sexual deviates (Mead 1992; Murray 1984). Their gendered, raced, and classed discourse has deep historical roots in the development of

American society. Throughout the nineteenth century, African American slave women and dark-skinned Mexican women were often defined as sexual predators. The representation of black and Latina women as whores served to legitimate sexual violence by white men against them. In addition, the social construction of Latina and black women as sexually dangerous served as the foundation for their depiction by white elites as out-of-control breeders (Almaguer 1994; Collins 2005). These women of color, along with poor white women, were defined by their unrestrained sexual appetites, legitimating their sexual exploitation. With the advent of mass media, particularly film and television, the historical image of overly sexualized black and Latina women proliferated and became part of the cultural fabric of contemporary American life. These historical images are prevalent in contemporary mass media and form the subtext of much neoconservative theorizing. Sexualized black and Latina bodies are ubiquitous in contemporary media (hooks 1992; Collins 2005) and in public policy debates. Poor white women, typically referred to as *white trash,* have also become identified with overt sexuality and to a lesser extent unrestrained fertility. As a result gendered and racialized representations of white women and women of color as sexual deviants resonate with an American public that has internalized these pejorative images. Constructing and maintaining images of Latinas and black women as promiscuous provides ideological justification for race, gender, and class oppression. Black and Latina single mothers have now become common symbols of racial ethnic inferiority signified by their uncontrollable sexuality (Roschelle 1999). The racialized discourse of poor women as out-of-control breeders maintains their social, political, and economic disenfranchisement resulting in social policy that further subordinates them. Ultimately, racialized gender ideology is used to justify patterns of oppression and discrimination that have significant economic ramifications (Almaguer 1994; Collins 2005). The pernicious image of black, Latina, and white homeless mothers as out-of-control sexual deviates continues unabated, absolving policy makers of providing housing and desperately needed meaningful social services.

TENUOUS TIES: THE CONSTRUCTION OF INFORMAL SOCIAL SUPPORT NETWORKS

Homeless women who lack extended kinship networks that can provide instrumental support often attempt to recreate those networks with other homeless families. Like traditional extended kinship networks, these relationships include both expressive and instrumental support and are based on exchange reciprocity. For most homeless women, the impetus for creating these new networks is primarily to obtain resources. Of course, as women enter into these exchange relationships, members also provide emotional support. The tenuous ties created by homeless families are very similar to what Desmond (2012) referred to as "disposable ties." Like the evicted tenants in his research, homeless women in San Francisco created networks with virtual strangers almost immediately upon meeting. These networks were extremely small and typically included two families. Intense levels of intimacy were quickly established among homeless mothers who shared a common bond of oppression. Although homeless women had very little to share, whatever meager resources they did have flowed in both directions, or the relationship was terminated. Because homeless families were tied together by their chaotic circumstances and they were essentially strangers, their ties were often fraught with turmoil and were extremely brittle. Most of these newly constructed informal social support networks only lasted a few months before they imploded. Nonetheless, these tenuous ties are a survival mechanism that represents an attempt by homeless mothers to exert their agency by replacing diminished familial support networks with alternative ones.

Not all homeless mothers created street-level informal social support networks. Some women were extremely distrustful of strangers, others of people outside their immediate family. Some women were so filled with self-loathing after years of abuse that they were extremely guarded and couldn't imagine anyone befriending them. Nonetheless, many women did try to recreate extended kinship networks with other homeless families. One such attempt was made by Tiffany and Pamela. Despite a lifetime of abuse and difficulty trusting anyone, Tiffany was desperate to find an exchange partner to help with Steph. When Pamela, her three teenaged kids, and their minivan showed up at the Franciscan Motel, Steph was elated. She immediately approached them and began to school them on being homeless in San Francisco. Pamela, John, Brian, and Rebecca had recently arrived from rural Oregon and were completely unfamiliar with the city. Tiffany, who had been homeless off and on for many years proved to be an outstanding source of information. Pamela told Tiffany about all the homeless service providers in San Francisco, showed her around the city, and brought her to Home Away. The two families became instant friends. When I asked Tiffany, a thirty-nine-year-old white woman, about why she came to San Francisco she replied:

> We came to San Francisco when my house in Oregon burned down. We lived in a rural part of the state in a house on five acres of land. It was my parents' house but I refinanced it so there was a monthly mortgage payment. Years ago, when I was pregnant with John, I hurt my back so badly that a few years later I couldn't work anymore and went on disability. We were doing okay. The kids were doing well in school and my disability covered most of the bills. I never had any money left after I paid the mortgage, utility bills, car insurance, and bought food—but we were hanging in there. Money was real tight though, so I had to cut back on some stuff—we couldn't afford any extras so I stopped paying my homeowner's insurance. There was nothing I could do about it, I

just didn't have any money to pay that bill. Then we had a fire, the house burned to the ground, and the bank took my land. Out of desperation we came to San Francisco to live with my sister. As you can see, that didn't exactly work out.

Pamela initially came to San Francisco to temporarily live with her sister until she could get back on her feet. She and her three kids crashed at her sister's place but after two weeks of incessant fighting her sister asked them to leave. This is not an uncommon scenario. Siblings often recreate dysfunctional childhood patterns, particularly under the highly stressful condition of doubling up in a small physical space. Pamela's sister claimed that Pamela was a lazy slob and used her back injury to avoid working. I asked Pamela about how she hurt her back and she said:

> When I was pregnant with John I fell and broke my back—or, cracked a bone in my back. I wouldn't let them take x-rays or wouldn't take any medication so I really didn't know that I'd cracked it. It wasn't until a couple of years after that when the pain got so bad that I went to the doctor. The doctor thought that I did crack it because she could feel swelling in there. So now because of when I fell it compressed my spine so hard that now I have degenerative spinal disease. So I can't stand on my feet. Like right now it hurts, you know? I've had one spinal surgery two years ago. They grafted bones from my hip and put a steel plate in my neck—the fourth, fifth, and sixth cervical vertebrae. I was told by that neurosurgeon that I had a spine like a seventy-year-old and you know sometimes that's how old I feel.

One of the reasons that Pamela was so empathetic to Steph was because they both suffered from intense bodily pain. John, Brian, and Rebecca were all close to their mother and witnessed the intense agony she suffered, so they too empathized with Steph. That bond solidified the relationship between the two families and they all became fast friends. The fact that Pamela had a minivan was an exceptional piece of luck for someone in a wheelchair. Pamela, Tiffany, and the kids would load Steph and her wheelchair into the van and drive to appointments around the city, to Market Street to sell bracelets, and to Home Away for some needed respite. In addition, the kids took turns pushing Steph around so that Tiffany could have a break. Tiffany, who weighed about eighty pounds, was so physically fragile she looked like she might break in half. A major load off Tiffany's mind and body was that Brian and Rebecca, the two oldest kids, would carry Steph up the stairs to her motel room. Apparently the Franciscan, a two-story motel, had a rule that only welfare recipients could live on the first floor. Given that Steph had aged out of the system and was no longer eligible for welfare, she and Tiffany were forced to live on the second floor. In fact, as soon as Steph turned eighteen the manager of the motel made them move upstairs from the room they had been living in for two years. I begged that manager to let Steph and Tiffany move back downstairs but he refused. He kept saying he would get fired if he broke the rules. Given the bureaucratic nightmare that is the poverty industry, I was never able to confirm that this was an actual rule. So—up they went and up they stayed. The motel had no elevator, and when Tiffany couldn't find anyone to help her she was forced to drag Steph up the stairs on her own. Imagine the pitiful image of this wisp of a woman dragging her dying daughter up a flight of stairs, going back to get the wheelchair, dragging the chair up the stairs, and then plopping her daughter into that wheelchair. This intensive and immediate bond was also helpful to Pamela and the kids who spent their lives in a rural community and needed help navigating San Francisco. These two families provided instrumental and emotional support to one another and even began referring to themselves as "a family."

Although this arrangement was mutually beneficial, Pamela wanted to get her kids into less dilapidated, more permanent housing. The entire family was living in one filthy cramped room on the outskirts of the city in Bayview Hunters Point. Like thousands of other homeless families, Pamela began her journey through the social service system by going to Compass Family Services. Compass Family Services has a program called Connecting Point for families experiencing a housing crisis, potential eviction, or homelessness. Connecting Point provides a variety of services, including finding emergency shelter for homeless families. After their initial intake, Pamela, John, Brian, and Rebecca were sent to the Hamilton Family Shelter. Pamela told her caseworker she wanted Tiffany and Steph to be sent to Hamilton along with them. Pamela explained that Steph was dying of bone cancer and that they had become a family during their short stay at the Franciscan; that they needed each other to survive. Pamela pleaded on behalf of Tiffany and Steph to no avail. The rules were quite clear; Steph was over eighteen so she and Tiffany were ineligible for housing in a family shelter. Pamela initially told me and the staff at Home Away that she would not go to Hamilton unless Tiffany and Steph could come. We all explained to her that this was simply impossible and implored Pamela to reconsider for the sake of her kids. Pamela had no choice but to relent and she finally agreed to take her family to Hamilton. She felt like she was abandoning Tiffany and Steph. Given that the families had only known each other for about a month it was remarkable how loyal they were to each other. They explained that their mutual survival depended upon each other. In a conversation with both women, they expressed the following:

> Pamela: We never would have figured out how to survive in San Francisco without Tiffany. She helped us learn our way around the city and took us to all our appointments—to Connecting Point and Home Away. Without her we would be lost.

Tiffany: Pamela and the kids have been a godsend. We usually have to drag our asses around using the bus which is really horrible because of how much pain Steph is in. Not to mention getting that damn wheelchair on and off the bus. I can't tell you how much easier it's been since Tiffany showed up with the minivan.

Pamela: Plus our families are super close. Tiffany is my sister now. She is hella more helpful than the one I came here to stay with. My sister is always judging me, acting like my back isn't killing me all the time. She thinks I am just trying to get out of working. I worked my whole life 'til my back injury. Before I hurt my back, I was an Inclusion Assistant for the Education Service District, working one on-one with developmentally disabled children. I worked with pre-school kids who were autistic and deaf, disabilities like that. My job was just to get them ready to enter school so they could interact with other kids. Before that I worked in restaurants, cooking, waitressing, and stuff like that. A lot of standing on your feet, a lot of heavy work—I can't do that anymore but I did that for years. Before that when I was in college—I did go but I never finished, I ran a business full-time with my aunt while I was in college full-time. We ran a restaurant. My aunt and I were partners in like a seventy-five-seat café for almost four years before it went out of business. So I don't know why my sister has to diss me so hard. With Tiffany it's different. She doesn't judge me, she accepts that I can't work, she understands my pain, she is kind, and we talk about all the problems we've had in our lives, we're sisters.

Tiffany: It's hard for me to trust anyone I've had such a shitty life. But I trust Pamela, she understands me and we are tight. I was so depressed before Pamela and the kids showed up. Now I feel less hopeless and that has been a godsend. I think I might just crumble up and die if we get separated.

Pamela: Don't worry. Even though we are going to Hamilton and you can't come, we'll still be a family. We'll keep helping each other survive.

Tiffany: I know we will!

Not surprisingly, after three weeks at the Hamilton Family Shelter, Pamela and her kids no longer had contact with Steph and Tiffany. They lost touch as quickly as they found each other. Although some homeless families had pagers, none of them had cell phones. Neither Tiffany nor Steph had pagers, and communicating required calling pay phones at pre-determined times. Steph, now in the Haight, was far from Bayview Hunters Point and had to drive herself and her kids to appointments all over the city. The cost of gas and the exhausting constraints of homelessness made it prohibitive for Pamela to continue to drive to the Franciscan. Tiffany stopped coming to Home Away because it was a long and torturous bus ride for Steph. She continued selling bracelets on Market Street but spent most of her days in abandoned isolation in her motel room with her dying daughter. Pamela and her kids made new friends who instantaneously became family and couldn't survive without each other, until they too moved on. This pattern was habitually repeated by many families as they negotiated the exigencies of homelessness in San Francisco. Although these newly formed kinship ties initially seemed unbreakable, they began to unravel almost immediately and proved to be profoundly unreliable.

TENUOUS TIES: INSTITUTIONAL SOCIAL SUPPORT NETWORKS

As disposable network ties disintegrated and homeless families found themselves on their own, they were forced to rely on institutional forms of social support for their survival. For families who were unable to recreate exchange networks in the first place, the local poverty infrastructure was their only source of help. Like homeless families across the country, families in San Francisco had frequent interactions with social service agencies and local service providers. Many of these interactions were fraught with discord and hostility. Some homeless mothers felt infantilized, disrespected, and even criminalized. Parents often articulated that service providers took pleasure in exerting arbitrary power over them. In addition, many homeless mothers felt an underlying racism among the primarily white middle-class social workers with whom they came into contact. Although many families were religious, those that weren't sometimes felt enormous pressure to feign religious fervor in order to receive services from particular faith-based agencies. At one transitional housing facility, residents were expected to attend weekly lectures on such topics as "The Myth of Evolution," and "How Jesus Can Lead You out of Temptation and Homelessness." Some mothers expressed antipathy at having to attend these lectures but were afraid of being denied services if they refused. One woman remarked that "you have to pretend to be a Jesus freak and go to these crazy talks, or they might throw you out!" Her friend concurred and added "The Myth of Evolution—are they insane? I don't want my kids growing up believing that science is a myth, but this is a stable safe place with lots of services. And that temptation bullshit—what the hell is that? I'm not homeless because of temptation; I'm homeless because I'm poor. But I don't really have a choice; I have to pretend to believe their bullshit." Homeless parents' frustration with inflexible and sometimes punitive service providers in San Francisco corroborates the research literature that indicates that homeless service agencies typically alienate their clients,

(Hoffman and Coffey 2008; Lyon-Callo 2000; Meanwell 2010; Sager and Stephens 2005; Williams 2003).[2] Clearly, attempting to replace historically based extended kinship networks with institutional forms of social support is extremely problematic. While these institutional forms of social support are essential for accessing services, they are absolutely inadequate for recreating culturally vital community kinship networks.

As homeless families made their way through the morass of bureaucracy that characterizes homeless social service agencies in San Francisco, they expressed their frustration, anger, and anxiety. From entrance into the social service system, through obtaining TANF, food, shelter, counseling, medical care, and schooling for their kids, homeless families were confronted with the draconian regulations inherent in the poverty industry. When I asked Carlos and Isabela to discuss how they became homeless and their experiences with social service agencies, it became clear that they immediately felt humiliated and disrespected. Their experience of going to Connecting Point to find emergency shelter was abysmal. The following conversation is indicative of their sojourn through the social service system:

Annee: Can you tell me about your experience with Connecting Point?

Isabela: The people at Connecting Point have been treating us really bad. They have no professional knowledge of what homeless people go through. They've never been homeless. They have people working there that haven't been homeless and don't know how to deal with people that are homeless, the stress we're going through, and what we have to do each day. And all they say is here's a list of food lines and we'll try to get you into a shelter. Then you have to come back to meet a case manager.

Carlos: They were very rude to us, very rude. They helped us find a soup kitchen the first day and after that it got bad. They've given us a very hard time. They don't help us with anything. I feel like they don't have compassion about people. The people who work there has never been homeless, you know? They don't know what it feels like and they treat you like it's your fault you are homeless. You know because I'm an immigrant they acted like I was trying to get out of working and scam the system. I've worked my entire life, in Guatemala and Mexico and then here. I came here legally and had a good job before I became homeless but I got injured on the job and got fired.

Annee: Can you tell me about that?

Carlos: I was trained as a carpenter in Guatemala and then moved to Mexico when I was nineteen. I worked there for six years and then came to the U.S. when I was twenty-five. Now I'm thirty-seven and I have never been out of work before. I worked as a contractor until last year when I started working for the company that makes those fancy French toilets. I work on the kiosks; you know the ones that have all the posters and advertisements on them. I helped assemble them and we moved some around the city—like from the Embarcadero to other places. Mostly I do maintenance on the lights—I keep them clean and change the posters every two weeks. I got paid $9.00 an hour which is barely enough to survive—but it is better than nothing, better than now. I got injured on the job and they fired me. I injured my foot six months ago. One of the kiosks got dropped on my foot and crushed it. I had surgery and missed work for a few days. The boss was pissed that I missed work and then I tried to get disability but the insurance company denied me. They said my injury was not work-related. But I went to a doctor and he said it is industrial, it's work-related, but they just said no. The fucking kiosk got dropped on my foot—how is that not work-related? The people at my job said I shouldn't get disability and the guy, my boss, he fired me. The doctor I went to is a specialist who works with insurance companies–he said the injuries were work-related and I have a right to have workers' compensation benefits. But instead I got fired, got no benefits, ran out of money, and now we are homeless. So we go to Connecting Point to get help and they treat us like criminals, like shit.

Annee: Tell me about that.

Carlos: When we went there for our second appointment we got kicked out. We were supposed to have an appointment at 2:00 in the afternoon. We got there at 2:00 and the door is locked. There is a sign on the door that says the staff is at a meeting and they will open at 2:00. Then we wait fifteen minutes and they don't open and I get really angry, my foot is killing me, I'm hungry, and worried about my kids. I was on medication and had my second surgery two days before. I was supposed to be in bed. So we ripped down the sign and left. The next day we come back and they say that we have don't have an appointment and have to come back. I told the woman what happened but she said we had to make an appointment and come back and she said it like she was happy, like it was funny. So I started yelling and shaking my cane at her. Then she told me we were suspended. I kept yelling at her and then I said I wanted to speak to Greg, the guy we met the first time we came in and Greg came out and he told me "You are suspended. Get out of here. You've got to get out of here now! If you don't leave now I'm calling the police." Then I blow up and I told him, you know, Fuck you! Fuck you asshole. So then he said we were suspended forever.

Annee: So if you get suspended from Connecting Point forever, does that mean you can never get into any of the city shelters?

Carlos: Yeah, you can't stay in any city shelters or housing. That's what they want to do—to keep us homeless. That's why we are living in that drug-infested motel in the Tenderloin, you know the Hartland.

Before becoming homeless, Isabela was a recipient of AFDC for two years. Once the welfare legislation was passed and the reforms were implemented, she was required to attend a series of orientation meetings and trainings. In addition, Isabela was required start looking for work in earnest. When I asked her about her experience with her new caseworker she replied:

Isabela: She was really good in the beginning but not anymore. Now she's really stuck up and nasty. She doesn't like me and tells me I'm not looking hard enough for work, that I'm late for meetings, that I don't pay attention and ask too many questions. She fights me on everything. She fights me every month on my child care. First she told me let's work on the homelessness. Then she says; no let's work on your job. It's like what do you want me to do here? And she's got me in a Catch-22 situation. I didn't do what I was supposed to do this month cuz I just plain didn't have the time. I'm trying to do the best I can and that's all I can promise you. She keeps holding my benefits—like she wants me to beg—she made me go through this big drama scene for a bus pass. She keeps threatening to hold back my check. I'm supposed to get it on the fifteenth but last month she held it up for a week, so that holds me up.

Annee: Why do you think she's doing that?

Isabela: I don't know, maybe she thinks I'm a bad mother. She probably thinks I do drugs. You know a lot of times these white women who work with poor people think bad of us—they don't see us as human beings. They think we are different because we are Black or Latino and poor. Oh we must be lazy. They never had to struggle for nothing and they don't understand how hard we work just to survive. How racist people are to us. She says it's because I'm not looking for work hard enough. She keeps saying that I have to look harder, that I have to contact her every week. I need to call her right now. I mean it is just so much to keep up with and I don't have a phone. I have to take care of my kids and since Carlos messed up his foot I have to take care of him too. I'm so overwhelmed. I feel like she is trying to push me off welfare. I feel like I'm at the end of the line.

After many conversations with Carlos about his inability to get workers' compensation for his work-related injury, and the unwillingness of service providers to help him, I took him to see an attorney who specialized in disability law. The attorney was the former boyfriend of one of my students. I initially met with Steven because I was considering doing research on the tightening of SSI eligibility requirements for poor and homeless individuals with physical and mental disabilities. I ultimately decided against this research project because the focus was too narrow and instead settled on my ethnography of homeless families. However, this contact proved to be useful as I was able to refer Carlos and several other individuals to him for legal advice. Steven was an extremely compassionate guy who dedicated his life to representing the disenfranchised who he felt were systematically denied disability benefits. He worked with Carlos for several months and was eventually able to get him workers' compensation for his crushed foot. Without my informal social support Carlos would not have met Steve, and would not have had me to drive him to Steve's office, which was an hour outside of San Francisco. Unfortunately, I was unable to help Isabela maintain a cordial relationship with her case manager and after several unpleasant meetings she was sanctioned. As previously discussed, caseworkers have absolute discretion regarding who they sanction and why. In Isabela's case her contentious relationship with her case worker and her inability to navigate the welfare-to-work bureaucracy ultimately resulted in her being expunged from the welfare rolls. Isabela's caseworker attributed her lateness to meetings and her failure to find a job as willful violations of the welfare reform, rather than as structural barriers that prevented Isabela from complying with the unyielding rules of the welfare state. Carlos and Isabela's frustration with representatives of social service agencies from their point of entry through later interactions is common among homeless families, as evidenced in the research literature. In addition, Isabela's inability to successfully navigate the new welfare reform is poignantly highlighted by homeless mothers in chapter 3.

One final place where homeless families often feel demoralized is in family shelters. Although employees at shelters are typically well-meaning, they are required to enforce a system of seemingly tyrannical rules. Although these rules are meant to keep order, families often experience them as punitive. Meals are served at a set time and if someone is late she/he/they are denied food. Family members are prohibited from opening the refrigerator to obtain food or milk for themselves or their children. Residents must return to shelters by 8:00 pm and are denied entry even if they are five minutes late. Everyone is forced out during the day regardless of individual circumstances, number of children, or health status. Residents who break the rules or whose children are too unruly are kicked out. While it is clear that shelter staff are trying to maintain order in an inherently chaotic environment, they regularly enforce rules that are detrimental to families. For example, when Allen, the trained chef and his wife Kathryn and daughter Phoebe showed up at Hamilton, they were initially told that Allen could not stay there with his family if he continued to work at his restaurant job. They simply refused to discuss the possibility of Allen returning home after curfew. Obviously, this policy is meant to create stability and prevent residents from coming in late and disturbing sleeping families. However, this rigid policy would have prevented Allen from working at the restaurant and would have forced him to choose between breaking up his family, sleeping on the streets, or losing his job. This rule embodies the inflexible structure of homeless family shelters, which is often experienced by clients as yet another form of oppression. It was only after we forcefully advocated with the staff on Allen's behalf that we convinced them to let him to continue working and return late to the shelter. Over the course of four years, I heard compelling stories of how families felt disrespected by the imposition of strict rules they encountered at shelters like Hamilton. Individuals repeatedly articulated that it was often adherence to the rules that made it difficult for them to find jobs, get back on their feet, and fulfill the requirements of welfare reform, ultimately miring them further in poverty.

RESILIENT TIES: A HOME AWAY FROM HOMELESSNESS

Jeanie, the Executive Director of Home Away, was profoundly aware of the heartless treatment that homeless families often received from social service providers throughout the city. Her initial impetus for creating Home Away was to create a place where children could experience a reprieve from the harsh realities of homelessness, feel respected, and be encouraged to reach their creative potential. She wanted children to experience moments of boundless joy. In addition, she wanted parents to have a safe and supportive space to escape the relentless pain of their lives. When parents came to the Club House they were allowed to freely use the computers and phones, do laundry, cook meals, watch T.V., read, or just hang out. The nonjudgmental and unrestricted atmosphere was a welcome alternative to the regimented and hostile environment of traditional social service agencies. Parents praised Home Away for their compassionate ethic and the warmth they felt from staff members and volunteers. The following comments from several different interviews over the course of four years represent the overwhelming fondness mothers had for Home Away:

Deborah: The staff at Home Away treats us with respect, and it's a decent place. It's not like—you know the awful shelters or social service offices we spend so much time in.

Jacinta: Home Away—oh it's a big relief you know? We can come here any time they're open, and get out from the burden of being homeless.

Keisha: We come here, a beautiful place, with a beautiful view, with beautiful people, to relax and eat a home-cooked meal and be with our kids without all the stress of daily survival.

Jalesa: Home Away is like—it's a great place. I mean, I don't feel like these people are staff. I feel like they're like one of us. I feel like they're really caring and compassionate towards everyone. They treat our children just wonderful. They come here and they're just open arms to our children. My kids love coming here. My daughter can't wait for a vacation. She goes I'm going to go to Home Away From Home every day, every day. And I'm telling her it's only open certain days so it's going to be a few days that she can't come here. But my daughter loves it. She's just like "I want a home like that." That makes it hard but at least for now she feels like this is her home.

Alma: They never let you down. You know, the other places you go to, they always let you down. You can't depend on no one except here.

Rendisha: It's a place you can come cry and get your feelings out and not feel ashamed, and not get back-talk. The social workers, they tell you it's your fault you're in the situation you're in. We left our motel because it was disgusting. The social worker told me—you should have kept your stable home. But they didn't understand our situation, that the place was falling apart, we were getting injured in our apartment, the cockroaches were like three inches big. And my son with asthma can't be around that. And he had so many flare-ups. We had to get out of there.

Janet: It just feels like family here. I mean, it really does. It feels like coming home.

Camilla: I live in the Tenderloin and crack addicts and drug addicts knock on your door all night and ask for weird things. That's really hard for me because I'm trying so hard to stay clean. I want my baby back. Sometimes they even ask to come in cuz they're hiding from somebody, It's crazy, it's terrifying. At night when you lay in bed you hear gunshots and sirens all the time and you know, you just don't know if you should walk out that door or not, you know? So when I come to Home Away I know I am safe and can relax for a moment. I don't have to be scared.

Barb: It's my lifeline.

Nicole: I like Home Away, I really do. And I'm really beginning to love them because they done something in my eyes that I never thought that I would ever see again. They are kind to me and they care about me. I haven't seen that in a long time. No one is kind to me. When I'm troubled I can talk to Sally and she tells me her problems and it like stays from my heart to her heart, you know, and I like it, I really like it. I can sit here. Just sit here. Like now I'm sitting here and I'm comfortable, you know what I'm saying? But I like them and I really like Jeanie and everyone who works here. It is such a relief to be around such kind people.

Pamela: For me, Home Away is relaxing. We can relax and just be ourselves. No one judges you. Once you leave it is all judgement and condescension.

Rochelle: There is room for the kids to play, there is room for me to breathe. I like that the only rules here are to be respectful and kind. It feels different. You can come in here and cook and enjoy a meal with other families and just sit and relax without having to ask permission.

Lydia: This place gives me a little sanity, a little hope. Yeah, it gives you a little hope, I don't get that anywhere else. And respect. I don't get that anywhere else either, I never feel ashamed here, only hope.

For chronically homeless families who spent years cycling in and out of homelessness or who were long term residents of motels, Home Away represented a stable, reliable, loving place they could come, with their children, to escape the violence of poverty and get access to much-needed services. In addition, Home Away was an effective alternative to the tenuous and ultimately futile kinship ties formed by San Francisco's homeless families. As an institutional form of social support, Home Away was far superior to most of the traditional social service agencies scattered throughout San Francisco. Nonetheless, even Home Away was not an adequate replacement for extended kin and fictive kin ties historically found among low-income white women and women of color. Race, class, and gender inequality prevented homeless women from creating suitable replacements for their disintegrated kin networks, propelling them further into poverty and desperation.

THE INEXORABLE STRUGGLE FOR SURVIVAL

As Jalesa pointed out, for homeless mothers, "life's a bitch." The relentless pursuit of health and mental health services, educational opportunities for their kids, housing, food, jobs, income, and compassion is thwarted by a callous poverty industry that stigmatizes and ultimately subjugates homeless families. Despite feeling utterly beaten down by their circumstances, homeless parents soldier on. The various survival strategies outlined in this chapter illustrate that homeless families in San Francisco are not merely passive victims of a heartless social structure. Rather, they resist. Some are forced to panhandle, sell their meager belongings, and in Tiffany's case, sell homemade crafts. Other homeless mothers engage in sexual bartering and prostitution. For these women the violence and sexual abuse of their childhoods is recreated in their adult interpersonal and economic exchange relationships. Given their brutal familial histories, homeless mothers recognized that a fundamental way of subordinating women is by controlling their sexuality (Collins 2005; Hurtado 2003). As a result, homeless mothers refused to passively accept racialized patriarchal norms about sexuality and made conscious decisions about their sexual and reproductive behavior. Women left abusive men, had children outside of marriage, and co-habitated with romantic partners. Some homeless women exerted their agency by using their sexualized bodies as an economic survival strategy. Unfortunately, this resistance strategy typically had the unintended consequence of reinforcing poor women's dependence on violent men and ultimately miring them further in poverty. In addition, this form of resistance perpetuates the gendered and racialized discourse of conservative policy analysts who argue that sexualized bartering is proof that poor white women and women of color are devoid of mainstream values and are, in fact, sexual deviants.

A more common survival strategy used by homeless families was the recreation of kin and fictive kin ties with other homeless families. Women of color drew upon their cultural traditions to empower themselves and their children by cultivating new extended kinship networks to replace the ones obliterated by their abject poverty. In addition to providing emotional and economic support, these tenuous ties allowed women of color to restore their historical role of kin keepers. In fact, one African American mother took bags of donated clothing back to her neighborhood to distribute among community members as a way of reasserting her role as *other mother*. Unfortunately, these newly created social support and fictive kinship networks were highly unstable and splintered almost as quickly as they were cobbled together. The unrelenting chaos of homelessness prevented the creation of enduring network ties. Ties that initially seemed unbreakable were unsustainable as race, class, and gender oppression forced women to fend for themselves and their children to the exclusion of anyone else.

In addition to constructing individual kinship networks, homeless mothers also tried to create institutional forms of social support with human services workers. Attempts at creating networks ties with social service agencies and service providers failed miserably. Homeless mothers felt disrespected by callous emissaries of the poverty infrastructure. The tendency to blame homeless women for their poverty was augmented by the raced, classed, and gendered ideological assumptions underlying service provision. As a result, it was almost impossible to create long-term supportive networks with service providers. One exception to this predicament was found at Home Away, where families felt welcomed and accepted. For families who were briefly homeless, Home Away was a lovely respite where they could bring their children while they were getting back on their feet. For chronically homeless families who spent years cycling between family shelters, residential motels, and transitional housing, Home Away was the one constant in their lives; the only place that felt like home. In addition to the programs offered at Home Away, staff members and volunteers frequently advocated on behalf the families at agencies and non-profits throughout the Bay Area. Home Away proved to be a vital alternative to the disposable kinship ties created by homeless families and was a vast improvement over traditional social service agencies that were unable to provide institutional social support. Nevertheless, Home Away could never adequately replace the extended kinship ties and informal social support networks endemic to low-income communities of color. Race, class, and gender inequality combined with the autocratic structure of the social service system prevented homeless women from creating and sustaining long-term social support networks even with the help of Home Away. Ultimately, homeless parents engaged in a variety of survival strategies in an attempt to sustain themselves and their children. Although some of these survival strategies had the unintended consequence of reproducing their poverty and recreating the sexual violence of their childhoods, they were important attempts at exerting their agency in an overwhelmingly hostile world.

NOTES

1. Under the PRWORA, food stamps were renamed the Supplemental Nutrition Assistance Program, commonly referred to as SNAP benefits. Most low-income women still use the colloquial term food stamps (see, for example, chapter 3). In order to honor their experience, when referring to SNAP, I will also use food stamps.

2. It should be made clear that there are also many wonderful therapists, social workers, case managers, and health care professionals working with welfare recipients and homeless families in San Francisco. Unfortunately, the structure of the welfare state is such that most service providers are excessively overworked and have too many clients. I interviewed several compassionate service providers who were incredibly frustrated by the structure of the system that impeded their ability to be effective. Nonetheless, there were many more representatives of the welfare state that were burned out, cynical, judgmental, and authoritarian, who blamed poverty on the individual failings of their clients, rather than on race, class, and gender inequality.

Chapter Six

Paradise Lost

The Lived Experiences of Homeless Kids

It sucks being poor and it sucks being homeless. Every day is a freakin'
struggle. —Olivia

WHAT ABOUT THE KIDS?

As painful as it is to be a homeless parent, there is nothing more heartbreaking than the toll poverty and homelessness takes on kids.[1,2] Therefore, as
women and children began to join the ranks of homeless adults in the 1980s,
and scholars became concerned with their well-being, research on homeless
kids proliferated. The initial phase of research focused on the causes of
family homelessness (Kozol 1988; Seltser and Miller 1993; Shinn and Weitzman 1996), life in homeless shelters (Arrighi 1997; Bassuk 1986; Liebow
1993; Kozol 1988), and the physical and mental health of homeless children
(Bassuk and Gallagher, 1990; Memmott and Young 1993). This research
provided the public with forewarnings about the devastating effects of childhood homelessness (Buckner 2008). As family homelessness continued to
rise throughout the 1990s and 2000s, scholars became increasingly concerned with the specific impact of homelessness on children. Subsequently, a
second phase of inquiry that examined the differential effects of poverty and
homelessness on children emerged (Buckner 2008). This research compared
the experiences of homeless children with low-income housed children, and
kids in the general population. A continuum of risk was identified in which
homeless kids had the worst physical health, mental health, and academic
performance followed by low-income kids. Not surprisingly, kids in the general population, who were not exposed to social structural inequality, suf-

fered the least amount of negative outcomes. Scholars hypothesized that exposure to community violence among low-income kids was exacerbated for kids also living in family shelters (Buckner et al. 1999; Masten et al. 1993). However, due to methodological limitations, researchers were unable to disentangle the specific effects of being homeless from the specific effects of being poor. Nonetheless, this research illustrated that whether housed or not, children living in poverty are exposed to a variety of devastatingly harmful life experiences (Buckner 2008).

POVERTY, VIOLENCE, AND HOMELESSNESS IN THE LIVES OF KIDS

Undoubtedly, low-income housed children and homeless children both face multiple risk factors as a result of living in poverty (Buckner et al., 1999; Buckner, 2008; Masten et al., 1993; Schmitz, Wagner, and Menke 2001). For many impoverished kids, homelessness simply becomes another traumatic event that intensifies the pain of being poor. For example, Schmitz, Wagner, and Menke (2001) found very few differences in levels of depression and behavioral problems among low-income kids regardless of whether they were housed or homeless. Similarly, the kids' fears of housing instability and neighborhood crime were not affected by whether or not they were housed. The reality of extreme poverty, housing instability, and poorly educated mothers had profound effects on both sets of kids. As Bruckner (2008) points out, problems associated with poverty may in fact be more profound than those associated with homelessness. He suggests that the persistently deplorable living conditions of low-income housed kids may be worse than the temporary conditions of living in a homeless shelter.

In order to delineate the impact of poverty from the impact of homelessness, Shinn et al. (2008) compared formerly homeless kids with their housed peers. Their results confirm earlier hypothesizing that poverty has a more profound effect on childhood development than homelessness per se. In fact, they found that negative life events, particularly exposure to family and community violence were more important to a child's emotional health than prior homelessness. Similarly, Gewirtz and Edleson (2007) found that exposure to intimate partner violence does affect a child's development. However, they also discovered that the context in which domestic violence occurs matters. Specifically, they illustrated that parental mental illness and substance abuse, exposure to familial and community violence, physical and sexual abuse, and feeling unsafe, are significant predictors of developmental problems among low-income kids. Gewirtz and Edleson (2007) argue that these risk factors are more detrimental to kids' development than short-term exposure to spells of homelessness. On a more positive note, Gewirtz and

Edleson (2007) did find that secure attachments to caregivers, healthy relationships with supportive peers, and living in close-knit communities with thriving extended kinship networks mitigate against the negative effects of these risk factors.

In a further attempt to disentangle the effects of homelessness from the effects of poverty, Huntington, Buckner, and Bassuk (2008) examined differences in behavior problems, adaptive functioning, and achievement among homeless kids. Their research identified two clusters of behavior in which higher functioning kids were doing better across all three domains and lower functioning kids were doing poorly across all three domains. Children who were exposed to high rates of physical and sexual abuse and had mothers with high rates of mental distress were clustered in the low functioning group. Homeless kids in the higher functioning group were not exposed to childhood trauma and had relatively calm family lives. Because kids in both groups had similar measures of residential stability and life experiences, it became clear that sexual and physical trauma caused behavior problems and hindered adaptive functioning and achievement. Ultimately, Huntington, Buckner, and Bassuk (2008) argue that early exposure to violence, maternal hardship, and exposure to stressors associated with poverty are more powerful predictors of maladaptive behavior than merely being homeless. Combined, these studies provide powerful support to earlier theorizing that the cumulative risks associated with poverty are more detrimental to the development of kids than prior homelessness (Masten et al. 1993) and that children suffer more from exposure to community and familial violence than from homelessness alone (Buckner, Beardslee, and Bassuk 2004). Not surprisingly, the devastating realities of poverty create cumulative harms that exacerbate one another producing painful outcomes for children. A more recent meta-analysis found that 10–26 percent of homeless preschool children had mental health problems that required clinical intervention. Among school age children, the percentage of kids with mental health problems increased to 24–40 percent. These rates were between two and four times higher than for impoverished housed children. Clearly, the added burden of homelessness and frequent exposure to violence has significant mental health consequences for children (Bassuk, Richard, and Tsetsvadze 2015).

This research has been invaluable in articulating the impact of poverty and homelessness on kids and distinguishing between the two. Maternal substance abuse and mental illness, community violence, sexual violence, physical abuse, and lack of community support networks have been systematically identified as predictors of maladaptive behavior among low-income kids. What is missing from this literature are the voices of kids. Except for very early qualitative accounts of homeless children (Kozol 1988; Shane 1996), there is very little research that focuses on how homeless kids experience poverty. In a previous study a colleague and I identified the stigma management strategies homeless kids in San Francisco use to protect their discredited self-identities (Roschelle and Kaufman 2004). Although we identified a variety of both successful and unsuccessful stigma management strategies, we did not examine the impact of family and community violence, physical and sexual abuse, maternal distress, or the loss of extended kinship networks on homeless kids. A more recent study in Australia identified how children construct meaning out of their experiences with homeless service providers (Moore, McArthur, and Noble-Carr 2011). However, this research lacked rich descriptive detail, focused specifically on kids' relationships with service providers, and did not convey their daily lived experiences. Currently, there are no systematic ethnographic accounts of how kids experience the intersection of poverty and homelessness and the meanings they construct out of their disenfranchised social location. Qualitative researchers have yet to identify how the home and family lives of impoverished kids impact them as they traverse the homeless landscape of urban America. By listening to the life stories of homeless kids, we can begin to understand how they endure the painful realities of their daily lives.

SITTING IN LIMBO:
INTERMITTENT CHILDHOOD HOMELESSNESS[3]

As the research literature indicates, kids who are newly or sporadically homeless and who have not lived in chronic poverty are typically not permanently damaged by the experience. These kids tend to have fewer gaps in their education, are less likely to have behavior problems, and have better coping skills then kids who've spent most of their lives in grinding poverty. Obviously, any episode of childhood homelessness is disorienting and terrifying. Nonetheless, kids who come from previously stable families with no substance abuse or violence, with a loving caregiver or parent, and intact social support networks, tend to bounce back once they are housed (Gewirtz and Edleson 2007). Over the course of my ethnography, I also found this assertion to be true. Kids who were homeless for brief periods of time and who hadn't lived in severe poverty were fairly well-adjusted and maintained some sense of optimism and joy. This was particularly true for kids who did not become homeless until their early teens. These kids were able to play together without constant fighting, followed the Beach House rules, were respectful of other kids and of adults, and did not hoard food (a common behavior among food-insecure kids). In fact, the newly homeless kids noticed how badly behaved some of the other kids were and sometimes commented on their conduct. Newly homeless kids had no way of knowing that the maladapted kids were chronically poor and were exposed to or suffered from violence and sexual assault. All they saw were homeless kids "just like them" who were misbehaving, slacking off in school, and generally disaffected. These kids were unaware that their own resiliency was a result of supportive families who had not lived in extreme poverty and had only recently experienced homelessness as a result of a crisis. For example, when Pamela, Brian, Rebecca, and John became homeless it was because their house in Oregon burned down. Although Pamela struggled financially, the kids spent their entire lives in a quaint home on five acres that their mother owned. Pamela had a network of friends and there was no significant violence in their community or in their interpersonal lives. Despite landing in the Franciscan Motel and being exposed to prostitution, pimps, drug use, and violence, Brian, Rebecca, and John remained relatively unscathed. John, who was only eleven and was frightened by the experience, was protected and nurtured by his two older siblings during their brief stay there. The family did not spend any significant time at the motel, traversing the city in search of social services and hanging out at Home Away during the day. Pamela and the kids only returned to the Franciscan to sleep. Within a month, they were placed at the Hamilton Family Shelter in the Haight, leaving Bayview Hunters Point far behind. Despite its history as a drug-riddled bastion for hippies and musicians, the Upper Haight had long since been gentrified and was a lovely neighborhood festooned with colorful Victorian homes.[4] Although living in a homeless family shelter is extremely unsettling, and the family missed Tiffany and Steph, at least they were safely housed. As soon as the kids got to the shelter they were enrolled in school and Pamela began looking for more permanent housing. Given their trauma-free upbringing, it was not surprising that John, Brian, and Rebecca were making friends and doing well in school. None of the kids exhibited behavior problems or seemed particularly angry. Understandably they were upset about being homeless and were resentful of a society that allowed them to fall through the cracks, but given the circumstances, they were remarkably well-adjusted. The kids were eager to talk about their family life prior to becoming homeless and how homelessness impacted them. The following conversation between seventeen-year-old Brian, fifteen-year-old Rebecca, and eleven-year-old John illustrates their guarded optimism and resiliency.

Annee: Tell me a little about your lives before you came to San Francisco.

Brian: You know we became homeless when our house burned down. Before that we lived a pretty normal life. We had lots of friends, we got along with our neighbors, and we went to church with the same kids we grew up with. At school, I was on the baseball team and Becca played soccer. We didn't get into too much trouble—you know, we'd sneak out at night sometimes to hang out with our friends and sometimes we smoked cigarettes or had a few beers, but mostly we are pretty good kids.

Rebecca: Yeah, especially compared to some of our friends who were doing drugs and having lots of sex. We didn't really do that. I was on the honor roll at school and was even thinking about going to community college. I always liked school. Even though John can be a pain in the butt sometime, you know how little brothers are; he's really a good kid too. We had a good relationship with each other and get along great with our mom.

John: Our mom is the best. She always played with me when Becca and Brian ignored me. She liked to bake cookies with me and she always tells me how much she loves me—and Becca and Brian too—even though she loves me the best!

Rebecca: Our home life was always pretty good, kind of calm. Sometimes we would fight about stupid shit, like any family, you know—brother-sister crap, silly arguments with mom, but it was a very loving environment. My parents got divorced when we were little and we didn't see my dad that much but when we did it was fine. There wasn't a lot of drama around my parents. They got a divorce and we all moved on. No fighting, no violence, it just didn't work out. Most of my friend's parents are divorced so it wasn't a big deal. Some of them had really messed up families, lots of drinking and fighting. Sometimes when mom's back was really bad and she was in a lot of pain she would get depressed, but she never took it out on us and she always bounced back. My best friend Ashley had to call the cops a few times to stop her father from beating her mother—it really messed her up. Sometimes Ashley would come and stay at our house when things got really bad. We didn't grow up like that.

Brian: That's for sure. Actually, our house was always the place to be. When we were little it was the fun house where all the kids hung out. When we got older and things were bad for some of our friends they would come stay with us. Our mom would talk to them about their problems and give them advice. She would let them stay a few days 'til things settled down with their parents. Even when her back was really bad, she took care of everyone else. She's really pretty cool that way.

Rebecca: She really is. To be honest the worst thing about being homeless is how bad I feel for my mom. She feels so guilty about not paying the insurance on the house. She keeps saying it's her fault that we're homeless. But it's not really her fault. She didn't have enough money to pay all the bills. She wanted to make sure we had enough food and clothes and she had to make sure we had electricity and stuff like that. You know, before she hurt her back, mom always worked hard. She paid all the bills and took care of everything. We never had a lot of money but we were okay. But after her back got so bad and she went on disability, she just couldn't afford to pay for everything. I guess she figured that we lived in the house our whole lives and nothing bad ever happened so she would take a chance and not pay that bill. It really pissed me off that after the fire they took our land and kicked us out. She paid insurance for so many years and never used any of it and then when the house burned down they basically said eff you—all that money you paid for all those years doesn't count. You don't have insurance now, so get out.

Brian: Yeah man, that is totally f'd up. I don't get how the money she paid all those years for nothing didn't count—but it didn't and here we are.

Annee: Can you tell me what your lives have been like since becoming homeless?

Brian: I can tell you it sucks! We stayed with our aunt for a little while but that didn't work out. She was pretty mean to our mom and they fought a lot so we left. The whole reason we came to San Francisco was to stay with her so that kind of screwed us up. I have an older brother back home. He's a mechanic but he lives in a small apartment with his girlfriend so we can't stay with him. We don't really have the money to go back to Oregon to live so I guess we're gonna stay here a while. After we left my aunt's, we stayed at the Franciscan motel. It was heinous.

John: I don't like being homeless, it's kind of scary. I didn't like staying in that motel. There were a lot of creepy people living there. I've never seen people like that before and they made me scared. I was glad we were all together it made me feel better. Brian and Becca watched out for me. They never left me alone and at night we all slept in the same room so I wasn't as scared. At first I couldn't sleep so good and at night if I heard a noise outside I would jump out of bed. Then Brian let me sleep with him so I felt safer. We did make friends though—with Steph and Tiffany—they were really nice and showed us around the city and taught us who to stay away from at the motel. I kind of miss them.

Rebecca: It was awful at the Franciscan. The place was filthy. It had peeling paint, bugs, and the most disgusting bathrooms ever. The people were heinous. John's too young to understand that some of those people were hookers and pimps. There were a lot of drug addicts too. He's right though—it was totally creepy. Some of the men would stare at me in a really gross way—like they wanted to have sex with me. It was awful. We tried to spend as little time there as possible, but when we were there we made sure never to be alone. We all stuck together so no one would hurt us.

Brian: I'm glad to be out of that rat-infested dump. You know, we grew up in the country, we never saw people like that before. There were some meth heads [methamphetamine addicts] where we lived but they kept to themselves and didn't really bother anyone. The shelter is so much better. Even though it's crowded and noisy, it's clean and the food isn't too bad. We all feel much safer there.

John: And there are a lot of nice kids to play with. Plus, I like my new school and my teacher is really nice.

Rebecca: Yeah, Hamilton is pretty decent. I wouldn't want to live there forever, but its fine for now. We go to school every day and go to the Beach House and the After-School Program. Luckily, I didn't miss that much school so I was able to catch up and am doing well in all my classes. That's important to me. I've made a couple of friends and am exploring the city, which is kind of cool. Right now the worst thing about being homeless is worrying about where we're going to live once we leave the shelter. It is so expensive in San Francisco I'm not sure how we will ever be able to afford an apartment. My mom is trying to find us a place, but if her social worker doesn't find us something I don't know what we're gonna do. Plus, we might end up in a bad neighborhood. I don't want to live in a place like the Tenderloin or South of Market. Those neighborhoods are dangerous and they don't seem much different from the Franciscan. The apartments are filthy and there are lots of addicts and prostitutes and pimps there. I don't want to be mean, I know people are struggling, but I'm not used to that and to be honest, I don't want to get used to it. The kids from those neighborhoods are so hard. Some of them come to the Beach House and they are so angry and disruptive. They get kicked out of school, are always fighting, and some of them are even in gangs. I don't want to be surrounded by that for the rest of my life. I'm trying to be optimistic, but it's hard. I just keep hoping for the best. Mom has always taken care of us and I know she is doing her best. But, I am kind of scared about where we will end up. I try not to think about the bad stuff too much, and stay positive, but it's not easy, and the longer we are homeless the harder it gets.

Brian: Yeah, it is pretty scary to think about where we will end up. We had a nice home life before the fire. Its f'd up that one bad thing can completely destroy your life. Something that isn't even your own fault and your whole life is ruined. It's not fair. We didn't do anything wrong.

We shouldn't have to live like this. I'm pissed but I try to stay positive. Hopefully we can find a place to live that isn't too bad. I am almost done with high school so next year after I graduate I can get a job and help pay the rent. I do wonder about our future though, it's not looking so good right now. We can only stay at the shelter for another month, so I'm worried about what's going to happen next. We can't sleep in our van, it's not safe and then we'd basically be like all the street homeless in the city. Can you imagine how that would be for John? He's a little kid; I don't think he'd ever get over that. Like Becca says, we gotta stay positive. At least we are all together.

As you can see from their conversation, these kids grew up in a stable and loving home. Despite Pamela's back injury, bouts of depression, and admitted overreliance on pain medication, her kids expressed appreciation for their supportive upbringing. Brian and Rebecca understood that their mom struggled economically, especially after she could no longer work. Prior to her back injury Pamela held a series of jobs that placed her solidly in the ranks of the working poor.[5] However, unlike most poor Americans, Pamela inherited her parents' home and raised her kids there for most of their lives. Living on five acres in a beautiful locale with supportive friends and neighbors buffered the family from the violence and chaos endemic to poverty. Brian, Rebecca, and John all had well-honed coping skills that served them well in their bout with homelessness. Nonetheless, homelessness is a disorienting and frightening experience. Despite their optimism, Brian, Rebecca, and John were terrified about their futures. The kids were angry about their predicament but underlying their anger was a critique of capitalism, not their mother. Brian and Rebecca recognized the absurdity of paying an insurance company year after year, essentially for nothing, and then losing their home because they briefly stopped making those payments. Despite their young age, they both understood that a country without a social safety net that prevented families from falling through the cracks was inherently flawed. After a three-month extension on their initial accommodation at Hamilton ran out, the family left San Francisco. I always wondered how the kids were holding up as they left the ranks of the newly homeless and possibly became members of the long-term homeless. As Rebecca articulated, the longer one remains homeless, the harder it is to stay optimistic. During the course of my four-year ethnography I met several kids like Brian, Rebecca, and John. Kids who came from economically disadvantaged but stable families that became temporarily homeless as a result of a crisis. These kids were also fairly resilient, had good coping skills, and managed to stay out of trouble while their families looked for permanent housing. For these kids the potential risk factors associated with their economic disenfranchisement was mitigated by loving caregivers and previously secure home lives.

ANGER IN THE STREETS: POVERTY, HOMELESSNESS,
AND COMMUNITY VIOLENCE[6]

Kids who grow up in neighborhoods fraught with brutality are often traumatized by their lifelong exposure to community violence. As Buckner (2008)
and Shinn et al. (2008) suggest, the unrelentingly wretched conditions of
poverty profoundly impacts kids and can result in multiple risk factors
(Schmitz, Wagner, and Menke 2001). Yet, kids do not act uniformly to these
conditions. Levels of depression, physical health, educational development,
substance use, and behavioral problems varied among the kids in my research. In fact, the behavior of homeless kids from San Francisco's most
impoverished neighborhoods ran the gamut from respectful and caring to
self-destructive to out-of-control to violent. Over the four years I spent in the
field, it became clear that when kids from destitute neighborhoods become
homeless, their ability to cope was determined by what happened inside their
homes, away from the chaos of the streets. Even under the worst conditions
of poverty, an emotionally stable, loving parent, relationships with well-
adjusted peers, or an intact social support network mitigated against the
effects of community violence (Gewirtz and Edleson 2007). Although Brian,
Rebecca, and John came from a lower-middle class rural community, that
was highly unusual. Some kids I worked with came from working-class
suburban neighborhoods in the Central Valley and others came from working-class urban neighborhoods. However, the majority of the homeless and
formerly homeless kids who participated in Home Away programs came
from impoverished neighborhoods in the Bay Area. These kids grew up in
unrelenting poverty surrounded by unthinkable violence and degradation.
The kids spoke unselfconsciously about growing up under these conditions
and the effect it had on them. The kids were keenly aware that the brutality
and exploitation they witnessed impacted every aspect of their lives. They
also recognized that some kids were devastated by their surroundings while
others were more resilient. The following conversation between Antoine, age
16; Kenny, age 15; Amari age, 14; Sasha, age 16; and Ediliana age, 15
poignantly depicts the ugly reality of growing up in poverty, the differential
effects it has on the kids, and the meanings they ascribe to their predicament.
Except for Ediliana who is Latina, the other kids are all African American.

Annee: Can you tell me what neighborhoods you grew up in?

Antoine: I'm from East Oakland, and I mean Deep East Oakland.[7]

Kenny: Yeah, I'm from Oakland too, but I grew up in Fruitvale.[8]

Amari: I lived in Hunter's Point my whole life.

Sasha: I grew up in the Tenderloin.

Ediliana: I grew up in the Mission District.

Annee: Describe what life in your neighborhood was like growing up.

Amari: Hunter's Point is a horrible place to grow up. There are drug addicts, whores, and pimps everywhere. Sometimes you see the pimps beating up their girls, it's fuckin' scary. But the worst thing is the gang violence. Man, you gotta keep your head down and stay out of it. Mind your own business and just keep your head down if you want to survive.

Sasha: I know what you mean. The Tenderloin is the same way. There's so much violence everywhere. One time when I was walking to school I saw a guy get shot. It freaked me out. I was only twelve when it happened. After that I was afraid to go out. I wouldn't walk anywhere alone. My mom had to take me to school for a month. If it weren't for her I don't think I would have ever left the apartment. And that's saying a lot because that place was horrible. Rats everywhere, the toilet always broke, water dripping from the pipes, no heat, used condoms and crack heads and junkies in the hallway. Always being scared, it takes it out of you. It's a bad way to live. Now I have to step over junkies and crack vials on the way to school, but I'm kind of used to it.

Amari: Yeah, our apartment was like that too. Totally disgusting. To be honest the shelter was better than that hellhole. Even with all the kids crying and running around it was like a palace compared to where I grew up. Even though being homeless sucks, at least we are out of the Point. It's amazing I got out of there alive.

Antoine: Oakland isn't much better. Same shit, different place. Gangs shooting up the neighborhood, people selling drugs on every corner, dudes beating up their girls. It ain't no place to grow up. It's stressful as shit. Every time you go outside you never know what to expect. Will you get shot, will you get stabbed? It's hard to grow up like that. It's hard to stay focused and keep out of trouble.

Kenny: I can relate dude. It's hella bad out there. One time I saw a bunch of kids light a building on fire. They just straight up lit the fucker up. No one lived there; it was like a shack, but what the fuck? Who does that? When we lived there I used to feel like I was living in a jungle or something—like it was the survival of the fittest.

Antoine: You mean survival of the craziest!

Kenny: Hell yeah! It is fucking crazy. I bet you didn't grow up like that Annee. Can you imagine how fucked up it is to be kid and live like this? I'm glad you're writing a book about us. People need to know how hard it is to live in these neighborhoods. How hard it is to stay out of trouble, to go to school, to keep off drugs, and to stay positive when you are surrounded by so much shit. It ain't easy! We should all get a medal.

Sasha: Right on Kenny, you be tellin' the truth.

Ediliana: The Mission was pretty bad but I think it felt a little safer than you guys because we had lots of family living there. My grandparents lived on the next block and I had lots of cousins nearby. Still, it was really scary a lot of the time. Like these guys said, there was a lot of violence everywhere, especially towards girls. Whenever I went out I saw girls getting hassled or beat up by their boyfriends and pimps. Me and my friends, we always had to be careful where we went so that we wouldn't get raped. At night if we were out my brother or a cousin would meet up with us so we wouldn't ever have to walk alone. Sometimes I felt like a prisoner in my own neighborhood, always having to think about being safe. I was always careful not to get in the way of the gangs or drug dealers or pimps. I tried to stay as invisible as possible, it was how I survived. Like Amari said, you mind your own business or you die. It's not right to grow up like that, it's not normal. It can make you crazy.

Annee: Wow. You guys amaze me. You've grown up surrounded by the worst conditions imaginable—poverty, violence, and horrific living conditions. Despite growing up with so much fear and then becoming homeless, you've all managed to, as Antoine put it, "keep out of trouble." You're all good kids, you do pretty well in school, and you've stayed away from gangs and drugs. Why do you think you've been able to keep out of trouble when some of your friends have not?

Sasha: For me, it's my mom. Even though she has a hard life she is my rock. My mom never did drugs and never hit any of us kids. She doesn't have a lot of boyfriends coming and going like some of my friends and she never let anyone beat her. Never. She always has a job and she works really hard. My mom taught me to respect myself and not to let any boys take advantage of me. She always tells me never to let any boy treat me bad no matter how much I like him. We talk a lot about that stuff. She loves us and tries to keep me and my brother safe no matter what. I look up to my mom.

Ediliana: I get along with my mom too. Plus I have my grandparents and aunts and uncles that live near us. They give me advice and make sure

I'm safe. We spend a lot of time with our family. We always have Sunday dinner together, ever since I was a little kid. Even when we were living in the shelter we spent a lot of time with them and had our Sunday dinner. We couldn't live with them when we lost our apartment because they might get evicted if they let us stay with them, but they helped us the best they could. Some of my friends come from really abusive homes and they are messed up. Their parents are alcoholics and when they get drunk they're really mean and beat up on the kids. One of my friends told me her mom was raped when she was young. That family is really messed up. Her mom does drugs and is always bringing creepy men home. They try to mess with my friend but she doesn't let them. I feel really sad for her; she doesn't have a good family like I do. Even though my family is poor no one takes drugs or beats on each other. We all look out for each other.

Kenny: When my dad was around he used to beat my mom. But he left when I was little and I don't really remember him. My mom kicked him out. She said she wasn't gonna be no punching bag. After my dad left, her sister moved in with us. I kinda had two moms. I call her aunty mom! My mom is strong, she's a survivor. She grew up poor too but she didn't let it beat her down. She never did drugs and she ain't crazy like some kids' moms. My one friend Keith that I grew up with, he's older than me, and his mom is bat-shit crazy. She came from a really bad family with hella violence and all kind of crazy shit. I don't know exactly what happened to her when she was growing up but it fucked her up big time. She used to get depressed and couldn't get out of bed. Sometimes she could barely move and Keith had to take care of his sisters. Then for a while she was doing drugs and would get all wired up. She had a different personality from one minute to the next. It was total chaos. It was just too much for Keith to take. He didn't have anyone looking out for him. He used to get into a lot of trouble and then he jumped a gang. Now he's in prison. I always felt bad for Keith; he was always on his own. Who wouldn't join a gang coming from a family like that? It's really sad. I'm lucky my mom takes such good care of me. She really loves me.

Antoine: Yeah, Keith is right. If you have someone looking out for you then you are less likely to get eaten alive by the streets. When we lived in Oakland, it was scary as shit. But I also had family close by to help my mom look after me. My grandparents lived in Oakland before they passed and my mom was very close to them. I always had someone to talk to and my grandpa kept me on the right path. Plus, we went to church and let me tell you, church folks have your back. Even though we're living in San Francisco now, sometimes me and my mom take the Bart and go to our church in Oakland. I also had friends who didn't have family to look after

them and they mostly ended up dropping out of school and joining gangs.
A bunch of them are in juvy [juvenile detention centers]. Don't get me
wrong, sometimes I feel like giving up too. Life is hard, but you gotta
keep going, you can't let it get you down, or you'll really be fucked.

Sasha: Antoine is right, I get depressed and overwhelmed sometimes too.
I don't always wanna go to school or do what my mom tells me. But, you
can't let the streets get you down; otherwise you'll never have a better
life. You gotta keep striving. That's why we come to Home Away. It
helps keep us out of trouble and work though our problems.

Kenny: I agree with what Sasha just said. It would be easy to just give up,
but in the long run it would make our lives worse. Plus, being homeless is
looked down upon in this city. Everyone hates the homeless and all these
young white dudes moving in and fucking up the city hate poor people.
They racist too. If we give in to the streets those fuckers will just use it as
ammunition to hate on us even more.

Sasha: Yup—all those weird white dudes who work on computers, they
just came in and took over the city.

Ediliana: Tell me about it. They own the Mission now, that's why we're
homeless. They treat us like we're all gang bangers and are even worse to
the homeless people on the streets. They treat them like shit, like they
have a disease. Like they don't belong. It was our city first.

Anne: What makes you think people don't like the homeless?

Kenny: I watch the news and there are always stories about how the
homeless are ruining the city and how lazy poor people are. They are
always talking shit about how lazy welfare mothers are; how they are
always scamming the system. That's a load of shit. My mother works
hard and she ain't never scammed anyone.

Antoine: Yeah, and the newspapers are always talking shit about the
homeless. Even though none of us live on the streets—we are homeless.
The only reason we don't live on the streets is because we live with our
moms so we get into shelters. If our moms were alone, they'd be on the
streets too. How fucked up is that?

Sasha: You know once we turn eighteen we can't stay in family shelters
and we could end up on the streets too.

Kenny: Fuck, I didn't think of that. Glad I'm only fifteen, got three more years.

Ediliana: Plus, the way people treat the homeless is horrible. I know they ask for money and some of them are crazy, but that doesn't give people the right to be so mean to them.

Amari: Did you hear that Da Mayor is gonna get a heat-seeking helicopter to find the homeless sleeping in the park?

Kenny: No way, you're full of shit man.

Sasha: That's crazy.

Kenny: No it's true. My mom said she read it in the paper.

Annee: Kenny's right, although I'm not sure about the heat-seeking part. But yeah, Mayor Brown tried to borrow a helicopter to find homeless people sleeping in the park at night. I think it has some kind of equipment that lets them see people hiding in the brush in the dark. He couldn't get it; the Oakland Police Department wouldn't let him use it.

Kenny: Wow, that's fucked up. See, I told you they hate us.

Sasha: What a dick!

Ediliana: People are so cruel. Don't they understand that people have problems; no one chooses to be homeless. Some of them are vets, some have mental problems, and drug problems or drink too much. I think a lot of the women left boyfriends who beat them. What kind of world do we live in that treats poor people like they deserve to be poor and homeless?

You can see from this exchange that Antoine, Kenny, Amari, Sasha, and Ediliana lived in deplorable conditions their entire lives. These kids witnessed unimaginable gang and interpersonal violence, drug abuse, sexual assaults, and institutionalized violence. Simply traversing their neighborhoods was fraught with danger. Imagine every time you stepped outside of your apartment you were worried about witnessing a violent crime. Imagine every time you stepped outside of your apartment you were terrified of being shot, stabbed, or raped. The rage endemic to impoverished neighborhoods that engulfed and threatened to devour these kids undoubtedly represents the sixth circle of hell. The one thing that buffered these kids from the horrors of their existence was a loving parent and intact extended kinship networks. Whether it was an aunt, a grandparent, a church member, or their mothers, all of these kids had adults they could rely on. Despite their external surroundings, these kids came from functional, loving families that protected them from the risk factors associated with poverty. Remarkably, these kids were self-reflexive enough to recognize their predicament. They articulated how living in extreme poverty impacted their daily lives. They recognized the race, class, and gender inequality that mired them in poverty and prevented them from finding safe and affordable housing. Yet, they acted, with agency and chose to avoid gangs, attend school, and stay out of trouble. Sometimes avoiding trouble was a struggle, but Antoine, Kenny, Amari, Sasha, and Ediliana persevered. In addition, they had a political critique of their circumstances deconstructing structural inequality. Their observations about how poor people are viewed and treated in San Francisco reflect their understanding of the social construction of poverty. Although they did not use this discourse, the subtext of their conversation reflects a visceral understanding of the derision society imposes on the impoverished. Nonetheless, these kids remained optimistic in the face of such derision. Kenny's comment that, "If we give in to the streets those fuckers will just use it as ammunition to hate on us even more," reflects his desire to avoid reinforcing pervasive stereotypes of the poor.

The comments made by the kids regarding the social construction of homelessness in San Francisco were particularly insightful. Throughout their young lives, the homeless problem intensified and a multitude of homeless people were visible throughout the city. The business community, the tourism board, and many local citizens were vocal about the scourge that was plaguing their beautiful City by the Bay. In 1992, when the former Police Chief, Frank Jordan, was elected Mayor, he inaugurated the Matrix Program. Matrix was aimed at cracking down on quality-of-life violations such as drinking, panhandling, urinating or sleeping in public. The program was criticized by religious leaders and homeless advocates as an attack on homeless people. When Willie Brown challenged Jordan for Mayor, he characterized the police patrols under the Matrix Program as occupation forces and vowed to discontinue Matrix. Despite espousing a more humane discourse toward the homeless, when Brown became Mayor in 1996, he continued Jordan's aggressive policies and more homeless street people were ticketed for quality-of-life violations than under Jordan's tenure. The kids frequently witnessed homeless people being rousted by the police. Mayor Brown fomented an increasingly vitriolic narrative that was epitomized by a November 4, 1997 *San Francisco Chronicle* headline that screamed "Crackdown on Riffraff At Golden Gate Park." Three days later there was an article in which Mayor Brown said that he had arranged for the police to conduct nighttime helicopter surveillance flights over Golden Gate Park using special equipment on loan from the Oakland Police Department to rid the park of homeless encampments. Despite outrage from homeless individuals and homeless advocates, the next day's headline read "Police Chief defends Helicopter Searches." Ultimately these searches never took place but only because the Oakland Police Department refused to lend the San Francisco Police Department their helicopter. Although this discourse was primarily aimed at homeless street adults, homeless kids were nonetheless wounded by these reports. The kids recognized that the only reason they were sheltered was because they were under eighteen and that their beloved moms would be on the streets if it weren't for them. For Antoine, Kenny, Amari, Sasha, and Ediliana, the pervasive narrative espoused by the Mayor and the *Chronicle* was irrefutable evidence that they were expendable and that the city only cared about rich, white residents. The kids made surprising interconnections between gentrification and increased development, racism, a lack of systematic poverty policy, and the inability of the city to provide them with stable housing. After long discussions about what we could do to change this discourse and promote political change, Antoine, Kenny, Amari, Sasha, and Ediliana decided to engage in political activism to make their voices heard. The six of us organized a group of kids and parents at Home Away to participate in a protest at City Hall. While the kids made signs the staff and I taught them about civil disobedience and the history of social movements in America. We discussed the Chicana/o and African American civil rights movements. Parents from Central America talked about their own experiences with protesting against right wing dictators. When we got to City Hall we were unexpectedly invited to speak to the City Council. The experience was incredibly empowering for the kids and their parents. The kids spoke powerfully about their value to the local community and the need for better more humane social services. They also articulated a desire for the cessation of the stereotypic depiction of poverty and homelessness that pervaded San Francisco.

TREACHEROUS BETRAYALS: WITNESSING FAMILY VIOLENCE[9]

For chronically poor kids who live in violent families, becoming homeless is a seemingly endless nightmare. When extremely impoverished, highly dysfunctional families become homeless, they typically move from apartments to residential motels to shelters to transitional housing and back again. These kids have a front-row seat to their parents' struggles with loss of housing, intimate partner violence, sexual degradation, drug and alcohol abuse, and physical and mental illness. Witnessing this kind of violence obviously has profound effects on kids and is more harmful to a child's emotional health than simply becoming homeless. However, according to Gewirtz and Edleson (2007) family violence is mitigated if the violence stops or the parent/ guardian protects the kids from being brutalized. In my experience risk factors associated with witnessing intimate partner violence are alleviated when the violence stops. However, even in families with a loving caregiver, kids who are exposed to sustained familial violence are likely to develop significant risk factors. Kids in my research who lived in persistently violent families were likely to have mental health problems, educational deficits, be substance abusers, and have significant behavior problems, even if they were not themselves physically abused. In chapter 2, I recounted the "hallway incident" in which Deborah teased me about being afraid of seeing someone get shot and told me to "toughen up." Deborah grew up in extreme poverty with a brutal father who habitually abused her mother. After her father left, Deborah's mom was battered and sexually abused by a series of boyfriends. As you may recall, Deborah told me "I seen violence my whole life Annee, it doesn't hardly affect me no more. My pops beat the crap out of my moms since I was a little kid. The only time I got some peace was when he took off. But you know, my moms had other boyfriends since my dad left and most of them beat her too." Deborah added that she had seen so much violence in her life that "it just doesn't bother me no more." Like many of the kids in my research Deborah, who was sixteen, spent her short life observing inexorable cruelty. The prospect of seeing yet another person get shot barely fazed Deborah. In order to survive the prolonged effects of exposure to community and intimate partner violence, Deborah became hardened, intentionally numbing herself to the pain of her surroundings. Yet, Deborah was amazingly resilient and once the domestic violence subsided she rebounded.

When I first met Deborah, her mom, with whom she was very close, had been without a boyfriend for two years. The two of them lived alone together in the Tenderloin, free of intimate partner violence for the first time in both of their lives. Over the course of a year, as I became close with Deborah, she opened up to me about how it felt to live in a violent home, to experience homelessness, and to ultimately persevere.

Deborah: My life has been hella hard. I seen way too much ugliness for a kid. My dad beat my moms ever since I could remember and after he left she got beat by a bunch of different boyfriends. I never got beat though. My moms always protected me. She never let my dad hit me. He would get drunk and just beat on her, but never me. She never let him. I always loved her for that—she protected me. But it was torture living like that, watching my moms get hit all the time. He raped her too. Before we were homeless, when we lived in an apartment, he would drag her into their bedroom and rape her. It was terrifying, especially when he was drunk. I was so angry then. I used to get into all kinds of trouble. I got suspended from school a few times, and I got into drinking and drugs. I started drinking when I was twelve; you know to shut out the pain. I stole shit, got into fights, and ran with a bad crowd. I smoked weed too. I was hella angry. I mouthed off to my teachers and didn't care about anything. After my dad left, things got better for a little while but then my moms would hook up with a new boyfriend and get beat by him. After all the abuse my moms couldn't hardly take no more. Then we got kicked out of our apartment. That was bad, we were so scared we were gonna end up on the street. But we got into a battered women's shelter for a few months and that was really good. The people who worked there were so caring and they didn't make you feel like it was your fault you were there. We both had counselors. I really liked my counselor; she was so kind. Plus, there were other kids and moms to talk to who went through the same things as us. It was really safe there and I felt less angry and stressed out. After we left the shelter we got a room in a hotel, not the one we live in now, and stayed there for a month then we got kicked out. Sometimes they kick you out after a month so they can raise the rent if they want to. Where we live now, they just make us move to a different room, they don't kick us to the curb.[10] Even though we were homeless, things were pretty good for a while. I was going to school, not getting into so much trouble. Then my moms got a new boyfriend. He was nice for a little while and then he started beating the crap out of her too. He made her do sexual things to him that she didn't want to. Sometimes I would sit in the hallway so I didn't have to listen. Once he tried to force himself on me so moms kicked him out but she just kept getting new boyfriends that hit her. I got really angry at my moms. I hated watching her get abused, I hated living like that—it's no way to live. Worrying about being homeless, living with violence, it ain't no way to live Annee. I started getting into trouble again and then I just kind of shut down. I sucked all the pain in and just shut it down. I mean, I'm just a kid, I can't do nothing to stop these guys from wailing on my moms. Her last boyfriend beat her so hard she had to go to the hospital. After she got out we went back to the battered women's shelter. I told my moms that she had to stop hooking up with those losers. I think her counselor helped her figure out why she always had a boy-friend who beat her up. When we left we never went back. My moms hasn't had a boyfriend in two years and I'm so proud of her. Our life is so much better now. Yeah, we are still basically homeless, I mean we have a room in the motel, but you never know when they're gonna kick you to the curb—so that's a little scary. But we're okay for now. It is so much more peaceful at home. We not moving around so much—I hated that. My moms and me we tight, we don't fight and we watch out for each other. I'm doing good in school again. It's not easy, but I'm trying my best. I don't drink or smoke weed no more and I even have a counselor at school who helps me stay out of trouble. She helps me figure out ways to talk about my anger so I don't get into fights. She says I can't keep all that painful stuff inside. I know she's right but sometimes it's hard, it hurts.

But if I don't talk about stuff one day it's gonna explode out of me. Also, talking to you helps a lot Annee, you never act like I deserve this shitty life or my mom is bad for staying with messed-up boyfriends. You always talking about society and inequality, all that stuff you teach. But I get it, I do, we not poor because my moms is lazy or doesn't try hard enough, its society right? It's unfair. I like when we have these conversations; it makes me feel respected. Most people just blame us for the way we live, like we chose to be poor. Who the hell would choose this life?[11] Going to the Beach House helps me too. It gives me stuff to look forward to and it feels good to have fun again—not always be so hard, so angry. Sometimes I even forget we are homeless and just feel joyful.

Over the course of the two years that they lived without familial violence, Deborah attended school consistently, participated in the Beach House and After-School Education Programs, stopped getting into fights, and refrained from abusing drugs and alcohol. Because of the educational deficits she accrued over the years, it was a constant struggle for Deborah to keep up in school. She often got frustrated and would sometimes have inappropriate outbursts of anger. Deborah worked hard to learn how to express her frustration and anger in more socially acceptable ways. Deborah's entire life was spent in poverty surrounded by brutality. Although she was emotionally scarred by her experiences, she was not annihilated by them. Deborah's close relationship with her mother and other supportive adults prevented her from being overtaken by negative life events. Once the familial violence ended, Deborah was able to draw upon these resources and became remarkably resilient. She even developed a sociological critique of the ways in which poverty and domestic violence impacted her life. Deborah's story illustrates the ability to rebound from the effects of witnessing brutalizing violence once it subsides. However, she was only able to maintain her resiliency because her mom refrained from entering into any more romantic partnerships. For kids who live in families where the violence returns, they are often unable to stave off negative risk factors for sustained periods of time.

Olivia's story is reflective of kids' inability to avoid problematic behavior and remain optimistic when the familial violence that had previously subsided returns. I met Olivia and her mom early in my field work. I spent several years getting to know both of them. In fact, Olivia was one of the kids I became closest to. As you may recall from chapter 3, when I first met Olivia's mom Marta, her husband Ricardo was incarcerated. Marta and Oliva had been homeless for several years, moving between shelters and residential motels throughout the city. After several months at Home Away, Marta began a training program at a vocational school and her daughter Olivia was reenrolled in school after a two-year absence. They were both doing extremely well. Marta was complying with all her TANF requirements and was succeeding in her training program. Olivia was doing exceptionally well in school and in her interpersonal life. Olivia was fourteen and was in the eighth grade. Despite having missed two years of school, Olivia quickly caught up. Her math skills were particularly astounding. She had no problem doing eighth-grade algebra, which was, embarrassingly, well beyond my comprehension. Her writing skills were a little rusty, but she worked hard and was making good progress. Olivia was well-liked by her teachers and by her fellow students. She spent a lot of time at the Club House and never missed her weekly Beach House trip. Olivia often took a leadership role at the Beach House and helped keep an eye on the younger kids. She especially loved to help with the cooking. When the After-School Education Program started she was an enthusiastic participant. Olivia was doing so well academically that Sarah, the Volunteer Coordinator, and I started looking into the possibility of her attending Lowell High School. [12] She was also making friends at school and became very close to an affluent classmate from the upscale Marina District. She spent a lot of time with her new friend Melissa and her family. Melissa's parents were extremely kind to Olivia, inviting her over for dinner and taking her with them on family outings. Olivia, who was always low-key, seemed much more upbeat and optimistic about her life. Despite living in a residential motel, Olivia began to once again experience the joy of being a free-spirited kid. She told me:

> Olivia: Things have been so good lately. I love being back in school and I am so much happier now. I don't have that weight on me I used to feel. My mom is going to school also, and she is doing really well. When my dad lived with us he beat the shit out of her all the time. It was brutal. I tried to stop him but he was too strong and threatened to beat me if I got between them. I hate him so much. He and my mom would do drugs all the time—I just checked out. I stopped going to school and couldn't deal with anything. I got so depressed I could barely get out of bed. It sucks being poor and it sucks being homeless. Every day is a freakin' struggle. There's just too much violence, too much pain. But it got better when my father left. I hate to say it, but I'm actually glad he's in prison. When he got arrested for dealing, it was the second time, so he got a longer sentence. Since he left, my mom has gotten clean and she's going to school to be a health care worker. We are both doing really good. I was a little scared to go back to school. When we were homeless and moving around the city all the time, I missed two years of school. I wasn't sure if I'd be able to catch up. I didn't want everyone to think I'm dumb, I'm not. I just missed so much school. I was kind of surprised when I went back and it wasn't as hard as I thought. I am doing great in math but writing is a little harder. I am getting tutored and that helps a lot. Plus Melissa helps me sometimes. She's my new friend. She is hella awesome. I go to her house

all the time now. Her family is really nice to me, they take me out with them to dinner, movies, and other family stuff. I never really had a family like that—they love each other and are so nice to each other. Her dad is hella respectful to her mom, not like how I grew up. It feels good to be around them. I wish my family was normal. At least for now things are good. I love going to school and the Beach House. It is so much fun to jump around in the water, ride bikes, and play games with the little kids. I love to cook for the kids. They are really cute and I can totally relate to how shitty their lives are. I try to be a good role model for them. Show them they can be good kids and go to school even though they are in shelters and foster care and stuff. I try to give them advice on how to deal with the bad shit in their lives. It makes me feel good to help them to show them they can survive. To not give up.

After a year of peaceful living, Oliva's father Ricardo was released on parole and moved back into the residential motel with Marta and Olivia. Immediately upon Ricardo's return, the domestic violence resumed. Ricardo forced Marta to start using drugs again and forced her to drop out of school. Ricardo began systematically abusing Marta. As the violence against Marta increased, Olivia became unglued. She became depressed and stopped going to school again. She would hang out all day in the city to avoid her parents. She kept coming to the Club House in the late afternoon but stopped coming to the After-School Education Program. Olivia was noticeably sullen and depressed. When I talked to her about how well she was doing and encouraged her to go back to school, she said, "I'm only a kid Annee, I just can't take anymore!" This was among the saddest days I spent at Home Away. Olivia had become so optimistic, and if she could just keep it together, she had a potentially bright future. Even in her darkest days, when I first met Olivia, she was adamant about not doing drugs or getting pregnant. She told me in no uncertain terms that she was not going to make her bleak life worse by becoming a teenage mother. In order to ensure that she would not get pregnant she refrained from having sex. She was not going to take a chance. Olivia didn't do drugs either, as she saw how it destroyed her parents' lives. When she started to excel at school everyone at Home Away was thrilled and did what we could to support her. However, once her father returned and the violence in her home resumed, she was doomed. She simply could "not take it anymore!" The violence was extreme and it frightened Oliva. Watching her mother descend back into drug abuse was devastating. Oliva could not sleep, was extremely anxious, and ultimately became utterly despondent. She was embarrassed about her family situation so she distanced herself from Melissa. Melissa's mom reached out to her, but Oliva was simply too humiliated to accept her help. When I asked Olivia about what it meant to have her abusive father back home and the impact it had on her, she told me:

Olivia: I just can't catch a break. I should have known better then to think me and my mom could be happy. Every time she gets her shit together somehow my father ruins everything. I wish he would go back to prison, then we'd have some peace again. But he always comes back. He's so filled with rage. I'm terrified of him. I wish I had a dad like Melissa. He loves his family. He doesn't beat his wife. Why couldn't I have a father like that? Parents aren't supposed to fight like that, with so much violence. I can't take it anymore. I just can't take it anymore. What's the point of going to school or getting out of bed? It's useless to even try to have a better life; it's never going to happen. My father will just keep showing up and beating my mother until she's dead. I got nothing to look forward to. My life sucks. I really just can't take it anymore. Sometimes I just want to die.

Oliva's story illustrates that despite being resilient enough to overcome family violence when it stops, once it resumes, kids simply cannot cope and often return to self-destructive behavior. In Olivia's case that meant dropping out of school and becoming withdrawn and utterly hopeless. Although Olivia did not engage in high-risk behavior like indiscriminate sexuality, lawbreaking, substance abuse, or violence, her response nonetheless had significant negative ramifications for her future. Dropping out of school and becoming mired in despair prevented Olivia from potentially overcoming her social structural location and from experiencing a life with even fleeting moments of joy. As bad as things were for Oliva, for the kids who were physically and sexually abused, life was a horror show.

ABANDON ALL HOPE: EXPERIENCING FAMILY VIOLENCE[13]

Kids who were physically and sexually abused had the most significant and profound problems coping with their lives. These kids were primarily from families with mothers who were tyrannized by extreme lifelong violence. These women were so physically and emotionally battered that they could barely function. As a result, these families cycled in and out of homelessness more frequently and had more sustained periods of homelessness than other families. Although they no longer lived with their victimizers, by the time I met these kids they had suffered from relentless brutality.[14] As the research indicates, kids who are physically and sexually abused, exposed to substance abuse, and whose mothers have high rates of mental distress, suffer from significant risk factors and are often profoundly damaged. In addition to emotional and behavioral problems, abused kids are often plagued by delayed adaptive functioning and impaired intellectual achievement (Huntington, Buckner, and Bassuk 2008; Gewirtz and Edleson 2007). These risk factors were common among the kids in my sample who were terrorized by emotional, physical, and sexual abuse.

One beautiful spring day I drove a group of kids to a baseball field to play softball. This particular group came from chronically impoverished families and grew up in violent neighborhoods with deplorable living conditions. In addition, some of the kids were viciously beaten by one or both of their parents. Most of the kids had cycled in and out of homelessness numerous times. As we were getting out of the mini-van, one of the boys, a ten-year-old African American named Lamar, accidently slammed my head in the sliding side door. As the door crashed against my head and I stumbled backward in a daze, Lamar freaked out. He dropped to the ground, grabbed his head, and curled up in the fetal position. He was whimpering and kept repeating "I'm sorry," "I'm so sorry," "I'm sorry," over and over again. Some of the kids looked terrified while others giggled. In order not to further traumatize them, I grabbed my head, started stumbling around, and said "Who am I? Where am I? What am I?" It was an old routine from the *Three Stooges* or some other silly movie culled from the recesses of my memory. As I lumbered about, I started laughing. The relief on the Lamar's face was palpable. He was obviously terrified. After I assured him that I knew it was an accident and that I was all right, I asked him why he was so upset. He told me that "whenever I fucked up, my dad beat the shit out of me. I thought I was going to get beat." When I asked him if he thought I would actually hit him he said, "no Annee, I know you'd never hit me. You cool. But, I just reacted, like out of fear from all the beatings he used to give me, you know, without thinking. That's one reason me and my moms left." Another kid who knew Lamar from the neighborhood said that Lamar's dad was "scary as shit." As we started talking about why some kids seemed frightened, and others were amused, it became clear that the kids from abusive families unconsciously expected a violent reprisal. For kids who witnessed family violence or were themselves brutalized, the event triggered their justifiable fear of being physically punished. When I asked the kids why they thought they would get in trouble when it was Lamar who slammed my head in the door, two kids told me that they often got punished for simply being in the room when their siblings misbehaved. Moisés, a sixteen-year-old Latino told me that "before my dad left he used to beat me just for being in the room when my brother got in trouble." Similarly, Laila, a fifteen-year-old African American girl said "Yeah, even when we didn't do nothing wrong if we were close by when there was trouble we got beat too." Her brother Joshua concurred "damn right." When I asked Moisés and Laila why they thought their parents punished them for their siblings' behavior they both indicated that their parents were angry and violent people. Laila said "my mom is so fucking angry all the time. She hates us kids and is just mean. She's had a shitty life and she takes it out on me and Joshua. When I was little and she got high she used to whip me and Joshua with a belt. She beat us our whole lives, that's why we're in foster care now." Joshua, Laila's thirteen-year-old brother, added "as much as I hate my foster family, at least we don't get beat anymore." Moisés agreed and said, "the best thing that ever happened to us was the day my father took off. He was an angry mother-fucker who beat us kids and my mom. It seemed like he enjoyed it."

The remaining kids in the group were not surprised by these stories, as they all lived in similar neighborhoods and many of their friends came from abusive homes. However, Stevie, Xavier, Mateo, and Sydney all had supportive caregivers and extended family network members throughout San Francisco that provided them with emotional support. Therefore, when my head got slammed in the car door, there was no past trauma to trigger a terrified response. In fact, once they realized I was okay, they all started laughing; the way we all laugh when someone falls and is not hurt. Despite the pounding headache and bump on my head, even I had to admit that it was pretty hilarious. So, after calming down Lamar, Moisés, Laila, and Joshua we went off to play softball. Ironically, despite everyone looking forward to the game all week, within fifteen minutes it descended into chaos. Stevie, Sydney Xavier, and Mateo took their positions on the ballfield, ready to rock and roll. However, it quickly became clear that Lamar, Laila, Moisés, and Joshua were incapable of controlling their behavior long enough to actually play the game. The four of them began running around, getting into arguments, and erupting into explosive outbursts of anger-fueled behavior. The smallest perceived slight, a missed pitch, or a poorly thrown ball resulted in threats of violence. We spent the entire game trying to calm them down and enjoy a lovely day of softball. Unfortunately, Lamar, Moisés, Laila, and Joshua simply couldn't control themselves enough to play an organized sport. The more out-of-control they acted, the more frustrated they became with their own behavior. Lamar, Moisés, Laila, and Joshua wanted to enjoy the game but they couldn't prevent themselves from acting out. This behavior was typical of the kids who were the most severely abused. Stevie, Sydney, Xavier, and Mateo were infinitely patient, but eventually became totally frustrated and gave up trying to play. Sydney, a sweet fourteen-year-old African American girl, summed up the experience when she said, "Looks like we're not playing softball today after all. Too bad, I was looking forward to it all week. Oh well, it's not that surprising this stuff happens all the time. Those kids are hella messed up. They can't seem to stop themselves from getting into trouble; they're so hotheaded. But who wouldn't be given their messed up lives? They got the worst families. Yeah, we're all homeless but they got drugged-out crazy parents and hella violence too." Ultimately, we all went home feeling a little sadder for Lamar, Moisés, Laila, and Joshua and disappointed that the day was ruined. On the surface this story seems fairly benign. However, it is indicative of the uncontrollable rage many of the most violated kids feel. Even the simplest pleasure is undermined by their inability to stay focused and just have fun. This type of behavior, so common among these kids, gets them in trouble in school, at the shelters, with case workers, and with law enforcement.

More disturbing are the actual experiences of sexual and physical exploitation these kids have been forced to endure. To provide insight into the kids' behavior and the meanings they ascribe to their abuse, I will present a conversation from an impromptu focus group that emerged one day when some of the girls opened up to me about their mistreatment. However, I am not going to provide details of the physical and sexual abuse they suffered at the hands of adults or foster siblings. In earlier chapters I provide vivid details of their mothers' sexual and physical abuse; but these are kids and I do not want to exploit them further. The point of presenting their voices is not to provide the prurient details of their exploitation, but rather, to illustrate the impact violence and sexual degradation has had on them. Shannon, Barb's fourteen-year-old daughter; Destiny, Jalesa's thirteen-year-old daughter; and Mia, Rochelle's sixteen-year-old daughter, poignantly expressed the excruciating realities of their lives:

Mia: You know us really well Annee. We don't have to tell you how messed up our families are. Our mothers have all been through it and so have we. We've all been beat up, we've all been molested, and when our mothers were too out of it to take care of us we were ignored and left to take care of ourselves and our younger brothers and sisters. When they get sick we have to take care of them. My brother has bad asthma. When he has an asthma attack, I'm the one who has to make sure he's okay and can breathe. If he needs to go to the hospital it's up to me to call. If he suffocates it's my fault. We all had to grow up real fast.

Shannon: You have to grow up fast to protect yourself. It's sad, you can't count on anyone to take care of you—not even your own parents. My mom, you know sometimes she works the streets. My brother Justin doesn't understand why she is out all night. He doesn't know what she does and I try to protect him from that. He's still kind of innocent. No one protected me. I knew she was a prostitute when I was twelve—I never got to be innocent.

Destiny: My mom works the streets sometimes too. She is so beaten down you can see it in her face. Her whole life has been violent and horrible and so has mine. You know they took my brother Zion away from her when he was little. When my mom was a kid she was in foster care. She said it was really bad. But she did the same thing to Zion. She was so high all the time they took him away and put him in foster care. I haven't seen him since I was real little. I wouldn't even know him if I saw him on the street. How messed up is that? All the bad stuff that happened to my mom, it is really sad, but now it's happening to me. Like Shannon says, I try to protect Malik, he's only nine—but I'm a kid too, I'm only thirteen. How am I supposed to protect anyone?

Mia: We never really got to be kids. We had to always be on the lookout to make sure we didn't get beat or worse. You had to be on your best behavior or some drunken boyfriend would take his rage out on you—or he would do sick sexual things to you. My mother's last boyfriend Gus used to beat and rape her and when he got bored with her he started to do it to me. We all lived through it and it fucked us up. The three of us, we struggle just to get through every day. Our lives are painful and no one seems to care. No one does anything about it. We keep getting into trouble all the time but no one understands why. I mean, it's hard to go to school and stay out of trouble when you are in so much pain. Our lives hurt!

Shannon: Mia's right. I always got in trouble in school, since I was in like third grade. I had trouble reading and every year I got more and more behind. My mom couldn't really help and the teachers just got sick of me asking questions all the time. Like I was doing it just to annoy them. I always felt stupid and after a while didn't want to participate. If the teacher would ask me to read I would throw a tantrum—I would actually start crying and kicking my feet—I actually threw tantrums in school! I think it was because I didn't want anyone to make fun of me or think I was dumb. I got sent to the principal's office all the time. When I was in sixth grade my teacher told me that she heard I was trouble and I better behave. So of course I acted even worse. Then I started smoking cigarettes and drinking after school. By the time I got to eighth grade I was smoking weed and drinking every day. I started shoplifting too. I got caught a couple of times and had to go to court. That scared me so I stopped. When I went to high school, things got worse. I only went for half the year. I was so angry all the time I wanted to kick everyone's ass. I kept getting into fights and I got suspended a few times. Then I just stopped going. The school didn't care and since we moved around so much they didn't know where to find me—not that they actually looked. They were probably happy to get rid of me.

Destiny: I get into fights at school too. I can't help it. I try to be good but I just get so angry sometimes I can't stop myself. I wish I could stay out of trouble but I talk back to my teachers, I pick fights with other kids. I don't know how to stop and no one helps me. I just get punished for being bad but I never get any help for how I've been treated, for the violence in my life. I get so sad sometimes I just want to sleep, to stop the pain I feel. I don't want to live like this anymore. Sometimes I just want to die.

Mia: Yeah, we really do have shitty lives. I got kicked out of school for cutting class and getting into fights. I got sent to the "alternative" school. You know, the one for poor black and Hispanic kids—where they send the throwaways—the kids no one wants. The teachers, they pretend like they are trying to help you but we all knew why we were there—we were the kids no one wanted to deal with. Our teachers were afraid of us and didn't want us to disrupt their classrooms. So, they sent us away. No one ever bothered to find out about my life, about why I was always in trouble. That I was raped, that I was beaten—they just didn't give shit. Who wouldn't be angry? Who wouldn't take drugs? Who wouldn't feel worthless? Who wouldn't fuck any boy who asks? Of course I do drugs and sleep around. Of course I steal shit. Sometimes I sell drugs to pay for stuff. If my mom doesn't have enough money for rent or food, what else can I do? Of course I'm depressed. What do I have to look forward to? I've been poor and homeless my whole life. I've been surrounded by violence everywhere I've lived. I'm only sixteen and I've been beaten and raped over and over again. Who wouldn't be a fuck up with a life like that? All we want is someone to help us, but no one ever does.

Not surprisingly, these girls and their peers who have also been viciously abused have the most miserable lives imaginable. They all struggled with mental health problems and had significant adaptive and educational deficits. Like Mia and Shannon, many kids who are physically and sexually debased never graduate from high school. Sexually, exploited girls are often filled with uncontrollable rage, get into fights, engage in criminality, abuse drugs and alcohol, and participate in unrestrained sexual behavior. All of these risk factors conspire to make their bleak lives even worse. Lacking a solid educational foundation is a barrier to employment and is a common precursor to a lifelong struggle for economic survival and reliance on the welfare state. Drug abuse, fighting, truancy, and minor criminality often precipitate introduction to the juvenile justice system and ultimately to the adult criminal justice system. Indiscriminate sexuality can cause emotional harm, sexually transmitted infections, and unwanted pregnancies. In addition, given the lack of self-worth often associated with sexual abuse (Gilfus, 2006), many young women will reproduce the behavior patterns of their mothers and also end up in violent, degrading relationships. For Mia, Shannon, Destiny, and girls like them throughout the United States, who have been brutally violated, and who continue to cycle in and out of homelessness, it is not unreasonable to think that they too might be forced to resort to prostitution to survive.

PARADISE LOST

The narratives presented throughout this chapter provide insight into how kids make sense of being impoverished, homeless, and maltreated. It is essential to deconstruct the perspectives of homeless kids to truly understand the profundity of their experience. Kids are remarkably self-reflexive and many of them articulate insightful analyses of social structural inequality. Kids are not passive receptacles of culture or of their social location. Rather, they are active agents in their own lives. Nonetheless, impoverished kids under eighteen are the most disenfranchised individuals in our society. They have no power and are at the mercy of adults who don't seem able or willing to rescue them from the wretched conditions of their lives. They are surrounded by violence, misery, and the degradation of poverty. The choices impoverished girls and boys make often seem irrational and self-destructive to members of the larger society. However, these choices are actually extremely rational given their life experiences and limited opportunities. For example, it makes perfect sense to misbehave in class rather than be publicly humiliated for being unable to read. It is totally logical to sell drugs to make money to pay for food or rent. For the most oppressed and damaged kids, their choices are also limited by their inability to control their behavior. Kids who were physically and sexually abused often developed maladaptive responses to life events. It was heartbreaking to see otherwise sweet, good-hearted kids getting into trouble over and over again because they didn't have effective coping mechanisms to draw upon. These kids desperately wanted to behave but were so damaged that they simply couldn't. It should now be clear how race, class, and gender are impacted by organizational inequality and the social structural arrangements that oppress these kids. The realities of the kids' race, class, gender, and age influence their daily experiences and shape subsequent life events that will inevitably mire them in poverty. Educational inequality, deplorable housing conditions, community and interpersonal violence, and racialized and gendered stereotypes all contribute to the reproduction of the kids' poverty. Like their mothers, many of these girls will end up in violent relationships and some will be forced to use their sexuality as a tool for survival. For the boys, the school-to-prison pipeline will lead to early involvement in the juvenile justice system and ultimately to the adult criminal justice system, where many of them will end up in prison (Mallett 2016; Meiners 2010).[15] For both boys and girls, their lives are constrained by their social structural location and a society unwilling to eradicate the causes of their oppression. As Bassuk DeCandia, Beach, and Berman (2014, 10) articulate, "Children experiencing homelessness are among the most invisible and neglected individuals in our nation."

NOTES

1. Although Paradise Lost refers to John Milton's epic poem, it has double meaning in this context where I continue the metaphor of *Dante's Inferno* begun in chapter 2. *Paradiso* (paradise) is the third and final part of Dante's *Divine Comedy*. Allegorically, paradise represents the state of innocence that existed before Adam and Eve fell from grace and is the place where the protagonist is redeemed.

2. I typically use the term "kids" instead of "children" because it is the colloquial term that homeless kids in San Francisco use to refer to themselves regardless of their age. I do sometimes use the term "children" when presenting other research or to improve the flow of my writing. For a more detailed explanation of Thorne's (1993) use of the term "kids," see Roschelle and Kaufman, 2004.

3. Limbo is the first Circle of Hell in *Dante's Inferno* and the place where the guiltless damned are punished by living in an imperfect form of Heaven. "Sitting in Limbo" is also the title of a Jimmy Cliff song.

4. It is true that there was a large population of street homeless in the Haight, but that was also common in many neighborhoods throughout San Francisco.

5. According to U.S. Department of Labor statistics, in 1996 and 1997 approximately 21 percent of the population, or 75 million people, were classified as the working poor. The working poor are defined as individuals who spent at least twenty-seven weeks in the labor force working (or looking for work) but whose income fell below the official poverty threshold (U.S. Department of Labor 1999). Although by 1997 Pamela was no longer working and was on disability, her previous low-wage jobs meant that for most of their lives, the family was in fact living below the poverty line.

6. Anger, the Fifth Circle of Hell, is the swampy waters of the river Styx. The enraged fight each other on the surface while the morose are stuck beneath the roiling water and are withdrawn into a murky sullenness, devoid of joy.

7. Deep East Oakland extends roughly from High Street to the San Leandro border and south to the Airport and north to 580 and Highway 13.

8. Fruitvale runs south from Foothill Blvd to 880 and east from Fruitvale to 35th Avenue.

9. The Ninth Circle of Hell is treachery. Among other things, treachery reflects the betrayal of family and community ties. Traitors are encased in a frozen lake of ice, unable to escape.

10. At the time, San Francisco had strict rent control laws that made tenants eligible for rent control after residing in a dwelling for a month. Many of the residential motels and SROs kicked the tenants out every month to avoid being effected by rent control. Some hotels allowed tenants to play "musical chairs" and switch rooms within the same hotel each month as long as they registered under a different name. Despite relinquishing their right to rent control, the residents happily agreed to this arrangement because it meant that they wouldn't be evicted every month.

11. Throughout my fieldwork, I spent countless hours hanging out and talking with the kids. Regardless of what cognitive or developmental deficits they had, the older kids (aged 12–18) typically had some comprehension of social structural inequality and the effect it had on their lives. Although the language they used to articulate their critique was not sophisticated, they clearly had an understanding of macro-level forces at work. The kids were sick of hearing adults blame their parents for their poverty and took pride in articulating their sociological imaginations.

12. Lowell High School is one of the best public schools in San Francisco. It is a public magnet school run by the San Francisco Unified School District. Students must apply to attend Lowell but it is free to accepted residents of the city. According to the school's website, "Admission to Lowell is competitive and merit-based, serving students from throughout the city who demonstrate academic excellence and are motivated to pursue a rigorous college preparatory program. "

13. "Abandon All Hope, Ye Who Enters Here" is the inscription above the entrance to Hell in *The Divine Comedy*.

14. Kids who were physically and/or sexually abused who participated in Home Away programs were typically no longer living with their abuser. Many of the women were homeless

because they left abusive men to protect themselves and/or their children. If anyone working or volunteering at Home Away suspected any type of abuse we immediately called Family and Children Services. Although their response was rarely prompt, we were required by law to report any suspected abuse and always did so.

15. The school-to-prison pipeline is a phenomenon that emerged beginning in the 1990s as schools and the juvenile court system became more punitive. Adopting zero tolerance policies, schools, particularly in low-income communities, criminalized acting out in class, truancy, fighting, and other minor offenses. The presence of police and safety officers in schools resulted in increased arrests and juvenile court referrals. Concomitantly, the number of African American and Latino boys who have been expelled from school has skyrocketed. As a result, millions of low-income boys of color have been forced out of public schools, into the juvenile justice system, and eventually into adult prisons. This school-to prison pipeline has contributed significantly to the current mass incarceration crisis in the United States (Mallett 2016). In San Francisco, 60 percent of the inmates in the county jail, most of them men of color, were students in San Francisco schools. Between 2002 and 2009 the suspension rate in the San Francisco Unified School District increased by 152 percent for a total of 4,341 suspensions. Although African American students comprised only one-tenth of the school district, they made up more than half of the expulsions. In an effort to curtail the school-to-prison pipeline, the San Francisco Board of Education mandated that schools find an alternative to suspension and expulsion. In 2009 a Restorative Justice Program was implemented and in the first two years of its inception expulsions fell 28 percent. In addition, non-mandatory referrals for expulsion (those not involving drugs, violence, or sexual assault) were down 60 percent (Smith 2011). In 2014 a policy against using "willful defiance" as a reason for suspension or expulsion was added, further reducing the number of suspensions for African American and Latinix students who continued to be disproportionally suspended. (Frey 2014).

Conclusion

Home Away is really structured to function as a family unit and because of that, the staff really became close with a lot of the families that came to the Club House.—Sarah

REFLECTIONS FROM THE FIELD

I began my research project in fall 1995. I spent my first year in the field doing weekly Beach House trips, hanging out at the Club House, and getting to know the families, the volunteers, Jeanie, Sally, and Jill Minkus, the Administrative Director. I met with case workers, service providers, shelter staff, and a myriad of folks throughout the city working in the poverty industry. As I became more involved in Home Away Jeanie asked my advice on the organizational structure of Home Away, unforeseen problems that emerged, and ideas for new programs. She expressed appreciation for my ability to be both analytical and kind. Jeanie particularly respected how I interacted with family members. The approach I took as a feminist ethnographer and anti-racist activist could not be more suited to Home Away. Jeanie appreciated that I purposefully moved beyond standard vocabularies of women's experiences and deconstructed conventional disciplinary topics to elicit new frames of knowledge. We talked about how the concepts I learned as a sociologist could potentially distort homeless women's experiences, so I crafted my interview questions around what I learned from women in the field rather than from established disciplinary categories (Devault 1999). Jeanie also appreciated my role as an activist-scholar, not a passive observer. I created a dialogic relationship with family members and constructed and reconstructed my field work based on those conversations; what Michael Burawoy (2005) would later refer to as Public Sociology. I let the families set the research agenda. I advocated tirelessly on behalf of San Francisco's homeless kids and their parents fully embracing my role as a scholar-activist. In addition, I worked closely with staff and volunteers to help better organize Home Away programs while maintaining their ethic of fostering creativity and self-determination. Structuring programs while simultaneously encouraging freedom is thorny. Jill and I had many conversations early on about how to be more systematic. We both agreed that the Beach House trips were wonderful but needed to be more organized. To a certain extent, we all flew by the seat of our pants. The following conversation is indicative of the organic way things developed at Home Away:

Jill: We need to be more organized, The Beach House trips are amazing but sometimes the training is totally haphazard. We want the kids to be free and have fun, but there needs to be some rules. Most of the time, we figure out the rules as we go. It is so messy.

Annee: Yeah, I went up with Jeanie on Saturday and as we were getting to the Beach House she stops the car and says "oh by the way, don't let the kids ride their bikes on this road," a road we rode up and down incessantly.

Jill: Or you know, "don't forget to bring the third pizza," or, "that reminds me, you can't go down the big hill," "stay away from that cliff," or "did you get in touch with the art teacher, I think she's coming to work with the kids today." That's how we roll, but it makes me nervous the way things unfold. I'm very structured and organized and Jeanie, she is a bit chaotic. That's why we need someone to help better organize things, to teach the volunteers what Jeanie calls "The Beach House Way" So the kids have fun but are safe.

Annee: I know what you mean. I was trained on the spot when I did the winter camp last year. I was there every day and I watched Jeannie intently so I could learn how she interacts with the kids and the way she does things. By the end of the week she made me a Maypole! I mean really? I was now supervising volunteers and had never worked with kids before and didn't really know what the hell I was doing. Obviously I am super responsible so I think that made Jeanie feel like I would be fine. Of course, at this point I realize that is how Home Away functions; we figure things out as we go, on the fly. Last week one kid climbed up a tree so fast I couldn't stop him. He climbed to the top and once he realized how high he was he was terrified, not as terrified as I was that he might fall. It took us almost an hour to coax him down. Guess what? I made a new rule—no tree climbing! [laughter]

As the first year unfolded, we began making plans for an after-school program. This idea also emerged organically from seeing what the kids needed. It seemed to me that this process was the social service equivalent of grounded theory. As Jill articulated, all of the programs emerged from our observations of what kids and parents needed:

> Well, as is true with just about everything that Home Away gets into, it really grew up from our observations of some of the needs of our kids. We have been noticing that a lot of the kids weren't in school because it's really hard for homeless families, who are going from shelter to motel to car to whatever, wherever they're living, to get their kids in school. There are a lot of barriers in their way. Instability is a big barrier. If they don't know where they're going to be, they don't know if they're going to be in one place long enough to register at the local school. School records are kind of loosey goosey, as Jeannie would say. Their records are lost; the families don't know what grade the kids should be in, how far along they are. A lot of these kids, just because their lives have been so nomadic, are quite behind in terms of their ability to read and write, you know, they don't have basic skills. So we realized that there really needed to be some sort of centralized way which we could help the kids get into school, get them tested so they're placed correctly, see if they have any learning disabilities, find out what grade they should be in, help the parents learn how to work within the school system to get their kids placed, and then also to give them the sort of remedial help they need. Plus, as you know, when we started the Beach House we had planned for there to be a tutorial component. We wanted kids to bring their homework out, get it done and then go play. You can imagine how well that worked! [laughter]. We don't do a lot of homework help with them out at the Beach House. Really, it was a pretty stupid idea to begin with. I mean, we should have known, but definitely within the first month we realized there was just no way. No one can ask a kid to go out to the middle of the Marin Headlands and do their math homework. That's the reason we wanted to start an offsite educational program, cuz the Beach House is—it's just a different thing. It's about exploration, creativity, and fun, not about school work. But during that first month we did notice that a lot of the kids seemed to be way behind and a few of them couldn't read at all. We knew we needed to do something about that.

Over the course of the next year, Jeanie galvanized a group of dynamic people to work together to make the After-School Educational Program a reality. Kay Timmer, a Board Member and appointee to the U.S. Commission on Child and Family Welfare, spearheaded the project along with Paula Minkus, who ran the Telegraph Hill Children's Center. Board Member Deidre English worked alongside Kay and Paula. They applied for grant money and coordinated local stakeholders. They enlisted the help of Gary Beringer, the Executive Director of San Francisco Educational Services, a nonprofit organization that ran the Youth Education Project for low-income high-risk kids in in Hunter's Point. Assemblyman John Burton who had been involved in the project from the beginning and persuaded Brian O'Neil, the Superintendent of the Golden Gate National Recreation Area, to donate the cottage to Home Away participated. Finally, the Superintendent of the San Francisco Unified School District, Bill Rojas, was consulted. The idea was to create a centralized After-School Education Program for homeless kids in San Francisco that did not recreate already existing programs. As the After-School Education Program was being funded and designed, the new Mentorship Program was also evolving. During this time Jill left Home Away for a several-month vacation to India.[1] Before she left, she told me how much she wanted Home Away to become more structured and streamlined. Jill said:

> The After-School Program is going to be a ton of work and we really want to do this up right. We need to hire more people to run the programs we already have and to promote the After-School Program. We need people to go to the shelters and schools to recruit kids and to make sure the kids can get here after school. We need a steady stream of volunteer tutors and we need materials. We've gotten enough grant money to get going, but we need to hire more staff. Plus, I'm leaving for my trip. We need to get things organized before I leave. Can you believe it? I actually wrote a nine-page memo explaining how everything works and what needs to be done for the new hires—so they can structure things better.

When I asked Jill how she felt about leaving after all the work she did systematizing the Beach House trips, working with the kids, and helping to get the After-School Program funded she told me:

> I'm really happy to be taking a trip. I've been sort of—I don't know—not frustrated with the work itself—I still really love the work itself— I love the kids but just the chaos around the Club House has really been getting to me lately. I've been just very frustrated with work and I think this is going to be such a good opportunity to step away and decide what I want to do with the rest of my life. It is so chaotic around the Club House and I think part of that is Jeannie wanting to have a place for these kids and the mom's to come but it's the office and it's kind of not really that appropriate. It gets out of hand. She's really sensitive to how we make the families feel, but it's too chaotic and it really been getting to me lately.

Shortly after this interview, Jill left Home Away for her adventure abroad. Over the course of the next several months three new people were hired. Sarah Kennedy (Watanabe), Wendy Guthrie (Harris), and Indira Culmback (Katan) all joined the staff. Wendy, who was hired as the Administrative Director, was in charge of the budget and wrote all the grants. Sarah was initially hired as the Volunteer Coordinator and at some point became the Beach House Coordinator and Mentor Program Coordinator. Given all the outstanding work she did with these programs, Sarah quickly became the

Program Director and oversaw them all. Indira was hired to run the After-School Educational Program immediately before it opened. I spent the next three years working closely with Sarah, Wendy, and Indira. All three of them were invaluable in solidifying already existing programs, getting the second Beach House cottage up and running, and expanding the new Mentorship and After-School Educational Programs. All three women were exceptionally competent, thoughtful, and embodied the Home Away ethic. Even Wendy, who was a hard core punk, had a soft spot for homeless families. It was my good fortune to work with them and for the three of us to become good friends.

IS A HOME AWAY FROM HOMELESSNESS POSSIBLE?

The problem of familial homelessness is a complex, multidimensional problem. Gentrification and housing policy, labor market conditions, welfare reform, intimate partner violence, institutional and community violence, substance abuse, poor physical and mental health, and educational inequality are all inextricably linked. Chronically poor and homeless individuals spend their lives enduring staggering hardships as a result of their social structural location. As the horrific conditions of their lives accumulate, many become despondent and self-destructive. Some people only see the outcomes of bad choices made by homeless mothers and their children without understanding the precipitating factors that led to those decisions. While it is true that every individual has agency and must take responsibility for their choices, it is also true that every choice a homeless parent or child makes is constrained by poverty and inequality. The degrading experiences recounted by homeless families throughout the book created significant physical and emotional damage. This damage presented unique challenges for Jeanie and the staff at A Home Away From Homelessness. Home Away was always intended to be different from traditional social service agencies. Jeanie's vision was to create a space where children could experience joy, be creative, and momentarily escape the ravages of poverty. She wanted parents to have a supportive place to unburden themselves; to escape the inexorable pain of poverty, to be respected, to feel love. Creating an alternative family rather than an institutionalized service agency is extraordinarily difficult. Jeanie, Sarah, Wendy, Indira, and I spent countless hours discussing how to organize and streamline things while maintaining the essence of Home Away. Creating a balance between safety and freedom, between autonomy and stability, between structure and self-determination among families who are ravaged by years of exploitation is inherently complicated. Sarah articulated this tension best when she opined:

Sarah: Home Away is really structured to function as a family unit and because of that, the staff really became close with a lot of the families that came to the Club House. We didn't really have a lot of boundaries set up and we were dealing with a lot of people who have significant problems. We wanted to trust people and to make them feel comfortable and at home, but there were a lot of really desperate people coming in. We tried to make it a home for people and we didn't really want them to feel like there were a lot of rules and that they were being watched. Family drop-in just sort of evolved out of the programs at Home Away and families that would come here had come to expect this sort of friendship and trust from the staff. We really struggled with how to create rules and boundaries without hurting anyone's feelings or making the place feel like a typical homeless service agency. We didn't want to be another agent of social control. People were free to come and go, to take food from the refrigerator or pantry, to cook meals, and do laundry, and play with their kids. We weren't interested in surveilling people–we wanted them to feel like this was their home. Most of the families who come here are emotionally damaged by the time we see them. Most of them have lived their entire lives in poverty and have dealt with violence and sexual abuse. Some of the mothers and fathers have been incarcerated, have drug and alcohol problems, and sometimes they make bad choices. We wanted them to trust us and stop seeing the world as something they needed to take advantage of to survive. Sally, the House Mom, was such a great model of that. We did have some problems with her in the beginning and there were a lot of trust issues. But now she's, you know, one of the most trustworthy people there is. After fourteen years of welfare and drug abuse and homelessness, she's one of the most valuable assets of Home Away. She's totally turned her life around and, you know, we can trust her with anything. So it is a process and we were sort of willing to take the risks. There were lots of thefts over the years, you know—PlayStations go missing, food is taken, clothing donations disappear—but we just sort of rolled with it and kept going because we didn't want to hurt the families who were trustworthy and didn't take advantage. We didn't want to lay down a bunch of rules because we didn't want to seem accusatory or militant. We wanted this to be their home. There are lots of families that are here for good reasons and not to rip us off and we didn't want to offend them. So we were constantly struggling with how do we set boundaries without turning into just another fascist service agency? Sometimes this didn't work out so well and there were several different things that happened. A big part of the problem was that we only had one working bathroom and it was in between the two offices. Families had to go through the office to get to the bathroom. Also, we had very limited phone lines and families had to come into the office to use the phone and fax machine, or a computer. We let families come and go, thinking we were fostering an environment of trust and trying to bolster self-esteem and all of that went along with it. But, some families took advantage; petty cash was stolen, items went missing, other stuff too.

Annee: Can you give me an example?

Sarah: Yeah. At some point we started getting a lot of calls for people to give donations. We hired one of the fathers to run errands and do other little jobs. One of his duties was to go and pick up the donations from people and bring them to the Club House. He was always very willing to go pick up donations. At some point, Wendy, the Administrative Director, noticed that when the people filled out their receipts for the tax break, the amount that they would put for their donation was far above and beyond the things that we were getting. We eventually realized that he was taking the valuable items and selling them at a pawn shop. We even located which pawn shop to make sure we weren't accusing him of something he didn't do. There was another family in particular that seemed really well intentioned and Home Away is very much about second and third and fourth chances for families. This one father, Morgan had a huge history of theft and other illegal behavior. He'd been incarcerated many times, he openly admitted that he'd made his living by stealing from people, he admitted to using drugs in the past. He explained that he wanted to get a fresh start. He wanted to be responsible, and get married. He wanted to totally do a life makeover and we were giving him his big chance. This is a man, who's like in his mid-forties, almost fifty, probably, and he'd lived a really long life of crime; trying to get away with whatever he could, abusing others, being in and out of jail. We saw it as a big chance to help him get his act together. While he was at the Family Drop-In Center, he met Ruthanne. They started a relationship and they got married. We even had a wedding for them here, in the backyard, overlooking the Bay. It was really beautiful and moving. The staff and volunteers came, lots of families, it really represented what Home Away is supposed to be. And it really did seem like a fresh start for both of them. Ruthanne started working in the office part-time. She needed a lot of training after so many years not working, but we were into mentoring her. In the beginning Morgan was all gung ho and we really started to entrust him with more and more things, but then as he started to get paychecks and have disposable cash, we noticed a decline in his behavior—he would come in really dirty and disheveled and he was very moody, especially with the kids. And we have seen people that have come from a background where, you know, it's all survival of the fittest, get what you can, get in where you can, and live for today. A lot of people that come to Home Away have that mentality and we know that it's a long process; it's going to take time for them to start processing the world differently. What goes along with that is that so many places for homeless families are not consistent. When you're in a shelter, you're there for four months, you get what you can, because in four months, when your time is up, they kick you out and services are suspended, friendships are gone, the relationships your kids have with the counselors and the children's program people, that's all gone. You make strong connections with those people and then you are out and those connections aren't there anymore. Those people disappear from your life. I can really see how families get into that mode of get what you can from who you can while you can because it's not going to be there forever. And Home Away isn't like that but I don't expect people to see it that way because that's just not their reality. So sometimes we were really naive. When Morgan started stealing from us it was pretty devastating. Even though we knew it was a possibility, we really thought he was getting his act together.

Annee: Did you feel that because Home Away wanted to be different from other homeless service agencies that it would be okay to have a lack of structure and not have the same kind of rules? Isn't that part of the philosophy, the ethic of Home Away?

Sarah: Yeah. But like I said, we were really naive. We knew people would take advantage but I think the staff didn't realize how much it would hurt when someone really took advantage of our generosity and really worked us. You know we developed a really close relationship with Morgan and Ruthanne, but it's like they had two sides to their life, the people they wished to be and the people they had been for so long. There was this whole underbelly of the people they were, which is living in extreme poverty, living in transient hotels, not having enough money to pay for rent, eating at Glide [Memorial Church], you know, that whole world. And then, the fact that Home Away tries to really befriend people, it was really hard for us to take when someone would hurt us in that way. Like what happened with the fire.

Annee: Tell me about the fire.

Sarah: It happened on December 28th, just after Christmas. Morgan and Ruthanne were there. Morgan was asleep on the couch. I very seriously suspect that he'd been using drugs for some time. Ruthanne was working in the office with the computer and her kids, who were our main connection to this family. Everyone was just doing their thing, coloring, homework, playing in the backyard, stuff like that. The fire started around two in the afternoon and it started in the back porch area. That's the area where people smoke, where they put out cigarettes, and that's where there are ashes, and matches could have been out there. The fire started in the back area and one of the girls noticed it and ran and told everybody and the family ran out the front door. When they opened the door it created a vacuum and sucked the fire through the house and it was all drywall. Morgan woke up but he didn't go for the fire extinguisher. He went outside and got the hose from the front of the house and tried to stretch it around and put the fire out, which didn't happen. But when the family ran to safety, which is perfectly normal and I'm glad they did, the fire really got sucked through the house because of the wind tunnel that was created. By the time the fire department got there the walls were gone, the house was completely gutted, and the roof and the house was basically destroyed. It was structurally sound but the whole house was destroyed. Morgan and Ruthanne disappeared for the next two days. We couldn't get ahold of them. Ruthanne had a pager that we bought for her and we paged her constantly but she didn't return the calls. We needed to talk to the fire department, we needed to talk to the insurance agents, and she was nowhere to be found. The day after the fire—they did come by briefly. Wendy was photographing the house, and Ruthanne offered Wendy our camcorder. Wendy said no that she didn't need it. Ruthanne had it in her backpack, somewhere in the car, or whatever. And Wendy said that's okay, I don't need it, but then the next day she did need it and she called to ask for it and Morgan told her they didn't have it, that it was destroyed in the fire. It was a thousand-dollar camcorder, brand new, on loan to us. But we knew she had it, we saw it the day before. Also, the fire department went through and there was no sign of it, and them lying, it created this weird tension between us and the family and they got very defensive and were making threatening phone calls. Ruthanne was making threatening phone calls saying "I hate you, fuck you," "fuck your program" to Jeannie. We heard Morgan say "If Jeannie fires me for this she's going to lose more than her Club House," and weird threats like that. They were really just going crazy with the calls and stuff. We were trying to regroup and get things together and they were totally obsessing over the fact that we were accusing them of having the camera. We later located the pawn shop where they sold it. He went back the next day and sold the resale ticket. And the pawn shop owner knew about many, many items that he had sold to him from us. We were missing a lot of computers and stuff like that that we had been storing in another building. That was the last we saw of them but then when we started doing clean-up in the other building, we found that they had stored a lot of their personal items there because they were homeless and living in a hotel. And we found a lot of pornography and a crack pipe and it was just really unnerving to us that he had been spending time there. It seemed as if he'd been living there at times or spending a lot of time there. Open food, that kind of thing, in this weird little nest area upstairs, sort of hidden away. So when we were cleaning we came across a lot of his personal items. The crack pipe was like the scariest thing of all. We'd all suspected that he was maybe using again but nobody really wanted to believe it and we all just gave him the benefit of the doubt. Part of the reason is whenever we confronted the family about the thefts and things that had gone on, Ruthanne got really defensive. And she seemed totally into Home Away. She had told us many times over, "You're the best friends I've ever had," she seemed very religious. And there's a part of me that thinks that she really wanted to live that life but he kind of pulled her down. Her insistence that she was not using and was working hard, she seemed very earnest and really trying to change her life and, I think, he had been lying to her as well, and eventually pulled the whole family down and by then all she could do was sort of defend herself and her family to us but it was way too late.

Annee: Do these experiences make you mistrustful of other families. How do you process these kinds of experiences so you don't become cynical and start seeing the bad in everyone?

Sarah: Well, I'm constantly on that fence. There's the side of me that wants to always be open and fresh to every face that walks through the door, but then there's a side that doesn't want to be a sucker. It goes along with the side that, you know, my heart goes out to every kid but I don't want to get heartbroken with every kid. So I'm constantly balancing and I'm always in check with that. And different people on the staff have, I think, a harder time of it than I do. I'm much more willing to give every person the benefit of the doubt and risk the loss than some other people. Wendy's a little more guarded. Jeannie has really become sort of hardened and it's just not like her. She used to be a lot more trusting of everyone and so willing to see the good. It's not easy. We have had to create more structure more rules over the years. But we always try to do it with the families, to make them part of the changes so they don't feel alienated. We want them to feel at home.

As evidenced by the narratives throughout the book, extremely impoverished families in San Francisco have very few places to go to escape the violence endemic to their lives. Many of these women and children have been significantly damaged by their life experiences. Home Away was the one place they felt loved and cared for. Families were welcome no matter what their circumstances. They came to cook, do laundry, chat with one another, have holiday meals, and even attend a wedding. As an institutional form of social support, Home Away was far superior to most of the traditional social service agencies in San Francisco. Nonetheless, creating an alternative family rather than a regulated service agency is incredibly difficult. Despite our desire to promote autonomy, we did have to implement rules over the years. Families could not reproduce the behavior of the streets at the Club House. Families were expected to adhere to certain policies like not taking food, or clothing back to their neighborhoods, or showing up after hours, or playing the television too loudly. While these rules seem benign, they are still restrictions on behavior; restrictions that would not exist in one's own home. Obviously there was no drinking, drug use, fighting, or stealing allowed on the premises. Although these behaviors are clearly more destructive, people who live in their own homes are free to engage in them whenever they like. As much as we tried to make families feel welcome and provide them with a safe haven from a hostile world, Home Away was not an adequate replacement for a permanent home, nor was it meant to be. Everyone at Home Away understood the profound impact of poverty, racism, and gender inequality on the families we served. We all understood that our programs, no matter how outstanding, could not replace safe and affordable housing, high quality public education, jobs that paid a living wage, or universal health care. Most heartbreaking of all was the realization that no matter how much love and compassion we exuded we could not eradicate the trauma of familial violence and abuse. Subsequently, we did the best we could. For families who were temporarily homeless, we provided the support they needed while they found permanent housing. For homeless kids, we provided desperately needed remedial educational assistance. For chronically homeless kids and their parents, we provided a supportive space to escape the ravages of their lives, even if only momentarily. The answer to the question, is a home away from homelessness possible, is yes, but only momentarily.

THE CITY BY THE BAY REDUX

My intention in writing this book was to make the experiences of homeless women and children visible and to give voice to a marginalized and frequently ignored population. Although San Francisco is a unique city, and I cannot generalize my findings to other regions, the rise in familial homelessness in the Bay Area in the 1990s is analogous to what was happening in metropolises throughout the country at the end of the twentieth century. Now that we are well into the new millennium it makes sense to take a brief look at what is currently happening economically in the San Francisco. Not surprisingly, things have gone from bad to worse, particularly for low-income families. An exhaustive study on poverty in the region by the Silicon Valley Institute for Regional Studies (2015) provides insight into the San Francisco Bay

Area.[2] Using data from 2013, the most recent available, they report that life in San Francisco and its surrounding counties is a struggle for many residents. The poverty rate for the Bay Area was 11.3 percent, with 829,547 people living below the poverty level. Although the poverty rate in the region decreased from the recession peak of 12.5 percent and was lower than for California (17%) and the nation as a whole (15.9%) it was much higher than the historical average of 9 percent. Given that the Bay Area is one the wealthiest regions in the world, such a high rate of poverty is astonishing. The city of San Francisco had the highest poverty rate, with 13.8 percent of the population living below the poverty level. Poverty rates for people of color reflect the stark racialized nature of inequality. In the region, whites make up approximately 41.1 percent of the population yet comprise only 26.8 percent of the poor. In contrast, African Americans make up 6.2 percent of the population but make up 26.8 percent of those living in poverty. Latinixs are 23 percent of the population yet have a poverty rate of 35 percent. Asians who comprise 24.4 percent of the population represent 19.5 percent of the poor (Silicon Valley Institute for Regional Studies 2015). For children and families, the widening gap between rich and poor is truly dire. High rates of poverty among children are typically a result of living with single mothers. About 27 percent of all children in the region live with a female parent and of these 30 percent live in poverty. The overall poverty rate for children in the Bay Area was 13.8 percent, and for kids between five and seventeen, it was 14.7 percent (Silicon Valley Institute for Regional Studies 2015). The percentage of children living below the poverty level in San Francisco between 2010 and 2014 was 9.8 percent for children under six, 11.9 percent for children between six and eleven, and 17.5 percent for children ages twelve to seventeen (San Francisco Health Improvement Partnership 2016). Among individuals with incomes below half the poverty line, 57 percent were women. Among children, who made up one-quarter of the population in California (24.3%), nearly one-third (32.7%) of them lived in deep poverty (Anderson 2015).[3] The number of homeless children in San Francisco continued to rise in the first decade and a half of the new millennium.

The homeless student population nearly tripled over the ten-year period between 2004 and 2014. According to the San Francisco Unified School District, in the 2004–2005 school year there were 844 homeless students compared to 2,352 in the 2013–2014 school year. Since 2010 more than 2,000 students were registered as homeless, peaking in 2014 at 2,094 (Sabatini 2014). Throughout the country, homelessness among children has increased since my data were collected. Nationwide there are 2.5 million children homeless each year, representing one in every thirty children. California is among the worst states when it comes to child poverty and homelessness. The National Center on Family Homelessness ranks states on a scale from one to fifty on four domains of child well-being, with one being the best and fifty being the worst. The overall state composite score includes the extent of childhood homelessness, child well-being, risk for child homelessness, and state policy and planning efforts.[4] For California, the composite score was an appalling forty-eight. These domains are also rated individually. California received a forty-eight for the extent of child homelessness, a thirty-nine on risk for child homelessness, a thirty-one for child well-being, and a forty-nine for state planning and policy (Bassuk, DeCandia, Beach, and Berman 2014). Current San Francisco residents with a graduate or post-graduate degree earn over $80,000 more than those with less than a high school diploma; therefore, it is essential to keep homeless kids in school (Silicon Valley Regional Studies 2019). Overall, the state of California is doing abysmally when it comes to child and familial homelessness.

Poverty rates tell us much about how individuals and children are living in the state, the region, and the city of San Francisco. However, these rates, based on federal guidelines, underestimate the extent of poverty. The method for measuring poverty was developed in the 1960s and has changed very little over time. Federal poverty rates do not account for geographic differences in the cost of living, receipt of non-cash benefits, or the current percentage of income individuals actually spend on housing. The cost of living in the Bay Area is exorbitant compared to other parts of the country. The federal poverty threshold for 2013 ranged from $12,119 for a one-person household to $24,028 for a family of four. However, in San Francisco, rents are 185 percent higher and home prices are 250 percent higher than for the rest of the county. In addition, the cost of goods and services in the city are 6 percent higher than they are nationwide. Accordingly, the poverty rate in the Bay area is probably about three or four percentage points higher than measured by the federal guidelines (Silicon Valley Institute for Regional Studies 2015). Because federal thresholds underestimate rates of poverty, the Stanford University Center on Poverty and Inequality developed a more sophisticated technique for measuring poverty in the state. Based on their California Poverty Measure (CPM), poverty in the Bay Area jumps from 11.7 percent to 19 percent in 2011 (Manfield and Wimer 2011). Another measure of economic hardship is the Self-Sufficiency Standard, which defines the amount of income necessary to meet basic needs without the help of public subsidies or private aid. This measure is more accurate than federal poverty calculations because it takes into account the cost of living and the daily expenses necessary to survive in a specific location. Essentially, this measure represents the proportion of households with incomes that are not high enough to be self-sufficient. For San Francisco, the Self-Sufficiency Standard reveals that 28 percent of families do not earn enough income to be self-sufficient (Silicon Valley Institute for Regional Studies 2015). In fact, according to the California Budget and policy Center (2013) two working adults with two children need $97,696 in household income in San Francisco to make ends meet!

Another yardstick of how difficult it is to live in San Francisco is income inequality. Not surprisingly, research indicates that the Bay Area is characterized by extreme and devastating income inequality. In fact, over the last thirty years income inequality grew faster in the Bay Area than in California and the country. A major factor contributing to this disparity was the rapid growth of extremely high and extremely low income households at the same time that middle-income households were disappearing. The most dramatic increases in income inequality occurred between 1989 and 1999 (during my data collection) and between 1999 and 2007. Although the Great Recession[5] brought about a decline in inequality in the region, the rapid recovery from the recession and the heavy concentration of employment in the high technology sector have once again produced rising levels of inequality. Among the top-earning 5 percent of households in the Bay Area, incomes in 2013 were $150,000 higher than they were for the rest of the nation. In fact, the average income among the top 5 percent of households in the Bay Area was $473,000 which is thirty-one-and-one-half times higher than the average income in the bottom quintile. Finally, average incomes among the highest-earning households in the Bay Area were $149,000 higher than they were nationwide ($489,000 compared to $340,000 nationwide) and the gap between high and low income households was also much wider ($263,000 compared to $178,000 nationwide) (Silicon Valley Institute for Regional Studies 2015b). In fact, the gap between the hourly earnings of California's high- and low-wage workers expanded over the last several years and in 2012 was the widest ever recorded (California Budget and Policy Center 2013). In San Francisco, the inequality ratio, which is the second highest in the nation, grew faster between 2007 and 2012 than in any other city. By 2012, the median income for skilled technology workers exceeded $111,000, while for low-skilled workers it was approximately $27,000 (Berube 2014; Berube and Holmes 2015; Hall 2015).

Exacerbating poverty and income inequality is the cost of housing. Although housing prices and rents plateaued during the Great Recession, they have rebounded with a vengeance. Between 2013 and 2014 San Francisco experienced a 20 percent increase in housing costs, with the median price for a home at just over one million dollars (Katz 2014). In fact, San Francisco had the least affordable home prices in the United States, with only 14 percent of homes being available to middle-class buyers (Jonas 2014). As of the completion of this book, San Francisco had the highest rental rates per square foot in the nation (Silicon Valley Institute for Regional Studies 2019). The recent growth in technology industries, Google, Facebook, Twitter, and Apple, led to unbridled gentrification in some neighborhoods and super-gentrification[6] in others. Super-gentrification in the city is characterized by rising rents, increasing evictions, the redevelopment of luxury condos, and the displacement of numerous nonprofit agencies serving neighborhood communities. Despite strict rent control laws and local legislation meant to prohibit evictions, property owners abused the Ellis Act to remove tenants from their buildings. The Ellis Act is a state law that gives landlords the right to evict tenants to go out of business (Katz 2014). Although the Ellis Act was initially meant to remove rental properties from the market altogether, it has been manipulated to undermine the city's rent control laws. Invoking the Ellis Act, property owners and land speculators converted rent-controlled properties into expensive condominiums and Tenancy-In-Common properties. As a result, low- and middle-income people have been systematically priced out of their own neighborhoods. According to the Anti-Eviction Mapping Project, there was a surge of evictions throughout San Francisco between 1999 and 2014. Specifically, there were a total of 11,766 no-fault evictions, including 3,693 Ellis Act evictions, 6,952 owner move-ins, and 1,121 demolitions. As was the case during my fieldwork, the Mission District was one again hit hard. In 2014, three-bedroom apartments in the Mission started at $4,800 per month and two-bedroom apartments cost between $3,500 and $8,900 a month (Stover 2014). According to the U.S. Census, San Francisco had the highest median rent between 2010 and 2012. As a result of rising rental and home prices, more Latinixs have been displaced from the Mission District. In 2000 Latinixs still made up 60.9 percent of the Inner Mission District but by 2012 they declined to 50 percent. For the broader Mission District the population of Latinixs decreased from 50 percent to 41 percent. At the same time, the white population increased from 47.3 percent in 2000 to 53 percent in 2010 (Jonas 2014). Similar stories of gentrification and super-gentrification are happening throughout San Francisco.

The cost of rent skyrocketed in San Francisco in the new millennium. According to Priceonomics (2014), the overall median rental price for an apartment was $3,600 in 2014. The median price was $2,300 for a studio apartment, $3,120 for a one-bedroom apartment, $4,000 for a two-bedroom apartment, and $4,795 for a three-bedroom apartment. Although rental apartments are becoming more expensive everywhere, the increase is not uniform. Tragically, the neighborhoods in which rents were increasing the fastest were previously the most affordable. For example, between 2011 and 2013 rents increased 46 percent in the Civic Center, 41 percent in the Mission, 39 percent in the Western Addition, 39 percent in the Haight, and 26 percent in the Castro. Even more disturbing is that rents in the cheapest and least desirable neighborhoods also increased substantially. Rents increased by 24 percent in SOMA, by 25 percent in the Tenderloin, and by 11 percent in Bayview Hunters Point (Priceonomics 2014). Except for the Castro, all of these neighborhoods have fairly high numbers of people living below the poverty level. Between 2010 and 2014, the poverty rate for Bayview Hunters Point was 23.5 percent, for the Tenderloin was 28.2 percent, for SOMA was 22.9, for the Western Addition was 14.8 percent, for the Mission was 13.3 percent, and for the Haight was 11.4 percent (San Francisco Heath Improvement Partnership 2016).[7] Most of the families highlighted in the book lived in these neighborhoods and were barely surviving when the rents were beginning to increase. No doubt, the ones who remained in San Francisco were trapped in a never-ending nightmare of residential motels, non-permanent substandard housing, shelters, and ultimately, long-term homelessness.

Further aggravating income inequality and skyrocketing rents was the continued dismantling of the welfare state. In 2009, at the end of the Recession, Congress passed the American Recovery and Reinvestment Act (ARRA), which increased the Supplemental Nutrition Assistance Program (SNAP) benefits by 13.6 percent.[8] This stop-gap measure was intended to help ease the devastating effects of the economic downturn and concomitant food insecurity. However, in 2013, when the economy was more stabilized, benefits were significantly decreased. The overall cuts amounted to $5 billion in 2014 and based on the Congressional Budget Office's projections for food inflation added an additional $6 billion in cuts for 2015 and 2016. These extensive cuts to the SNAP Program caused considerable suffering for participants, including 22 million children living below the poverty level and 10 million children living in deep poverty. The initial cuts were the equivalent of taking away twenty-one meals per month for a family of four, or sixteen meals per month for a family of three. Prior to these cuts, the United States Department of Agriculture (USDA) estimated that in 2009 benefits from the ARRA reduced the number of households in which one or more individuals had to skip a meal or eat less by 500,000. In addition, boosting SNAP benefits during the summer for households with school-aged children who didn't have access to the USDA's summer food program cut very low food security among these households by almost 20 percent. Given the excessive cuts to SNAP and the inadequacy of the current benefit allotments, researchers estimate that the number of poor households that cannot afford sufficient food will significantly increase (Dean and Rosenbaum 2013).

In addition to cuts to the federal SNAP program, California reduced state welfare benefits for poor women and children. During his term as Governor, Arnold Schwarzenegger proposed major changes to CalWORKs sanctions and time limits in an attempt to increase the number of adult recipients who were working. During the time of my field work, state law allowed cash assistance to be provided to children even if their parents had been sanctioned for failing to meet work requirements. Similarly, although the law limited adults to a maximum of five years of cash assistance, their children's eligibility was not limited. In 2009 Governor Schwarzenegger recommended eliminating grants to families of parents who exceeded their five-year limit and were not working an adequate number of hours. He also recommended eliminating a family's welfare grant if adults not working the required number of hours failed to attend a biannual self-sufficiency review. Essentially the proposal aimed to eliminate benefits to the entire family, including children, if the parents were not working enough hours (Danielson and Reed 2009). Although the Governor was unable to implement these changes, he did cut the time limit from five years to four and imposed stricter sanctions. Jerry Brown, the iconic liberal Governor, made even more devastating cuts in his 2012 state budget. He cut Healthy Families, the program that provided health care to 880,000 low-income families and shifted it to the already overburdened Medi-Cal program. In 2012 Medi-Cal provided health services to 3.6 million children whose families had even lower incomes than the recipients of Healthy Families. In addition, he imposed stricter rules on how long adults could spend on CalWORKs, decreasing recipiency from four years to two to meet harsher federal requirements (Buchanan and Lagos 2012). Finally, Brown cut grants by 8 percent, lowering the monthly maximum payment for a family of three from $694 to $638, which was lower than the $663 a family of three received in 1988 (Yamamura 2012). As rents increased, housing stock declined, prices soared, inequality widened, and the social safety net unraveled, disenfranchised families in San Francisco were pushed farther and farther into the margins of society.

RACE, CLASS AND GENDER: THEORIZING THE INTERSECTIONS REDUX

Throughout the book, the experiences of homeless mothers, fathers, and children have been analyzed from the perspective of intersectionality theory. Rather than offer a grand overarching theoretical framework, intersectionality allows for the analysis of the particularities of everyday experience in the context in which it occurs. It should now be clear that race, class, and gender are fundamental organizing principles of society and the way they are structured form the basis of both privilege and oppression. For the elite super-gentrifiers and for homeless families in San Francisco the ways in which race, class, and gender organize social institutions and social structural arrangements profoundly impacts their lived experiences. The narratives contained throughout the book illuminate how socially structured race, class, and gender inequality influences the daily lives of homeless families in San Francisco and how their subsequent experiences are then shaped by race, class, and gender inequality in an interactive process. In addition, it should now be evident that race, class, and gender are shifting categories of oppression and that that homeless families do not react uniformly to social structural constraints. In addition, family members are not simply passive repositories of social structure. Rather, individuals have the ability to intervene in their world and make choices about their actions; they have agency. Throughout the book, homeless men, women, and children, made choices as they attempted to survive in a heartless city. Yet, every attempt to exert their agency was constrained by their social structural location and by their habitus. Clearly, where people are situated in the social hierarchy shapes their perspectives on life. This is not only true for homeless families but for the mostly white middle-class service providers, case managers, and policy makers, who make decisions on their behalf based on their own normative perspectives. Because these normative perspectives shape the social structure which in turn shapes individuals' lives, they have the unintended consequence of reproducing inequality (Alcoff 1994; Anzaldúa 1990; DeVault 1994 Mohanty 1991; Bannerji 1995; Giddens, 1984; Ken 2010; Bourdieu 2003; Bourgeois 1995; Ritzer and Goodman 2004). In San Francisco, individuals' perspectives shaped the structural locations of race, class, and gender and impacted the institutional forces that contributed to their continued formation. The interrelationship between social structural inequality and everyday oppression profoundly impacted the daily lives of homeless families in San Francisco. This interrelationship became appallingly clear when, in March 2019, a group of affluent residents from Rincon Hill, South Beach, Mission Bay, and other neighborhoods calling themselves "Safe Embarcadero for All" created a GoFundMe page to raise money to hire legal counsel to contest the building of a 200-bed Homeless Navigation Center on an Embarcadero parking lot. In less than a month the anti-homeless group raised over one hundred thousand dollars (Fracassa 2019). Although this center is not intended for homeless families, the vitriol with which San Francisco residents greeted the proposal provides insight into the ways in which homeless residents are demonized and subsequently marginalized. By giving voice to their lived experiences and refraining from homogenizing those experiences, readers should have a more sophisticated and visceral understanding of the ways race, class, and gender function in the City by the Bay.

NOTES

1. When Jill returned to the United States, she did not come back to Home Away.
2. The Bay Area includes Alameda, Contra Costa, Marin, Napa, San Francisco (city and county), San Mateo, Santa Clara, and Solano counties.
3. Deep poverty is defined as those with cash income below half the official poverty threshold, and is associated with higher levels of maternal food insecurity, and longer spells of poverty (Schaefel, Mattingly, and Edin 2018). For a family of three, deep poverty is defined as struggling to survive on less than $200.00 per week (Edin and Schaefer 2015).
4. The extent of child homelessness is the number of homeless children in the state. Measures of child well-being include health problems (one or more chronic conditions, asthma, ADD/ADHD), food insecurity, and educational proficiency in reading and math. Risk for child homelessness includes home foreclosures, percentage of children in poverty, percentage with-

out health insurance, percentage of teenage-headed households, birth rate per 1,000 teens, state minimum wage, and income needed for a two-bedroom apartment. State policy and planning include housing units for homeless families (emergency shelter, transitional housing, permanent supportive housing), whether or not there is an active Interagency Council on Homelessness, and a state plan that includes children and families.

5. According to the Stanford Center for the Study of Poverty and Inequality (2011), the Great Recession lasted from December 2007 through June 2009 (Wimer and Guo, 2011).

6. Super-gentrification is a term that refers to intensified regentrification in cities that have substantial increases in investment and conspicuous consumption by a new generation of super-rich financiers who are subsidized by fortunes from global finance and corporate service industries and, in the case of San Francisco, the technology industry. This latest resurgence of gentrification is different from previous urban revitalization when middle-class residents moved in and displaced the working class residents, artists, and activists. In this round of regentrification in San Francisco, those original gentrifiers are now being displaced by wealthy and super-rich employees of the technology industry (Lees 2003).

7. Rents for apartments in some of the most impoverished neighborhoods for 2014 were as follows: In Bayview Hunters Point a one-bedroom was $1,425, a two-bedroom was $2,650 and a three-bedroom was $3,500. In the Tenderloin a one-bedroom was $1,595, a two-bedroom was $1,605, and a three-bedroom was $3,395. In the Western Addition a studio was $1,725, a one-bedroom was $2,400, a two-bedroom was $3,400, and a three-bedroom was $3,950. In SOMA (where Barb was forced to prostitute herself) a studio was $2,197, a one-bedroom was $3,359, a two-bedroom was $4,800, and a three-bedroom was $6,999 (Priceonomics 2014).

8. SNAP was previously referred to as the Food Stamp Program.

References

Alcoff, Linda. 1994. "The Problem of Speaking for Others." In *Feminist Nightmares Women at Odds: Feminism and the Problem of Sisterhood,* edited by Susan Ostrov Weisser and Jennifer Fleischner, 285–309. New York: New York University Press.

Alejandrino, Simon Velasquez. 2000. "Gentrification in San Francisco's Mission District: Indicators and Policy Recommendations." *Mission Economic Development Association Report,* summer 2000, 17–18.

Allen, Walter. 1979. "Class Culture and Family Organization: The Effects of Class and Race on Family Structure in Urban America." *Journal of Comparative Family Studies* 10 (3): 301–313.

Almaguer, Tomás. (1994). *Racial Fault Lines: The Historical Origins of White Supremacy in California.* Berkeley: University of California Press.

Anderson, Elijah. 1999. *Code of the Street: Decency, Violence, and the Moral Life of the Inner City.* New York: W.W. Norton & Company.

Anderson, Alissa. 2015. *Five Facts Everyone Should Know About Deep Poverty.* Sacramento, CA: California Budget and Policy Center. http://calbudgetcenter.org/wp-content/uploads/Five-Facts-Everyone-Should-Know-About-Deep-Poverty_Issue-Brief_06.05.2015.pdf.

Anderson, Margaret L. 1992. *Race, Class, and Gender: An Anthology.* California: Wadsworth Publishing Company.

Andrade, Sally J. 1982. "Family Roles of Hispanic Women: Stereotypes, Empirical Findings, and Implications for Research." In *Work, Family, and Health: Latina Women in Transition,* edited by Ruth E. Zambrana, 95–106. New York: Hispanic Research Center, Fordham University.

Anooshian, Linda A. 2005. "Violence and Aggression in the Lives of Homeless Children." *Journal of Family Violence* 20 (6): 373–87.

Anzaldúa, Gloria, ed. 1990. *Making Faces, Making Souls/Haciendo Caras: Creative and Critical Perspectives by Women of Color.* San Francisco: Aunt Lute Books.

Arnold, Kathleen R. 2004. *Homelessness, Citizenship, and Identity: The Uncanniness of Late Modernity.* Albany: State University of New York Press.

Arrighi, Barbara A. 1997. *America's Shame: Women and Children in Shelter and the Degradation of Family Roles.* Westport, CT: Praeger.

Atkinson, Paul. 1990. *The Ethnographic Imagination: Textual Construction of Reality.* New York: Routledge.

Baker, Charlene K., Sarah L. Cook, and Fran N. Norris. 2003. "Domestic Violence and Housing Problems: A Contextual Analysis of Women's Help-seeking, Received Informal Support, and Formal System Response." *Violence Against Women* 9: 754–83.

Bane, Mary Jo, and David T. Ellwood. 1994. *Welfare Realities: From Rhetoric to Reform.* Cambridge: Harvard University Press.

Bannerji, Himani. 1995. *Thinking Through: Essays on Feminism, Marxism, and Anti-Racism.* Toronto: Women's Press.

Bassuk, Ellen L. 1986. "Homeless Families: Single Mothers and Their Children in Boston Shelters." In *The Mental Health Needs of Homeless Persons*, edited by E.L. Bassuk, 45–54. San Francisco: Josey Bass.

Bassuk, Ellen L. 2010. "Ending Child Homelessness in America." *The American Journal of Orthopsychiatry* 80 (4): 496–504.

Bassuk, Ellen L., Carmela J. DeCandia, Corey Anne Beach, and Fred Berman. 2014. *America's Youngest Outcasts: A Report Card on Child Homelessness.* Waltham, MA: The National Center on Family Homelessness.

Bassuk, Ellen L., and Ellen M. Gallagher. 1990. "The Impact of Homelessness on Children." *Child and Youth Services* 14 (1):19–33.

Bassuk, Ellen L., Molly K. Richard, and Alexander Tsertsvadze. 2015. "The Prevalence of Mental Illness in Homeless Children: A Systematic Review and Meta-Analysis." *Journal of the American Academy of Child & Adolescent Psychiatry* 54 (2): 86–96.

Bassuk, Ellen L., Linda F Weinreb, John C. Buckner, Angela Browne, Amy Salomon, and Shari S. Bassuk. 1996. "The Characteristics and Needs of Sheltered, Homeless, and Low-Income Housed Mothers." *JAMA* 276 (8): 640–46.

Bermúdez, María E. 1955. *La vida familiar del Mexican.* Mexico City: Robredo.

Blea, Irene I. 1992. *La Chicana and the Intersection of Race, Class, and Gender.* Westport, CT: Praeger.

Berube, Alan. 2014. *All Cities Are Not Created Unequal.* Washington, D.C.: The Brookings Institution. https://www.brookings.edu/research/all-cities-are-not-created-unequal/.

Berube, Alan and Natalie Holmes. 2015. *Some Cities are Still More Unequal than Others—An Update.* Washington, D.C.: The Brookings Institution. https://www.brookings.edu/research/some-cities-are-still-more-unequal-than-others-an-update/.

Borsook, Pualina. 1999. "How the Internet Ruined San Francisco," Silicon Valley, *Salon.com,* Oct. 28, http://www.salon.com/1999/10/28/internet_2/.

Bourdieu, Pierre. 2003. *Outline of a Theory of Practice.* Cambridge: Cambridge University Press.

Bourdieu, Pierre. 1996. "Understanding." *Theory, Culture, and Society* 13 (2):17–37.

Bourgois, Philippe. 1995. *In Search of Respect: Selling Crack in El Barrio.* Cambridge: Cambridge University Press.

Brandwein, Ruth A. 1999. "Family Violence, Women, and Welfare." In *Battered Women, Children, and Welfare Reform: The Ties That Bind*, edited by Ruth Brandwein, 3–14. Thousand Oaks: Sage Publications Inc.

Branswein, Ruth A., and Diana M. Filiano. 2000. "Toward Real Welfare Reform: The Voices of Battered Women." *Affilia* 15(2): 224–43.

Browne, Angela, and Shari S. Bassuck. 1997. "Intimate Violence in the Lives of Homeless and Poorly Housed Women: Prevalence and Patterns in an Ethnically Diverse Sample." *American Journal of Orthopsychiaty* 6 (2): 261–78.

Brush, Lisa D. 2006. "Safety and Self-Sufficiency: Rhetoric and Reality in the Lives of Welfare Recipients." In *The Promise of Wlfare Reform: Political Rhetoric and the Reality of Poverty in the Twenty-First Century*, edited by Keith M. Killy and Elizabeth A. Segal, 183–92. Binghamton, NY: The Haworth Press.

Buckner, John C. 2008. "Understanding the Impact of Homelessness on Children: Challenges and Future Research Directions." *American Behavioral Scientist* 51 (6): 721–36.

Buckner, John C., Ellen L. Bassuk, Linda F. Weinreb, Margaret G. Brooks. 1999. "Homelessness and its Relation to the Mental Health and Behavior of Low-Income School Age Children." *Developmental Psychology* 35: 246–57.

John C. Buckner, William R. Beardslee, and Ellen L. Bassuk. 2004. "Exposure to Violence and Low-Income Children's Mental Health: Direct, Moderated, and Mediated Relations." *American Orthopsychiatric Association* 74 (4): 413–23.

Buchanan, Wyatt and Marissa Lagos. 2012. " CA budget: Big Cuts to Welfare, Kids' Health Care." *SF Gate*. http://www.sfgate.com/news/article/CA-budget-big-cuts-to-welfare-kids-health-care-3668717.php.

Burawoy, Michael. 2005. "2004 Presidential Address: For Public Sociology." *American Sociological Review* 70: 4–28.

Burt, Martha. 1992. *Over the Edge: The Growth of Homelessness in the 1980s*. New York: Russell Sage Foundation

Burt, Martha, Laudan Y. Aaron, Toby Douglas, Jesse Valente, Edgar Lee, Britta Iwen. 1999. *Homelessness: Programs and the People they Serve*. Summary Report of the National Survey of Homeless Assistance Providers and Clients. Washington, D.C.: The Urban Institute.

Burt, Martha, Laudan Y. Aaron, Edgar Lee, and Jesse Valente. 2001. *Helping America's Homeless: Emergency Shelters or Affordable Housing?* Washington, D.C.: The Urban Institute Press.

California Budget and Policy Center. 2013. *Uneven Progress: What the Economic Recovery has Meant for California's Workers*. Sacramento, CA: California Budget and Policy Center, Economy Brief. http://calbudgetcenter.org/wp-content/uploads/130901_Uneven_Progress_Labor%20Day.pdf.

Casey, Timothy. 2010. "The Sanction Epidemic in the Temporary Assistance for Needy Families Program." *The Women's Legal Defense and Education Fund*, www.legalmomentum.org. New York: Legal Momentum.

Charmaz, Cathy. 2000. "Grounded Theory: Objectivist and Constructivist Methods." In *Handbook of Qualitative Research*, edited by Norman.K. Denzin and Yavonna. S. Lincoln, 509–35. Thousand Oaks: Sage Publications Inc.

Charmaz, Cathy. 2002. "Qualitative Interviewing and Grounded Theory Analysis." In *Handbook of Interview Research: Context & Method*, edited by Jaber F. Gubrium and James A. Holstein, 675–94. Thousand Oaks: Sage Publications Inc.

Charmaz, Cathy. 2006. *Constructing Grounded Theory: A Practical Guide Through Qualitative Analysis*. Thousand Oaks: Sage Publications Inc.

Cherlin, Andrew J., Karen Bogen, James M. Quane, and Linda Burton. 2002. "Operating within the Rules: Welfare Recipients' Experiences with Sanctions and Case Closings." *Social Services Review* 76 (3): 387–405.

Cherlin, Andrew J. 2013. *Public and Private Families: An Introduction*. New York: McGraw Hill.

Choo, Hae Y., and Myra M. Ferree. 2010. "Practicing Intersectionality in Sociological Research: A Critical Analysis of Inclusions, Interactions, and institutions in the Study of Inequalities." *Sociological Theory* 28 (2): 129–49.

Chow, Esther N., Doris Y. Wilkinson, and Maxine B. Zinn. 1996. *Race, Class, and Gender: Common Bonds, Different Voices*. Thousand Oaks: Sage Publications Inc.

Clifford, James, and George E. Marcus. 1986. *Writing Culture: The Poetics and Politics of Ethnography*. Berkeley: University of California Press.

Cohen, Robert B. 1981. "The New International Division of Labor, Multinational Corporations and Urban Hierarchy." In *Urbanization and Urban Planning in Capitalist Society*, edited by Michael Dear and Allen J. Scott, 287–318. New York: Methuen.

Collins, Patricia H. 1986. "Learning From the Outsider Within: The Sociological Significance of Black Feminist Thought." *Social Problems* 33 (6): S14–S32.

Collins, Patricia H. 1990. *Black Feminist Thought: Knowledge, Consciousness, and the Politics of Empowerment*. New York: Routledge.

Collins, Patricia H. 1998. *Fighting Words: Black Women and the Search for Justice*. Minneapolis: University of Minnesota Press.

Collins, Patricia H. 2005. *Black Sexual Politics: African Americans, Gender, and the New Racism*. New York: Routledge.

Collins, Patricia Hill and Sirma Bilge. 2016. *Intersectionality*. Cambridge: Polity Press.

Conley, Dalton C., 1996. "Getting it Together: Social and Institutional Obstacles to Getting Off the Streets." *Sociological Forum* 11: 25–40.

Copp, Jennifer E. et al. 2015. "Intimate Partner Violence in Neighborhood Context: The Roles of Structural Disadvantage, Subjective Disorder, and Emotional Distress." *Social Science Research* 53: 59–72.

Culhane, Dennis P., and Stephen Metraux. 2008. "Rearranging the Deck Chairs or Lifeboats? Homelessness Assistance and Its Alternatives." *Journal of American Planning Association* 74 (1): 111–21.

Danielson, Caroline and Deborah Reed. 2009. *Sanctions and Time Limits in California's Welfare Program*. San Francisco, Public Policy Institute of California. http://www.ppic.org/content/pubs/other/409CDR_appendix.pdf.

Davis, Angela. 1981. *Women, Race, and Class*. New York: Random House.

Davis, Kathy. 2008. "Intersectionality as Buzzword: A Sociology of Science Perspective on What Makes a Feminist Theory Successful." *Feminist Theory* 9: 67–85.

Davis, Martha F. 1999. "The Economics of Abuse: How Violence Perpetuates Women's Poverty." In *Battered Women, Children, and Welfare Reform: The Ties That Bind Us*, edited by Ruth Brandwein, 17–30. Thousand Oaks: Sage Publications Inc.

Davis, Martha F., and Susan J. Kraham. 1995. "Beaten then Robbed." *New York Times*, January 13. A31.

Dean, Stacy and Dottie Rosenbaum. 2013. *SNAP Benefits Will Be Cut for Nearly All Participants In November 2013*. Washington, D.C.: Center on Budget and Policy Priorities.

Desmond, Matthew. 2012. "Disposable Ties and the Urban Poor." *American Journal of Sociology* 117 (5): 1295–1335.

DeVault, Marjorie. 1999. *Liberating Method: Feminism and Social Research*. Philadelphia: Temple University Press.

Dick, Kirby and Amy Ziering. 2015. *The Hunting Ground*. DVD. Directed by Dick Kirby. New York: The Weinstein Company.

Dill, Bonnie T. 1983. "Race, Class, and Gender: Prospects for an All-Inclusive Sisterhood." *Feminist Studies* 9 (1): 131–50.

Dodson, Jualynne. 1988. "Conceptualizations of Black Families." In *Black Families*, edited by Harriette Pipes McAdoo, 77–90. Newberry Park: Sage Publications.

Dordick, Gwendolyn E. 1997. *Something Left to Lose: Personal Relations and Survival Among New York's Homeless*. Philadelphia: Temple University Press.

Eder, Donna, and Laura Fingerson. 2002. "Interviewing Children and Adolescents." In *Handbook of Interview Research: Context & Method*, edited by Jaber F. Gubrium and James A. Holstein, 181–201. Thousand Oaks: Sage Publications Inc.

Edin, Kathryn, and Laura Lein. 1997. *Making Ends Meet: How Single Mothers Survive Welfare and Low-Wage Work*. New York: Russell Sage Foundation.

Edin, Kathryn and H. Luke Schaefer. 2015. *$2.00 a Day: Living on Almost Nothing in America*. New York: Houghton Mifflin.

Eggebeen, David J. 1992. "Family Structure and Intergenerational Exchanges." *Research on Aging* 14:427–47.

Eggebeen, David J., and Dennis P. Hogan. 1990. "Giving Between Generations in American Families." *Human Nature* 1:211–32.

Ellwood, David T. 1988. *Poor Support: Poverty in the American Family*. New York: Basic Books.

Evans, Rhonda D., and Craig J. Forsyth. 2004. "Risk Factors, Endurance of Victimization, and Survival Strategies: The Impact of Structural Location of Men and Women on Their Experiences within Homeless Milieus.'" *Sociological Spectrum* 24: 479–505.

Fosse, Nathan Edward. 2010. "The Repertoire of Infidelity among Low-Income Men: Doubt, Duty, and Destiny." *ANNALS, AAPSS* 629: 125–43.

Fracassa, Dominic. 2019. "Opponents to Navigation Center on SF's Embarcadero Gearing up for Legal Fight." *San Francisco Chronicle*, March 2019. https://www.sfchronicle.com/bay-area/article/Opponents-to-new-homeless-Navigation-Center-on-13721606.php.

Frank, Darcy. 1999. *Housing San Francisco's Workforce: Strategies for Increasing the Supply of Affordable Housing*. Berkeley: Program on Housing and Urban Policy Professional Report Series, University of California Institute of Business and Economic Research.

Frazier, E. Franklin. 1939. *The Negro Family in the United States.* Chicago: University of Chicago Press.

Frey, James H. and Andrea Fontana. 1993. "The Group Interview in Social Research." In *Successful Focus Groups: Advancing the State of the Art*, edited by David L. Morgan, 20–34. Thousand Oaks, CA: Sage Publications Inc.

Geissler, Lisa J., Carol A. Bormann, Carol F. Kwiatkowski, G. Nicholas Braucht, and Charles S. Reichardt. 1995. "Women, Homelessness, and Substance Abuse: Moving Beyond the Stereotypes." *Psychology of Women Quarterly* 19: 65–83.

George, Christine. 2006. "Welfare Reform and the Safety Needs of Battered Women." In *The Promise of Welfare Reform: Political Rhetoric and the Reality of Poverty in the Twenty-First Century*, edited by K. Kilty and E. Segal, 193–203. Binghamton, NY: The Haworth Press.

Gerson, Jill. 2007. *Hope Springs Maternal: Homeless Mothers Talk About Making Sense of Adversity.* New York: Gordian Knot Books.

Gerstel, Naomi, and Natalia Sarkisian. 2008. "The Color of Family Ties: Race, Class, Gender, and Extended Family Involvement." In *American Families: A Multicultural Reader* 2nd Edition, edited by Stephanie Coontz, Maya Parson, and Gabrielle Raley, 447–53. New York: Routledge.

Gewirtz, Abigail H., and Jeffrey Edleson. 2007. "Young Children's Exposure to Intimate Partner Violence: Towards a Developmental Risk and Resilience Framework for Research and Intervention." *Journal of Family Violence* 22: 151–63.

Giddens, Anthony. 1984. *The Constitution of Society: Outline of the Theory of Structuration.* Los Angeles: University of California Press.

Gilfus, Mary. 2006. "From Victims to Survivors to Offenders: Women's Routes of Entry and Immersion into Street Crime." In *In Her Own Words: Women Offender's Views on Crime and Incarceration*, edited by L. Alarid and P. Cromwell, 5–14. Los Angeles: Roxbury.

Glaser, Barney G., and Anselm L. Strauss. 1967. *The Discovery of Grounded Theory: Strategies for Qualitative Research.* Chicago: Aldine.

Glenn, Evelyn N. 1985. "Racial Ethnic Women's Labor: The Intersection of Race, Gender, and Class Oppression." *Review of Radical Political Economics* 17 (3): 86–108.

Glenn, Evelyn N. 1999. "The Social Construction of Gender and Race: An Integrative Framework." In *Revisioning Gender*, edited by Myra Marx Ferree, Judith J. Lorber. and Beth Hess, 1–42. Thousand Oaks: Sage Publications Inc.

Goldberg, Heidi, and Liz Schott. 2000. *A Compliance-Oriented Approach to Sanctions in State and County TANF Programs.* Washington, D.C.: Center on Budget and Policy Priorities.,

Gottschalk, Peter, Sara McLanahan, and Gary D. Sandefur. 1994. "The Dynamics and Intergenerational Transmission of Poverty and Welfare Participation." In *Confronting Poverty: Prescriptions for Change*, edited by Sheldon H. Danziger, Gary D. Sandefur, and Daniel H. Weinberg, 85–108. New York: Russell Sage Foundation.

Gowen, Teresa. 2000. "Excavating 'Globalization' from Street Level; Homeless Men Recycle Their Pasts." In *Global Ethnography: Forces, Connections, and Imagination in a Postmodern World*, edited by Michael Burrawoy, Joseph A. Blum, Sheba George, Zsuzsa Gille, Teresa Gowen, Lynne Hanney, Maren Klawiter, Steven H. Lopez, Seán O'riain, and Millie Thayer, 74–105. Berkeley: University of California Press.

Gowen, Teresa. 2010. *Hobos Hustlers and Backsliders: Homeless in San Francisco.* Minneapolis: University of Minnesota Press.

Guarino, Kathleen, Lenore Rubin, and Ellen Bassuck. 2007. "Trauma in the Lives of Homeless Families." In *Health and Illness.* Vol. 2 of *Trauma Psychology: Issues in Violence, Disaster, Health, and Illness*, edited by Elizabeth K. Carl, 231–58. London: Praeger.

Gubrium, Jaber F. and James A. Holstein. 1997. *The New Language of Qualitative Method.* New York, Oxford: Oxford University Press.

Hartman, Chester. 2002. *City For Sale: The Transformation of San Francisco.* Berkeley: University of California Press.

Hayes, Maureen, Megan Zonneville, and Ellen L. Bassuk. 2013. *The SHIFT Study Final Report: Service and Housing Interventions for Families in Transition.* Newton, MA: National Center on Homeless Families.

Hays, Sharon. 2003. *Flat Broke With Children: Women in the Age of Welfare Reform*. Oxford: Oxford University Press.

Hearn, Marcellene E. 2000. "Dangerous Indifference: New York City's Failure to Implement the Family Violence Option." A Joint Project of the NOW Legal Defense Fund, The Legal Aid Society, The Women, Welfare, and Abuse Task Force, and The Urban Justice Center. NOW Legal Defense and Education Fund. Web Edition. https://vawnet.org/publisher/now-legal-defense-and-education-fund.

Hedden, Sara L., Joel Kennet, Rachel Lipari, Grace Medley, Peter Tice, Elizabeth A. P. Copello, Larry A. Kroutii. 2015. "Behavioral Health Trends in the United States: Results from the 2014 National Survey on Drug Use and Health." http://store.samhsa.gov

Heller, Celia. 1966. *Mexican American Youth: Forgotten Youth at the Crossroads*. New York: Random House.

Heyl, Barbara. 2001. "Ethnographic Interviewing." In *Handbook of Ethnography*, edited by Paul Atkinson, Amanda Coffey, Sara Delamont, John Lofland, and Lyn Lofland, 369–83. Thousand Oaks, CA: Sage Publications Inc.

Hicks-Coolidge, Anne, Patricia Burnside-Eaton, and Ardith Peters. 2003. "Homeless Children: Needs and Services." *Child and Youth Forum* 32 (4): 197–210.

Hill, Shirley A. 2005. *Black Intimacies: A Gender Perspective on Families and Relationships*. Walnut Creek, CA: AltaMira Press.

Hofferth, Sandra. 1984. "Kin Networks, Race, and Family Structure." *Journal of Marriage and the Family* 46:791–806.

Hoffman, Lisa and Brian Coffey. 2008. "Dignity and Indignation: How People Experiencing Homelessness View Services and Providers." *The Social Science Journal* 45 (2): 207–22.

Hogan, Dennis P., David J. Eggebeen, and Clifford C. Clogg. 1993. "The Structure of Intergenerational Exchanges in American Families." *American Journal of Sociology* 98:1428–58.

Holstein, James A., and Jaber F. Gubrium. 1995. *The Active Interview*. Thousand Oaks: Sage Publications.

hooks, bell. 1981. *Aint I a Woman: Black Women and Feminism*. Boston: South End Press.

Huey, Laura. 2010. "False Security or Greater Social Inclusion? Exploring CCTV use in Public and Private Spaces Accessed by the Homeless." *British Journal of Sociology* 61: 63–82.

Huey, Laura, and Eric Berndt. 2008. "'You've Gotta Learn How to Play the Game': Homeless Women's Use of Gender Performance as a Tool For Preventing Victimization." *The Sociological Review* 56 (2): 177–94.

Huntington, Nicholas, John C. Bruckner, and Ellen L. Bassuk. 2008. "Adaptation in Homeless Children: An Empirical Examination Using Cluster Analysis." *American Behavioral Scientist* 51 (6): 737–55.

Hurtado, Aida. 2003. *Voicing Chicana Feminisms: Young Women Speak Out on Sexuality and Identity*. New York, New York: NYU Press.

Institute for Children, Poverty, & Homelessness. 2012. *Intergenerational Disparities Experienced by Homeless Black Families: A National Survey Policy Brief from ICPH*. New York: ICPH.

Jasinski, Jana L., Jennifer K. Wesely, James D. Wright, and Elizabeth E. Mustaine. 2010. *Hard Lives, Mean Streets: Violence in the Lives of Homeless Women*. New England: Northeastern University Press.

Jencks, Christopher. 1994. *The Homeless*. Cambridge: Harvard University Press.

Jonas, Susanne. 2014. "Hard Times for Low-Wage Latino Immigrants in San Francisco's Mission District." *Footnotes* 42 (5): 1–3.

Kalil, Ariel, Kristen S. Seefeldt, and Hui-ChenWang. 2002. "Sanctions and Marital Hardship Under TANF." *Social Service Review* 76 (4): 642–62. https://doi.org/10.1086/342998.

Katz, Sheila M. 2014. "Hard Times and Inequality San Francisco Bay Area Style." *Footnotes* 42 (2): 1–3.

Keating, Kevin. 2007. "Mission Yuppie Eradication Project: A Critical Re-Examination of an Ultra-Left Effort Against the Gentrification of San Francisco in the Late 1990's." Love and Treason, *Infoshop.org*, December, http://infoshop.org/myep_criticism.html.

Ken, Ivy. 2007. "Race-Class-Gender Theory: An Image(ry) Problem." *Gender Issues* 24: 1–20.

Ken, Ivy. 2010. *Digesting Race, Class, and Gender: Sugar as a Metaphor.* New York: Palgrave Macmillan.

Kozol, Jonathan. 1988. *Rachel and Her Children.* New York: Ballantine Books.

Krakauer, Jon. 2015. *Missoula: Rape and the Justice System in a College Town.* New York: Anchor Books.

Lamont, Michèle, Stefan Beljean, and Matthew Claire. 2014. "What is Missing? Cultural Processes and Causal Pathways to Inequality." *Socio-Economic Review* 12: 573–608.

Lee, Barrett, A. and Christopher J. Schreck. 2005. "Danger on the Streets: Marginality and Victimization Among Homeless People." *American Behavioral Scientist* 48: 1055–81.

Lees, Loretta. 2003. "Super-gentrification: The Case of Brooklyn Heights, New York City" *Urban Studies* 40: 2487–2509.

Lens, Vicki. 2008. "Welfare and Work Sanctions: Examining Discretion on the Front Lines." *Social Service Review* 82 (2): 197–222.

Letiecq, Bethany, Elaine Anderson, and Sally Koblinsky. 1998. "Social Support of Homeless and Housed Mothers: A Comparison of Temporary and Permanent Housing Arrangements." *Family Relations* 47 (4): 415–21.

Levin, Rebekah. 2001. "Less Than Ideal: The Reality of Implementing a Welfare-to-Work Program for Domestic Violence Victims and Survivors in Collaboration with the TANF Department." *Violence Against Women* 7: 211–21.

Lewis, Oscar. 1959. *Five Families: Mexican Case Studies in the Culture of Poverty.* New York: Basic Books.

Lewis, Oscar. 1966. *La Vida: A Puerto Rican Family in the Culture of Poverty-San Juan, New York.* New York: Random House.

Liebow, Elliot. 1993. *Tell Them Who I Am: The Lives of Homeless Women.* New York: Penguin.

Litwak, Eugene. 1960. "Occupational Mobility and Extended Family Cohesion." *American Sociological Review* 25: 9–21.

Los Angeles Coalition to End Hunger and Homelessness. 2005. CalWORKs: The People's Guide. Los Angeles Coalition to End Hunger and Homelessness. Available at www.lacehh.org/tpcg/pdf/calworksen.pdf.

Lyon, Eleanor. 2000. "Welfare, Poverty and Abused Women: New Research and Its Implications." Harrisburg, PA: National resource center on domestic violence. http://www.vawnet. org/NRCDVPublications/BCSDV/Paers/BCS10_POV.php. Accessed 2002 .

Lyon-Callo, Vincent. 2000. Medicalizing Homelessness: The Production of Self-Blame and Self-Governing Within Homeless Shelters." *Medical Anthropology Quarterly* 14: 328–45.

MaCurdy, Thomas, David C. Mancuso, Margaret O'Brien-Strain. *Does California's Welfare Policy Explain the Slower Decline of Its Caseload?* San Francisco: Public Policy Institute of California. https://www.ppic.org/content/pubs/report/R_102TMR.pdf.

Madriz, Esther. 2000. "Focus Groups in Feminist Research." In *Handbook of Qualitative Research,* edited by N. K. Denzin and Y. S. Lincoln, 835–50. Thousand Oaks: Sage Publications Inc.

Majors, Richard, and Janet Mancini Billson. 1992. *Cool Pose: The Dilemmas of Black Manhood in America.* New York: Lexington Books.

Mallett, Christopher. 2016. "School-to-Prison Pipeline: A Critical Review of the Punitive Paradigm Shift." *Child & Adolescent Social Work.* 33 (1): 15–24.

Manfield, Lucas and Christopher Wimer. 2011. *Estimating Poverty Thresholds in San Francisco: An SPM-Style Approach.* Palo Alto, CA: Stanford Center for the Study of Poverty and Inequality. http://inequality.stanford.edu/sites/default/files/manfield_wimer_SPM.pdf.

Masten Ann S., Donna Miliotis, Sandra Graham-Bermann, A. MaryLouise Ramirez, Jennifer Neemann. 1993. "Children in Homeless Families: Risks to Mental Health and Development." *Journal of Consulting and Clinical Psychology* 61: 335–43.

Masten Ann S., Arturo Sesma Jr., Rekhet Si-Asar, Catherine Lawrence, Donna Miliotis, and Jacqueline A. Dionne. 1997. "Educational Risks for Children Experiencing Homelessness." *Journal of Social Psychology* 35: 27–46.

Mathis, Arthur. 1978. "Contrasting Approaches to the Study of Black Families." *Journal of Marriage and the Family* 40: 667–76.

Martin, Elmer P., and Joanne M. Martin. 1978. *The Black Extended Family*. Chicago: University of Chicago Press.

Maurin, Judith T., Leslie Russell, and Rae Jeanne Memmott. 1989. "An Exploration of Gender Differences Among the Homeless." *Research in Nursing and Health* 12 (5): 315–21.

McAdoo, Harriette P. 1980. "Black Mothers and the Extended Family Support Network." In *The Black Woman*, edited by La Frances Rodgers-Rose, 125–44. Beverly Hills: Sage.

McCall, Leslie. 2001. *Complex Inequalities: Gender, Class, and Race in the New Economy*. New York: Routledge.

Mead, Lawrence. 1992. *The New Politics of Poverty: The Nonworking Poor in America*. New York: Basic Books.

Meanwell, Emily. 2012. "Experiencing Homelessness: A Review of Recent Literature." *Sociology Compass* 6 (1): 72–85.

Meier, Joan. 1997. "Domestic Violence, Character, and Social Change in the Welfare Reform Debate." *Law and Social Policy* 19 (2): 205–63.

Meiners, Erica R. and Maisha T. Winn. 2010. "Resisting the School to Prison Pipeline: The Practice to Build Abolition Democracies." *Race, Ethnicity, & Education* 13 (3): 271–76.

Memmott, Rae Jeanne, and Laurie Ann Young. 1993. "An Encounter With Homeless Mothers and Children: Gaining and Awareness." *Issues in Mental Health Nursing* 14: 357–65.

Menjivar, Cecilia. 2000. *Fragmented Ties: Salvadoran Immigrant Networks in America*. Berkeley: University of California Press.

Miner, Sonia. 1995. "Racial Differences in Family Support and Formal Service Utilization Among Older Persons: A Non-Recursive Model." *Journal of Gerontology: Social Sciences* 50 (3): S143–S153.

Miner, Sonia, and Peter Uhlenberg. 1997. "Intragenerational Proximity and the Social Role of Sibling Neighbors After Mid-Life." *Family Relations* 46 (April): 145–53.

Mirabel, Nancy Raquel. 2009. "Geographies of Displacement: Latina/os, Oral History, and The Politics of Gentrification in San Francisco's Mission District." *The Public Historian* 31 (2): 7–31.

Mirandé, Alfredo. 1985. *The Chicano Experience: An Alternative Perspective*. Indiana: University of Notre Dame Press.

Mohanty, Candra Talpade. 1991. "Cartographies of Struggle: Third World Women and Politics of Feminism." In *Third World Women and the Politics of Feminism*, edited by Chandra T. Mohanty, Ann Russo, and Lourdes Torres, 1–47. Bloomington: Indiana University Press.

Moore, Tim, Morag McArthur, and Debbie Noble-Carr. 2011. "Lessons Learned from Children Who Have Experienced Homelessness: What Services Need to Know." *Children & Society* 25: 115–26.

Morgan, David L. 2002. "Focus Group Interviewing." In *Handbook of Interview Research: Context & Method*, edited by Jaber F. Gubrium and James A. Holstein, 141–59. Thousand Oaks: Sage Publications Inc.

Moyniham, Daniel P. 1965. *The Negro Family: A Case for National Action*. Washington D.C.: Government Printing Offices.

Murray, Charles. 1984. *Losing Ground: American Social Policy, 1950–1980*. New York: Basic Books.

National Alliance to End Homelessness. 2018. *Children and Families*. Washington, D.C.: National Alliance to End Homelessness. Web Edition. https://endhomelessness.org/homelessness-in-america/who-experiences-homelessness/children-and-families/

National Center for Children in Poverty. 2010. *Basic Facts About Low-Income Children, 2009*, New York: Mailman School of Public Health Columbia University.

Nieves, Evelyn. 1999. "Homeless Defy Cities' Drive to Move Them." *New York Times*, December 7.

North, Carl S. and Elizabeth M. Smith. 1993. "A Comparison of Homeless Men and Women: Different Populations, Different Needs." *Community Mental Health Journal* 29 (5): 423–31.

Ong, Paul M. and Douglas Houston. 2005. "CalWORKs Sanction Patterns in Four Counties: An Analysis of Administrative Data." *WPRP Briefing Paper*. University of California, Berkeley: California Policy Research Center.

Parker, Ashley. 2011. "Lawsuit Says Military Is Rife With Sexual Abuse." *New York Times*, February 16. A18.

Passaro, Joanne. 1996. *The Unequal Homeless: Men on the Streets and Women in Their Place*. New York: Routledge.

Patil, Vrushali. 2011. "Transnational Feminism in Sociology: Articulations, Agendas, Debates." *Sociology Compass* 5/7: 540–50.

Pearson, Jessica, Esther Ann Griswold, and Nancy Thoennes. 2001. "Balancing Safety and Self-Sufficiency: Lessons on Serving Victims of Domestic Violence for Child Support and Public Assistance Agencies. *Violence Against Women* 7: 176–92.

Personal Responsibility and Work Opportunity Reconciliation Act of 1996, Pub. L. No. 104–93, 110 Stat. 2105 (1996).

Postmus, Judy. 2004. "Battered and on Welfare: The Experiences of Women With the Family Violence Option." *Journal of Sociology and Social Welfare* 2: 113–23.

Priceonomics. 2014. "The San Francisco Rent Explosion: Part II." Priceonomics. http://priceonomics.com/the-san-francisco-rent-explosion-part-ii/.

Rafferty, Yvonne. 1991. "Developmental and Educational Consequences of Homelessness on Children and Youth." In *Homeless Children and Youth*, edited by Julee H. Kryder-Coe, Lester M. Salamon, and Janice M. Molnar, 105–39. New Jersey: Transaction Publishers.

Rafferty, Yvonne and MaryBeth Shinn. 1991. "The Impact of Homelessness on Children *American Psychologist* 46: 1170–79.

Rainwater, Lee. 1966. "Crucible of Identity: The Negro Lower-Class Family." *Daedalus* 95: 172–216.

Raley, Kelly R. 1995. "Black-White Differences in Kin Contact and Exchange among Never-Married Adults." *Journal of Family Issues* 16 (1): 77–103.

Raphael, Jody. 2000. *Saving Bernice: Battered Women, Welfare, and Poverty*. Boston: Northeastern University Press.

Reichmann, Nancy E., Julien O. Teitler, and Marah A. Curtis. 2005. "TANF Sanctioning and Hardship." *Social Service Review* 79 (2): 215–36.

Reskin, Barbara F., and Heidi I. Hartmann. 1986. *Women's Wok, Men's Work: Sex Aggregation on the Job*. Washington, D.C.: National Academy Press.

Richie, Beth E. 2012. "The Matrix: A Black Feminist Response to Male Violence and the State." In *Arrested Justice: Black Women, Violence, and America's Prison Nation*, edited by Beth E. Richie, 125–56. New York: NYU Press.

Riger, Stephanie and Susan L. Staggs. 2004. "Welfare Reform, Domestic Violence, and Employment: What Do We Know and What Do We Need to Know?" *Violence Against Women* 10: 961–90.

Ritzer, George, and Goudlas J. Goodman. 2004. *Sociological Theory*, 6th ed. New York: McGraw Hill.

Roschelle, Anne R. 1997. *No More Kin: Exploring Race, Class, and Gender in Family Networks*. Thousand Oaks: Sage Publications.

Roschelle, Anne. R. 1999. "Gender, Family Structure, and Social Structure: Racial Ethnic Families in the United States." In *Revisioning Gender*, edited by Myra Marx Ferree, Judith Lorber, and Beth B. Hess, 311–40. Thousand Oaks, CA: Sage Publications.

Roschelle, Anne R. 2002. "The Tattered Web of Kinship: Black White Differences in Social Support in A Puerto Rican Community." In *The New Politics of Race: From DuBois to the 21st Century*, edited by Marlese Durr, 113–36. Westport, CT: Praeger.

Roschelle, Anne R. 2008. "Welfare Indignities: Homeless Women, Domestic Violence, and Welfare Reform in San Francisco." *Gender Issues* 14: 357–80.

Roschelle, Anne R, 2017. Our Lives Matter: The Racialized Violence of Poverty Among Homeless Mothers of Color." *Sociological Forum* 32 (S1): 998–1017.

Roschelle, Anne R., and Peter Kaufman. 2004. "Fitting In and Fighting Back: Stigma Management Strategies Among Homeless Kids." *Symbolic Interaction* 27 (1): 23–46.

Roschelle, Anne R., Maura I. Toro-Morn, and Elisa Facio. 2010. "Toward a Feminist Methodological Approach to the Intersection of Race, Class, and Gender: Lessons From Cuba." *Advances in Gender Research* 14: 357–80.

Rosenthal, Rob. 1994. *Homeless in Paradise: A Map of the Terrain.* Philadelphia: Temple University Press.

Rossi, Peter. 1989. *Down and Out in America: The Origins of Homelessness.* Chicago: The University of Chicago Press.

Russell, Diana E. H. 1986. *The Secret Trauma: Incest in the Lives of Girls and Women.* New York: Basic Books.

Sabatini, Joshua. 2014. "Thousands of SF Public-School Students are Homeless." *The Examiner.* http://archives.sfexaminer.com/sanfrancisco/thousands-of-sf-public-school-students-are-homeless/.

Sacks, Karen B. 1989. "Toward a Unified Theory of Class, Race, and Gender." *American Ethnologist* 16 (3): 534–50.

Sager, Rebecca and Laura Susan Stephens. 2005. "Serving Up Sermons: Clients' Reactions to Religious Elements at Congregation-Run Feeding Establishments." *Non-Profit and Voluntary Sector Quarterly* 34 (3): 297–315.

San Francisco Health Improvement Partnership. 2016. "People Living Below the Poverty Level." San Francisco Health Improvement Partnership. http://www.sfhip.org/modules.php?op=modload&name=NS-Indicator&file=indicator&iid=14103282.

Sarkisian, Natalia, and Naomi Gerstel. 2004. "Kin Support among Blacks and Whites: Race and Family Organization." *American Sociological Review* 69: 812–37.

Schmitz, Cathryne L., Janet D. Wagner, and Edna M. Menke. 2001. "The Interconnection of Childhood Poverty and Homelessness: Negative Impact/Points of Access." *Families in Society* 82 (1): 69–77.

Scott, Ellen K., Andrew S. London, and Nancy A. Myers. 2002. "Dangerous Dependencies: The Intersection of Welfare Reform and Domestic Violence." *Gender & Society* 16 (6): 878–97.

Seltser, Barry Jay, and Donald E. Miller. 1993. *Homeless Families: The Struggle for Dignity.* Chicago: University of Illinois Press.

Schaefer, Luke H., Marybeth Mattingly, and Kathryn Edin. 2018. *The State of the Union 2018: Poverty.* Stanford, CA: The Stanford Center for the Study of Poverty and Inequality. Web Edition. https://inequality.stanford.edu/sites/default/files/Pathways_SOTU_2018_poverty.pdf.

Shane, Paul G. 1996. *What About America's Homeless Children? Hide and Seek.* Thousand Oaks, CA: Sage Publications.

Shaw, Linda L. John Horton, and Manuel H. Moreno. 2008–09. "Sanctions as Everyday Resistance to Welfare Reform." *Social Justice* 35(4): 83–98.

Similanick, Paul. 2006. "CalWORKs Safety Net Program: What we Know from Administrative Data." Paper presented at the meeting of the National Association for Welfare Research and Statistics, Jackson Hole, WY.

Shinn, Marybeth, Judith S. Schteingart, Nathanial Chioke Williams, Jennifer Carlin-Mathis, Nancy Bialo-Karagis, Rachel Becker-Klein, and Beth Weitzman. 2008. "Long Term Association of Homelessness with Children's Well-Being." *American Behavioral Scientist* 51 (6): 789–809.

Shinn, Marybeth, and Beth C. Weitzman. 1996. "Homeless Families are Different." In *Homelessness in America,* edited by J. Baumhohl, 109-122. Phoenix: Oryx Press.

Sidel, Ruth. 1986. *Women and Children Last: The Plight of Poor Women in Affluent America.* New York: Penguin.

Sigle-Rushton, Wendy, and Sara McLanahan. 2002. "For Richer or Poorer? Marriage as an Anti-Poverty Strategy in the United States." *Population* 57 (3): 509–26.

Silicon Valley Institute for Regional Studies. 2019. *2019 Silicon Valley Index.* San Jose, CA: Silicon Valley Institute for Regional Studies. https://jointventure.org/images/stories/pdf/index2019.pdf.

Silicon Valley Institute for Regional Studies. 2015. *Poverty in the San Francisco Bay Area.* San Jose, CA: Silicon Valley Institute for Regional Studies, Research Brief. http://www.jointventure.org/images/stories/pdf/poverty-brief-2015-03.pdf

Silicon Valley Institute for Regional Studies. 2015b. *Income Inequality in the Bay Area*. San Jose, CA: Silicon Valley Institute for Regional Studies, Research Brief. http://www.jointventure.org/images/stories/pdf/income-inequality-2015-06.pdf.

Simmons, Ronald L., and Les B. Whitbeck. 1991. "Sexual Abuse as a Precursor to Prostitution and Victimization Among Adolescent and Adult Homeless Women." *Family Issues* 12: 361–79.

Small, Mario Luis, David J. Harding, and Michèle Lamont. 2010. "Reconsidering Culture and Poverty." *ANNALS, AAPSS* 629: 6–27.

Smith, Barbara. 1983. "Introduction." In *Home Girls: A Black Feminist Anthology*, edited by B. Smith, XIX–IVI. New York: Kitchen Table Press.

Smith, Jeremy Adam. 2011. "Bucking a Punitive Trend, San Francisco Lets Students own up to Misdeeds Instead of Getting Kicked Out of School." *San Francisco Public Press*, Dec 11. Web Edition https://sfpublicpress.org/news/2011-12/bucking-a-punitive-trend-san-francisco-lets-students-own-up-to-misdeeds-instead-of-getting-kicked-out-of-school.

Snow, David A., and Leon Anderson. 1993. *Down on Their Luck: A Study of Homeless Street People*. Berkeley: University of California Press.

Snow, David A. and Michael Mulcahy. 2001. "Space, Politics, and the Survival Strategies of the Homeless." *Behavioral Scientist* 45: 149–69.

Snow, David A., Louis Zurcher, and Gideon Sjoberg. 1981. "Interviewing By Comment: An Adjunct to the Direct Question." *Qualitative Sociology* 5:285–311.

Sokoloff, Natalie J., and Ida Dupont. 2005. "Domestic Violence at the Intersections of Race, Class, and Gender." *Violence Against Women* 11(1): 38–64.

Stacey, Judith. 1988. "Can There be Feminist Ethnography?" *Women's Studies International Forum* 11 (1):21–27.

Stack, Carol. 1974. *All Our Kin: Strategies For Survival in a Black Community*. New York: Harper & Row.

Staggs, Susan L. and Stephanie Riger. 2005. "The Effects of Intimate Partner Violence on Low-Income Women's Health and Employment." *American Journal of Community Psychology* 36 (1/2): 133–45.

Stanfield, John H., ed. 1993. *Race and Ethnicity in Research Methods*. Newbury Park: Sage Publications Inc.

Staples, Robert. 1981. "The Myth of Black Matriarchy." In *The Black Woman Cross Culturally*, edited by Filomena Steady, 335–48. Cambridge: Schenkman Publishing Company.

Staples, Robert, and Alfredo Mirandé. 1980. "Racial and Cultural Variations Among American Families: A Decennial Review of the Literature of Minority Families." *Journal of Marriage and the Family* 42 (4): 157–73.

Steinberg, Stephen. 2011. "Poor Reason." Boston Review January 13 www.bostonreview.net/BR36.1/Steinberg.php.

Stewart, David W., and Prem N. Shamdasani. 1990. *Focus Groups: Theory and Practice*. Thousand Oaks: Sage Publications Inc.

Stover, John. 2014. "Understanding Super-Gentrification in San Francisco." *Footnotes* 42 (4): 1–3.

Sussman, Marvin B. 1965. "Relationships of Adult Children With Their Parents in the United States." In *Social Structure and the Family: Generational Relations*, edited by E. Shanas and G.F. Streib, 62–92. Englewood Cliffs, NJ: Prentice-Hall.

Swanson, Henry. 2008. "Hotel Review: The Covered Wagon in San Francisco." https://archive.is/20130622152650/www.associatedcontent.com/article/602233/hotel_review_the_covered_wagon_in_san.html#selection-34.0-183.373.

Taylor, Mary Jane, and Amanda Smith Barusch. 2004. "Personal Family and Multiple Barriers of Long Term Welfare Receipt." *Social Work* 49 (2): 175–83.

Thomas, Adam, and Isabel Sawhill. 2002. "For Richer or Poorer: Marriage as an Antipoverty Strategy." *Journal of Policy Analysis and Management* 21 (3): 587–99.

Tolman, Richard, and Jody Raphael. 2000. "A Review of Research on Welfare and Domestic Violence." *Journal of Social Issues* 56 (4): 655–82.

Toohey, Siobhan M., Marybeth Shinn, and Beth C. Weitzman. 2004. "Social Networks and Homelessness Among Women Heads of Household." *American Journal of Community Psychology* 13 (1/2): 7–20.

Tucker, Joan S., David Kennedy, Gery Ryan, Suzanne L. Wenzel. Daniela Golinelli, James Zazzali, and Christopher McCarty. 2009. "Homeless Women's Personal Networks: Implications for Understanding Risk Behavior." *Human Organization* 68 (2): 129–40.

Turner, Jason A. and Thomas Main. 2001. "Work Experience Under Welfare Reform." In *The New World of Welfare*, edited by Rebecca. Blank and Ron Haskins, 291–310. Washington D.C.: Brookings Institution Press.

U.S. Census Bureau. 1996. *Money Income in the United States: 1996*. Washington, D.C.: U.S. Census Bureau.

United States Conference of Mayors. 2001. *A Status Report on Hunger and Homelessness in America's Cities: A 21-City Report*. Washington, D.C.: The United States Conference of Mayors.

U.S. Department of Housing and Urban Development. 2007. *The 2007 Annual Homeless Assessment Report to Congress*. Washington, D.C.: U.S. Department of Housing and Urban Development.

U.S. Department of Housing and Urban Development. 2009. *The 2008 Annual Homeless Assessment: Report to Congress*. Washington D.C.: U.S. Department of Housing and Urban Development.

U.S. Department of Housing and Urban Development. 2018. *The 2018 Annual Homeless Assessment Report to Congress*. Washington D.C.: U.S. Department of Housing and Urban Development.

U.S. Department of Justice. 1991. *Female Victims of Violent Crimes 5*. Washington D.C.: Government Printing Office.

U.S. Department of Labor. 1999. *A Profile of the Working Poor, 1997*. Report 936. Bureau of Labor Statistics.

Vaisey, Stephen. 2010. "What People Want: Rethinking Poverty, Culture, and Educational Attainment." *ANNALS, AAPSS* 629: 75–101.

Wacquant, Loïc. 2002. "Scrutinizing the Street: Poverty, Morality, and the Pitfalls of Urban Ethnography." American Journal of Sociology 107(6): 1468–1532.

Warren, Carol A. B. 2002. "Qualitative Interviewing." In *Handbook of Interview Research: Context & Method*, edited by Jaber F. Gubrium and James A. Holstein, 83–101. Thousand Oaks: Sage Publications Inc.

Wasserman, Jason A. and Jeffery M. Clair. 2010. *At home on the Street: People, Poverty, & A Hidden Culture of Homelessness*. Boulder: Lynn Rienner Publishers, Inc.

Wasserfall, Rahel R. 1997. "Reflexivity, Feminism, and Differences." In *Reflexivity and Voice*, edited by Rosanna Hertz, 151–62. Newbury Park: Sage Publications.

Wenzel, Suzanne L., Barbara D. Leake, and Lillian Gelberg. 2001. "Risk Factors for Major Violence Among Homeless Women.' *Journal of Interpersonal Violence* 16 (8): 739–52.

Wenzel, Suzanne L. Paul Koegel, and Lillian Gelberg. 2000. "Antecedents of Physical and Sexual Victimization Among Homeless Women: A Comparison to Homeless Men." *American Journal of Community Psychology* 28 (3): 367–90.

Wesley, Jennifer K. 2009. "'Mom Said we Had a Money Maker': Sexualization and Survival Contexts Among Homeless Women." *Symbolic Interaction* 32 (2): 91–105.

Wesley, Jennifer K. and James D. Wright 2005. "The Pertinence of Partners: Examining the Intersections between Women's Adult Homelessness and Their Adult Relationships." *The American Behavioral Scientist* 48: 1082–1101.

West, Carolyn M., Linda M. Williams, and Jane A. Siegel. 2000. "Adult Sexual Revictimization Among Black Women Sexually Abused in Childhood: A Prospective Examination of Serious Consequences of Abuse." *Child Maltreatment* 5 (1): 49–57.

Whitbeck, Les B. and Dan R. Hoyt. 1999. *Nowhere to Grow: Homeless and Runaway Adolescents and their Families*. New York: Aldine De Gruyter.

Whitbeck, Les B. and Ronald L. Simmons. 1993. "A Comparison of Adaptive Strategies and Patterns of Victimization Among Homeless Adolescents and Adults." *Violence and Victims* 8 (2): 135–52.

Williams, Jean Calterone. 2003. *A Roof Over My Head: Homeless Women and the Shelter Industry*. Boulder: University Press of Colorado.

Wilson, William J. 1987. *The Truly Disadvantaged: The Inner City, the Underclass, and Public Policy*. Chicago: University of Chicago Press.

Wimer, Christopher and Jean Guo. 2011. *Updating the San Francisco Distress Index: July, 2010-February 2011*. Stanford, CA: The Stanford Center for the Study of Poverty and Inequality. Web Edition. https://inequality.stanford.edu/.

Wyatt, Gail E., Donald Guthrie, and Cindy M. Notgrass. 1992. "Differential Effects of Women's Child Sexual Abuse and Subsequent Sexual Revictimization." *Journal of Consulting and Clinical Psychology* 60 (2): 167–73.

Yamamura, Kevin. 2012. "California Gov. Brown Proposes Big Cuts for Welfare." Sacramento Bee. http://www.mcclatchydc.com/news/politics-government/article24722248.html.

Yancey Martin, Patricia, and Robert A. Hummer. 1998. "Fraternities and Rape on Campus." In *Race, Class, and Gender: An Anthology*, edited by Margaret L. Anderson and Patricia Hill Collins, 413–29. Belmont, CA: Wadsworth Publishing Company.

Ybarra, Lea. 1983. "Empirical and Theoretical Developments in the Study of Chicano Families." In *The State of Chicano Research on Family, Labor, and Migration: Proceedings of the First Stanford Symposium on Chicano Research and Public Policy*, edited by Armando Valdez, and Albert Camarillo, 91–110. Stanford, California: Stanford Center for Chicano Research.

Zedlewski, Sheila R. and Pamela Loprest. 2001. "Will TANF Work for the Most Disadvantaged Families?" In *The New World of Welfare*, edited by Rebecca Blank and Ron Haskins, 311–34. Washington D.C.: Brookings Institution Press.

Zinn, Maxine B. 1989. "Family, Race, and Poverty in the Eighties." *Signs* 14: 856–74.

Zinn, Maxine B. 1990. "Family, Feminism, and Race in America." *Gender and Society* 4 (1): 68–82.

Index

About the Author

Anne R. Roschelle received her PhD in Sociology from the University at Albany, State University of New York. Anne is Professor of Sociology and Chair of the Department of Women's, Gender, and Sexuality Studies at the State University of New York at New Paltz. Dr. Roschelle is the author of *No More Kin: Exploring Race, Class, and Gender in Family Networks*, which was a recipient of Choice Magazines 1997 Outstanding Academic Book Award.

Anne is a feminist ethnographer whose research publications focus on racial ethnic families, poverty and homelessness, race, class, and gender inequality, welfare reform and domestic violence, and gender, work, and tourism in Cuba. Anne has recently published her new research on unaccompanied minors in the Hudson Valley and is conducting research on Central American immigrants in the Hudson Valley and deportees in Guatemala. In addition, Anne is writing a book (with Sharina Maillo-Pozo) on the legacy of Dominican scholar Camila Henriquez Ureña.